Steven P. Schacht, PhD
with Lisa Underwood
Editors

D0082664

The Drag Queen Anthology:
The Absolutely Fabulous
but Flawlessly Customary World
of Female Impersonators

The Drag Queen Anthology: The Absolutely Fabulous but Flawlessly Customary World of Female Impersonators has been co-published simultaneously as *Journal of Homosexuality*, Volume 46, Numbers 3/4 2004.

Pre-publication
REVIEWS,
COMMENTARIES,
EVALUATIONS . . .

"Indispensable. . . . For more than a decade, Steven P. Schacht has been one of the social science's most reliable guides to the world of drag queens and female impersonators. . . . This book assembles an impressive cast of scholars who are as theoretically astute, methodologically careful, and conceptually playful as the drag queens themselves."

Michael Kimmel
Author of The Gendered Society
Professor of Sociology
SUNY Stony Brook

HPP

Harrington Park Press®
An Imprint of The Haworth Press, Inc.

The Drag Queen Anthology:
The Absolutely Fabulous
but Flawlessly Customary World
of Female Impersonators

The Drag Queen Anthology: The Absolutely Fabulous but Flawlessly Customary World of Female Impersonators has been co-published simultaneously as *Journal of Homosexuality*, Volume 46, Numbers 3/4 2004.

The *Journal of Homosexuality* Monographic "Separates"

Below is a list of "separates," which in serials librarianship means a special issue simultaneously published as a special journal issue or double-issue *and* as a "separate" hardbound monograph. (This is a format which we also call a "DocuSerial.")

"Separates" are published because specialized libraries or professionals may wish to purchase a specific thematic issue by itself in a format which can be separately cataloged and shelved, as opposed to purchasing the journal on an on-going basis. Faculty members may also more easily consider a "separate" for classroom adoption.

"Separates" are carefully classified separately with the major book jobbers so that the journal tie-in can be noted on new book order slips to avoid duplicate purchasing.

You may wish to visit Haworth's website at . . .

http://www.HaworthPress.com

. . . to search our online catalog for complete tables of contents of these separates and related publications.

You may also call 1-800-HAWORTH (outside US/Canada: 607-722-5857), or Fax 1-800-895-0582 (outside US/Canada: 607-771-0012), or e-mail at:

docdelivery@haworthpress.com

The Drag Queen Anthology: The Absolutely Fabulous but Flawlessly Customary World of Female Impersonators, edited by Steven P. Schacht, PhD, with Lisa Underwood (Vol. 46, No. 3/4, 2004). *"Indispensable. . . . For more than a decade, Steven P. Schacht has been one of the social science's most reliable guides to the world of drag queens and female impersonators. . . . This book assembles an impressive cast of scholars who are as theoretically astute, methodologically careful, and conceptually playful as the drag queens themselves." (Michael Kimmel, author of* The Gendered Society; *Professor of Sociology, SUNY Stony Brook)*

Queer Theory and Communication: From Disciplining Queers to Queering the Discipline(s), edited by Gust A. Yep, PhD, Karen E. Lovaas, PhD, and John P. Elia, PhD (Vol. 45, No. 2/3/4, 2003). *"Sheds light on how sexual orientation and identity are socially produced–and how they can be challenged and changed–through everyday practices and institutional activities, as well as academic research and teaching. . . . Illuminates the theoretical and practical significance of queer theory–not only as a specific area of inquiry, but also as a productive challenge to the heteronormativity of mainstream communication theory, research, and pedagogy." (Julia T. Wood, PhD, Lineberger Professor of Humanities, Professor of Communication Studies, The University of North Carolina at Chapel Hill)*

Gay Bathhouses and Public Health Policy, edited by William J. Woods, PhD, and Diane Binson, PhD (Vol. 44, No. 3/4, 2003). *"Important. . . . Long overdue. . . . a unique and valuable contribution to the social science and public health literature. The inclusion of detailed historical descriptions of public policy debates about the place of bathhouses in urban gay communities, together with summaries of the legal controversies about bathhouses, insightful examinations of patrons' behaviors and reviews of successful program for HIV/STD education and testing programs in bathhouses provides. A well rounded and informative overview." (Richard Tewksbury, PhD, Professor of Justice Administration, University of Louisville)*

Icelandic Lives: The Queer Experience, edited by Voon Chin Phua (Vol. 44, No. 2, 2002). *"The first of its kind, this book shows the emergence of gay and lesbian visibility through the biographical narratives of a dozen Icelanders. Through their lives can be seen a small nation's transition, in just a few decades, from a pervasive silence concealing its queer citizens to widespread acknowledgment characterized by some of the most progressive laws in the world." (Barry D. Adam, PhD, University Professor, Department of Sociology & Anthropology, University of Windsor, Ontario, Canada)*

The Drag King Anthology, edited by Donna Troka, PhD (cand.), Kathleen Le Besco, PhD, and Jean Bobby Noble, PhD (Vol. 43, No. 3/4, 2002). *"All university courses on masculinity should use this book . . . challenges preconceptions through the empirical richness of direct experience. The contributors and editors have worked together to produce cultural analysis that enhances our perception of the dynamic uncertainty of gendered experience." (Sally R. Munt, DPhil, Subject Chair, Media Studies, University of Sussex)*

Homosexuality in French History and Culture, edited by Jeffrey Merrick, PhD, and Michael Sibalis, PhD (Vol. 41, No. 3/4, 2001). *"Fascinating . . . Merrick and Sibalis bring together historians, literary scholars, and political activists from both sides of the Atlantic to examine same-sex sexuality in the past and present." (Bryant T. Ragan, PhD, Associate Professor of History, Fordham University, New York)*

Gay and Lesbian Asia: Culture, Identity, Community, edited by Gerard Sullivan, PhD, and Peter A. Jackson, PhD (Vol. 40, No. 3/4, 2001). *"Superb. . . . Covers a happily wide range of styles . . . will appeal to both students and educated fans." (Gary Morris, Editor/Publisher, Bright Lights Film Journal)*

Queer Asian Cinema: Shadows in the Shade, edited by Andrew Grossman, MA (Vol. 39, No. 3/4, 2000). *"An extremely rich tapestry of detailed ethnographies and state-of-the-art theorizing. . . . Not only is this a landmark record of queer Asia, but it will certainly also be a seminal, contributive challenge to gender and sexuality studies in general." (Dédé Oetomo, PhD, Coordinator of the Indonesian organization GAYa NUSANTARA: Adjunct Reader in Linguistics and Anthropology, School of Social Sciences, Universitas Airlangga, Surabaya, Indonesia)*

Gay Community Survival in the New Millennium, edited by Michael R. Botnick, PhD (cand.), (Vol. 38, No. 4, 2000). *Examines the notion of community from several different perspectives focusing on the imagined, the structural, and the emotive. You will explore a theoretical overview and you will peek into the moral discourses that frame "gay community," the rift between HIV-positive and HIV-negative gay men, and how Israeli gays seek their place in the public sphere.*

The Ideal Gay Man: The Story of Der Kreis, by Hubert Kennedy, PhD (Vol. 38, No. 1/2, 1999). *"Very Profound. . . . Excellent insight into the problems of the early fight for homosexual emancipation in Europe and in the USA. . . . The ideal gay man (high-mindedness, purity, cleanness), as he was imagined by the editor of Der Kreis, is delineated by the fascinating quotations out of the published erotic stories." (Wolfgang Breidert, PhD, Academic Director, Institute of Philosophy, University Karlsruhe, Germany)*

Multicultural Queer: Australian Narratives, edited by Peter A. Jackson, PhD, and Gerard Sullivan, PhD (Vol. 36, No. 3/4, 1999). *Shares the way that people from ethnic minorities in Australia (those who are not of Anglo-Celtic background) view homosexuality, their experiences as homosexual men and women, and their feelings about the lesbian and gay community.*

Scandinavian Homosexualities: Essays on Gay and Lesbian Studies, edited by Jan Löfström, PhD (Vol. 35, No. 3/4, 1998). *"Everybody interested in the formation of lesbian and gay identities and their interaction with the sociopolitical can find something to suit their taste in this volume." (Judith Schuyf, PhD, Assistant Professor of Lesbian and Gay Studies, Center for Gay and Lesbian Studies, Utrecht University, The Netherlands)*

Gay and Lesbian Literature Since World War II: History and Memory, edited by Sonya L. Jones, PhD (Vol. 34, No. 3/4, 1998). *"The authors of these essays manage to gracefully incorporate the latest insights of feminist, postmodernist, and queer theory into solidly grounded readings . . . challenging and moving, informed by the passion that prompts both readers and critics into deeper inquiry." (Diane Griffin Growder, PhD, Professor of French and Women's Studies, Cornell College, Mt. Vernon, Iowa)*

Reclaiming the Sacred: The Bible in Gay and Lesbian Culture, edited by Raymond-Jean Frontain, PhD (Vol. 33, No. 3/4, 1997). *"Finely wrought, sharply focused, daring, and always dignified. . . . In chapter after chapter, the Bible is shown to be a more sympathetic and humane book in its attitudes toward homosexuality than usually thought and a challenge equally to the straight and gay moral imagination." (Joseph Wittreich, PhD, Distinguished Professor of English, The Graduate School, The City University of New York)*

Activism and Marginalization in the AIDS Crisis, edited by Michael A. Hallett, PhD (Vol. 32, No. 3/4, 1997). *Shows readers how the advent of HIV-disease has brought into question the utility of certain forms of "activism" as they relate to understanding and fighting the social impacts of disease.*

Gays, Lesbians, and Consumer Behavior: Theory, Practice, and Research Issues in Marketing, edited by Daniel L. Wardlow, PhD (Vol. 31, No. 1/2, 1996). *"For those scholars, market* *researchers, and marketing managers who are considering marketing to the gay and lesbian community, this book should be on required reading list." (Mississippi Voice)*

Gay Men and the Sexual History of the Political Left, edited by Gert Hekma, PhD, Harry Oosterhuis, PhD, and James Steakley, PhD (Vol. 29, No. 2/3/4, 1995). *"Contributors delve into the contours of a long-forgotten history, bringing to light new historical data and fresh insight. . . . An excellent account of the tense historical relationship between the political left and gay liberation." (People's Voice)*

Sex, Cells, and Same-Sex Desire: The Biology of Sexual Preference, edited by John P. De Cecco, PhD, and David Allen Parker, MA (Vol. 28, No. 1/2/3/4, 1995). *"A stellar compilation of chapters examining the most important evidence underlying theories on the biological basis of human sexual orientation." (MGW)*

Gay Ethics: Controversies in Outing, Civil Rights, and Sexual Science, edited by Timothy F. Murphy, PhD (Vol. 27, No. 3/4, 1994). *"The contributors bring the traditional tools of ethics and political philosophy to bear in a clear and forceful way on issues surrounding the rights of homosexuals." (David L. Hull, Dressler Professor in the Humanities, Department of Philosophy, Northwestern University)*

Gay and Lesbian Studies in Art History, edited by Whitney Davis, PhD (Vol. 27, No. 1/2, 1994). *"Informed, challenging . . . never dull. . . . Contributors take risks and, within the restrictions of scholarly publishing, find new ways to use materials already available or examine topics never previously explored." (Lambda Book Report)*

Critical Essays: Gay and Lesbian Writers of Color, edited by Emmanuel S. Nelson, PhD (Vol. 26, No. 2/3, 1993). *"A much-needed book, sparkling with stirring perceptions and resonating with depth. . . . The anthology not only breaks new ground, it also attempts to heal wounds inflicted by our oppressed pasts." (Lambda Book Report)*

Gay Studies from the French Cultures: Voices from France, Belgium, Brazil, Canada, and The Netherlands, edited by Rommel Mendès-Leite, PhD, and Pierre-Olivier de Busscher, PhD (Vol. 25, No. 1/2/3, 1993). *"The first book that allows an English-speaking world to have a comprehensive look at the principal trends in gay studies in France and French-speaking countries." (André Bèjin, PhD, Directeur, de Recherche au Centre National de la Recherche Scientifique (CNRS), Paris)*

If You Seduce a Straight Person, Can You Make Them Gay? Issues in Biological Essentialism versus Social Constructionism in Gay and Lesbian Identities, edited by John P. De Cecco, PhD, and John P. Elia, PhD (cand.) (Vol. 24, No. 3/4, 1993). *"You'll find this alternative view of the age old question to be one that will become the subject of many conversations to come. Thought-provoking to say the least!" (Prime Timers)*

Gay and Lesbian Studies: The Emergence of a Discipline, edited by Henry L. Minton, PhD (Vol. 24, No. 1/2, 1993). *"The volume's essays provide insight into the field's remarkable accomplishments and future goals." (Lambda Book Report)*

Homosexuality in Renaissance and Enlightenment England: Literary Representations in Historical Context, edited by Claude J. Summers, PhD (Vol. 23, No. 1/2, 1992). *"It is remarkable among studies in this field in its depth of scholarship and variety of approaches and is accessible." (Chronique)*

Coming Out of the Classroom Closet: Gay and Lesbian Students, Teachers, and Curricula, edited by Karen M. Harbeck, PhD, JD, Recipient of Lesbian and Gay Educators Award by the American Educational Research Association's Lesbian and Gay Studies Special Interest Group (AREA) (Vol. 22, No. 3/4, 1992). *"Presents recent research about gay and lesbian students and teachers and the school system in which they function." (Contemporary Psychology)*

Homosexuality and Male Bonding in Pre-Nazi Germany: The Youth Movement, the Gay Movement, and Male Bonding Before Hitler's Rise: Original Transcripts from Der Eigene, the First Gay Journal in the World, edited by Harry Oosterhuis, PhD, and Hubert Kennedy, PhD (Vol. 22, No. 1/2, 1992). *"Provide[s] insight into the early gay movement, particularly in its relation to the various political currents in pre-World War II Germany." (Lambda Book Report)*

Monographs "Separates" list continued at the back

The Drag Queen Anthology:
The Absolutely Fabulous
but Flawlessly Customary World
of Female Impersonators

Steven P. Schacht, PhD
with
Lisa Underwood
Editors

The Drag Queen Anthology: The Absolutely Fabulous but Flawlessly Customary World of Female Impersonators has been co-published simultaneously as *Journal of Homosexuality*, Volume 46, Numbers 3/4 2004.

HPP

Harrington Park Press®
An Imprint of The Haworth Press, Inc.

New York • London • Victoria (AU)
www.HaworthPress.com

Published by

Harrington Park Press®, 10 Alice Street, Binghamton, NY 13904-1580 USA

Harrington Park Press® is an imprint of The Haworth Press, Inc., 10 Alice Street, Binghamton, NY 13904-1580 USA.

The Drag Queen Anthology: The Absolutely Fabulous but Flawlessly Customary World of Female Impersonators has been co-published simultaneously as *Journal of Homosexuality*, Volume 46, Numbers 3/4 2004.

PUBLISHER'S NOTE: Steven P. Schacht passed away in 2003. This volume has been published posthumously.

Cover image provided by Manstouch.com.

Cover design by Marylouise E. Doyle

Library of Congress Cataloging-in-Publication Data

The drag queen anthology : the absolutely fabulous but flawlessly customary world of female impersonators / Steven P. Schacht, Lisa Underwood, editors.
    p. cm.
    "Co-published simultaneously as Journal of homosexuality, volume 46, numbers 3/4 2003."
    Includes bibliographical references and index.
    ISBN 1-56023-284-6 (hardcover : alk. paper) – ISBN 1-56023-285-4 (softcover : alk. paper)
    1. Transvestism. 2. Transvestites. 3. Female impersonators. I. Schacht, Steven P. II. Underwood, Lisa. III. Journal of homosexuality.
HQ77.D68 2003
305.3–dc22
                                            2003022188

Indexing, Abstracting & Website/Internet Coverage

This section provides you with a list of major indexing & abstracting services. That is to say, each service began covering this periodical during the year noted in the right column. Most Websites which are listed below have indicated that they will either post, disseminate, compile, archive, cite or alert their own Website users with research-based content from this work. (This list is as current as the copyright date of this publication.)

(continued)

(continued)

(continued)

Special Bibliographic Notes related to special journal issues (separates) and indexing/abstracting:

- indexing/abstracting services in this list will also cover material in any "separate" that is co-published simultaneously with Haworth's special thematic journal issue or DocuSerial. Indexing/abstracting usually covers material at the article/chapter level.
- monographic co-editions are intended for either non-subscribers or libraries which intend to purchase a second copy for their circulating collections.
- monographic co-editions are reported to all jobbers/wholesalers/approval plans. The source journal is listed as the "series" to assist the prevention of duplicate purchasing in the same manner utilized for books-in-series.
- to facilitate user/access services all indexing/abstracting services are encouraged to utilize the co-indexing entry note indicated at the bottom of the first page of each article/chapter/contribution.
- this is intended to assist a library user of any reference tool (whether print, electronic, online, or CD-ROM) to locate the monographic version if the library has purchased this version but not a subscription to the source journal.
- individual articles/chapters in any Haworth publication are also available through the Haworth Document Delivery Service (HDDS).

The Drag Queen Anthology: The Absolutely Fabulous but Flawlessly Customary World of Female Impersonators

CONTENTS

ABOUT THE EDITOR

Steven P. Schacht, PhD (1960-2003), served as Professor in the Department of Sociology at Plattsburgh State University of New York. The bulk of his research over the past 10 years was ethnographic in approach, exploring issues of gender identity and gender construction. He also served as co-editor of *Feminism and Men: Reconstructing Gender Relations* with Doris Ewing and *Forging Radical Alliances Across Difference: Coalition Politics for the New Millennium* with Jill Bystydzienski. Dr. Schacht was involved in an ongoing ethnography of drag settings since 1993 and published nearly a dozen articles and book chapters on drag queens and drag kings.

Preface

Judith Lorber

I have been puzzling over what distinguishes drag from other forms of occasional or long-term cross-dressing. Where does drag fit into the larger pantheon of transgendered behavior? What are its core elements?

It is clear from reading the papers in this anthology that drag is not private cross-dressing, nor is it publicly passing for a member of the opposite gender for occupational or other reasons. It does not necessarily involve homosexuality, and it is not a form of transitioning for people planning to change genders permanently.

Drag's core elements are *performance* and *parody*. Drag exaggerates gendered dress and mannerisms with enough little incongruities to show the "otherness" of the drag artist. In the exaggeration lies the parody. Drag is performance because it needs an audience to appreciate the underlying joke. The joke is that a man can be a woman or a woman a man convincingly enough that the "unmasking"–or "unwigging"–at the end of the performance gives a pleasurable *frisson* and evokes laughter, even though the audience has been in on the joke from the beginning. (They have come to see a drag act, after all.)

The laughter is the giveaway. A joke is being played out. What is the joke in drag? Not that someone can pass convincingly as a member of the opposite gender–transgenders and permanent cross-dressers do not

---

Judith Lorber is affiliated with the Graduate School and Brooklyn College, City University of New York (Emerita).

Correspondence may be addressed: 319 East 24 Street, Apt 27E, New York, NY 10010 (E-mail: judith.lorber@verizon.net).

[Haworth co-indexing entry note]: "Preface." Lorber, Judith. Co-published simultaneously in *Journal of Homosexuality* (Harrington Park Press, an imprint of The Haworth Press, Inc.) Vol. 46, No. 3/4, 2004, pp. xxv-xxvi; and: *The Drag Queen Anthology: The Absolutely Fabulous but Flawlessly Customary World of Female Impersonators* (ed: Steven P. Schacht, with Lisa Underwood) Harrington Park Press, an imprint of The Haworth Press, Inc., 2004, pp. xv-xvi. Single or multiple copies of this article are available for a fee from The Haworth Document Delivery Service [1-800-HAWORTH, 9:00 a.m. - 5:00 p.m. (EST). E-mail address: docdelivery@haworthpress.com].

want to be unmasked. The joke in drag is to set up "femininity" or "masculinity" as pure performance, as *exaggerated* gender display–and then to cut them down as pretense after all.

One of the current issues in drag is whether it transgressively undercuts conventional gender categories or bolsters them. Since the whole concept of drag is a parody of otherness, it needs visible contrasts of dress and behavior, as many of the papers point out. In an era of gender fluidity, as Western societies seem to be experiencing, these contrasts are already being undercut by everyday behavior of ordinary women and men who are only passing as postmodern. Does this mean that as time goes on there will be no contrasts to parody, no future for drag? Not as long as there is tabooed gender behavior.

Drag plays with the forbidden–that's part of its appeal. In India, hijras transgress proper gendered and sexual behavior. In Western societies, it is acceptable for a woman to wear a tux at a formal occasion but taboo for a man to wear an evening gown. So there is still a place for drag queens to masquerade in formal makeup, elaborate hairdos, ballgowns, high heels, long gloves and big jewelry–to parody exaggerated femininity.

The papers in this anthology show us that in different cultures, times, and places, as long as there are clear-cut categories to transgress and send up, drag lives.

Acknowledgments

This edited volume has truly been a collaborative project. All submitted papers were sent out to two to four reviewers. Both contributors and outside parties served as reviewers with many of these individuals reviewing several papers. We sincerely thank all of the following people for the obvious thought and time that went into the reviews they provided for this project (and apologize to anyone whom we have neglected to mention): David Keys, Vivian E. Zazzau, Carlton Parks, John Stoltenberg, Doris Ewing, Mary Kirk, Sandeep Bakshi, Nancy Barta-Smith, Bassam Romaya, Moe Meyer, Stephanie Gilmore, Elizabeth Swain, Carol Burbank, Thomas Pointek, Nancy Tuana, S. J. Hopkins, Leila J. Rupp, Carsten Balzer, Tom King, Sky Gibert, Regan Rhyne, Richard Niles, Amanda Lock Swarr, and Jennifer Spruill. Thanks are also due to all the wonderful contributors whom have made this project possible. Finally, special thanks to John De Cecco for ultimately making this anthology on drag queens/female impersonators possible.

The Absolutely Fabulous
but Flawlessly Customary World
of Female Impersonators

Steven P. Schacht, PhD

Plattsburgh State University of New York

Lisa Underwood

Washington State University

SUMMARY. Our editorial introduction to this volume on drag queens highlights what we believe are some of the most prominent and important themes of female impersonation in the past and today. Building on contributors' articles, a substantial body of literature on female impersonators/drag queens and the social construction of gender, and our own extensive ethnographic experiences in a multitude of drag settings, we first suggest that such individuals can be seen as symbolic representatives of the cultural ideals associated with the feminine and women and how they have changed over time. We next argue that the notion of the

---

Steven P. Schacht (1960-2003) served as Associate Professor of Sociology at Plattsburgh State University of New York.

The authors thank Leila J. Rupp for her helpful comments and suggestions on an earlier draft of this paper.

[Haworth co-indexing entry note]: "The Absolutely Fabulous but Flawlessly Customary World of Drag Queens and Female Impersonators." Schacht, Steven P., and Lisa Underwood. Co-published simultaneously in *Journal of Homosexuality* (Harrington Park Press, an imprint of The Haworth Press, Inc.) Vol. 46, No. 3/4, 2004, pp. 1-17; and:*The Drag Queen Anthology: The Absolutely Fabulous but Flawlessly Customary World of Female Impersonators* (ed: Steven P. Schacht, with Lisa Underwood) Harrington Park Press, an imprint of The Haworth Press, Inc., 2004, pp. 1-17. Single or multiple copies of this article are available for a fee from The Haworth Document Delivery Service [1-800-HAWORTH, 9:00 a.m. - 5:00 p.m. (EST). E-mail address: docdelivery@haworthpress.com].

effeminate drag queen is more a myth than a reality with the contextual benefits many performers receive–status and power–being indicative of the hegemony of masculinity in male-dominated societies. We next explore how additional social identities, such as race, class, nation, and religion, often impact drag performances and how others interpret them. We end our introduction by offering a model that delineates what are some of the present transgressive limits and subversive possibilities of female impersonation. *[Article copies available for a fee from The Haworth Document Delivery Service: 1-800-HAWORTH. E-mail address: <docdelivery@ haworthpress.com> Website: <http://www.HaworthPress.com> © 2004 by The Haworth Press, Inc. All rights reserved.]*

KEYWORDS. Drag queen, female impersonator, transgressive, subversive, transgendered, third gender, female impersonation in a historical framework, cross-dressing, effeminate, masculinity, race, class, nation, religion

What the hell, I'm a drag queen. And we don't always deal in reality. You can say we deal in something kind of realer. We deal in dreams. We're as American as apple pie. (From the movie *Stonewall*, 1997).

Wanting to look like a man is as big a joke as wanting to look like a woman. It's just another set of rules to play with. Gender's still the game. (Mathu Anderson quoted from an interview in Chermayeff, David, and Richardson, 1995, p. 62)

Some champion drag queens as fearless urban street fighters at the "battle" of Stonewall (Duberman, 1994; Feinberg, 1998). A few conceptualize drag queens as failed men and symbolic representatives of the stigma associated with all gay men (Newton, 1979; Perkins, 1996; Tewksbury, 1994). Many view drag queens as transgendered provocateurs of dichotomous notions of gender (Brubach, 1999; Butler, 1990; Garber, 1992; Lorber, 1994; Rupp and Taylor, 2003), apt proponents of queer politics (Feinberg, 1996; Muñoz, 1999; Schacht 2000a), and/or as gender-benders, gender-fuckers, and gender-anarchists (Bullough and Bullough, 1993; Fleisher, 1996; Hilbert, 1995; RuPaul, 1995). Yet others argue that drag queens are often gender royalists and aspirants to masculine power (Schacht, 1998, 2000b, 2002a, 2000b) and ultimately misogynists (Hawkes, 1995; Tyler, 1991). Dependent on the observer, drag queens and female impersonators[1] in our society are seen as representing an array of disparate, often contradictory cultural values, limitations and possibilities.

Both in the media and academic circles there has been a proliferation of interest in drag queens in recent years. While the female impersonator is in many ways a very old cultural form with a long recorded history (Ackroyd, 1979; Baker, 1994; Bulliet, 1928; Bullough and Bullough, 1993; Feinberg, 1996; Herdt, 1994; Hirschfeld, 1991; Senelick, 2000; Thompson, 1974), our contemporary society's quite public and sustained preoccupation with the drag queen very much seems to be unprecedented. In the past ten years there have been numerous "drag queen" movies (some quite popular), including *Torch Song Trilogy, Priscilla, Birdcage, Flawless, Too Wong Foo, Midnight in the Garden of Good and Evil, Wigstock,* and *Paris Is Burning*; some drag queens have emerged as celebrated cultural icons exemplified by The Lady Chablis (Chablis, 1996) and RuPaul, self-proclaimed supermodel of the world (RuPaul, 1995); several nonfiction popular press books on drag queens have been published like *Drag Diaries* (Chermayeff, David, and Richardson, 1995), *The Drag Queens of New York* (Fleisher, 1996), *Girlfriend: Men, Women, and Drag* (Brubach, 1999), *Guy to Goddess* (Richardson, 1994) and *Ladies, Please!* (Camerilla, 1994); and drag queens have been the fodder of several important academic texts such as *Gender Trouble* (Butler, 1990), *Vested Interests* (Garber, 1992), and *Paradoxes of Gender* (Lorber, 1994).

This collection on drag queens represents many of the multiple, often contradictory cultural impulses found in female impersonation and looks to celebrate what increasingly can be seen as an institutionalized form of gender itself. In this editorial introduction we highlight what we see are some of the most important themes of female impersonation, as reflected in both the articles included herein and the larger literature upon which they build. In undertaking this task we recognize the inherent biases found in our thematic selection and are in no way suggesting that these are exhaustive ways of exploring drag queens. More so, the framework that follows is based on a mixture of our read of the contributors' articles and related literature combined with our over eight years of ethnographic involvement in nearly two dozen cities throughout North America with a multitude of drag performers (for more detailed discussions of the type and depth of our involvement in all these various settings, please see the teaching piece included in this volume and Schacht, 1998, 2000b, 2002a, 2002b, 2002c).

In editing this volume and writing this introduction, as stated in our original call for papers, drag queens/female impersonators are simply defined as individuals who publicly perform being women in front of an audience that knows they are "men," regardless of how compellingly female–"real"–they might otherwise appear. Thus, this working definition is inclusive of drag queens, female impersonators, and some preoperative transsexuals, but does not include transvestites (largely straight men who wear women's attire often for erotic purposes) or postoperative transsexuals. At the root of this conceptualization is the explicit recognition that the individual publicly performing femininity and *being a woman* is also simultaneously acknowledged to be a man and *not a woman*. An inevitable tension arises when one can successfully be what one is not, nor is ever supposed to be. Drag queens, like their drag king brothers, put a paradoxical spin on the notion of "to be or not to be" by demonstrating that "being" need not be an either/or proposition and that there are actually multiple ways that gender can be performed and experienced. As very much found in each of the articles in this volume, it is exactly these ironies, contradictions, limitations and possibilities that are explored in this introduction.

FEMALE IMPERSONATION IN A HISTORICAL CONTEXT: A SIGN OF THE TIMES

Female impersonation realistically began when clothing started to take on gendered meanings in cultures as a form of cross-dressing behavior. Important cross-dressing figures are found in the mythology of all the earliest known cultures, many of which held festivals and rituals to celebrate such behavior (Ackroyd, 1979; Baker, 1994; Bulliet, 1928; Bullough and Bullough, 1993; Feinberg, 1996; Herdt, 1994; Hirschfeld, 1991; Senelick, 2000; Thompson, 1974). Contemporary examples of institutionalized cross-dressing events are found in Halloween and Mardi Gras celebrations. Females who cross-dressed throughout history often did so to undertake behaviors and pursuits allowed only of men (Thompson, 1974; Wheelwright, 1989). Joan of Arc is one of the most famous examples of a woman who dressed as a man. Historical accounts of male cross-dressers, on the other hand, often portray such individuals as undertaking the behavior for erotic purposes (an early form of the contemporary transvestite) and/or losing status for doing so (Bullough and Bullough, 1993; Thompson, 1974). Some cultures, however, created special third gender categories, such as the "winkte," "bote," and "nadle" found by the European colonizers of North America and the hijras of present day India, wherein cross-dressing individuals were, and still are, widely accepted and, in some cases, held in high regard (Bakshi in this volume; Feinberg, 1996; Herdt, 1994; Thompson, 1995, p. 447).

Because of various prohibitions against women appearing in public places, some cultures dictated that men played the roles of women in theatrical productions (Ackroyd, 1979; Baker, 1994; Bulliet, 1928; Senelick, 2000). For example, in England, men (often boys) playing women's roles became an institutionalized mainstay of the Elizabethan playhouse of the early 1600s, and made possible the emergence of the professional female impersonator. More recently, due to bans on women in the military serving in combat areas, female impersonators in both World War I and II played important roles in military entertainment (Bérubé, 1990). Laurel Halladay's article in this volume, "A Lovely War: Male to Female Cross-Dressing and Canadian Military Entertainment in World War II," illuminates how entertainment units were established to increase the morale of the troops and how representations of femininity changed over the course of the war. While little is definitely known about the sexual orientation of many of these performers, prior to and during World War II, female impersonation was increasingly associated with homosexuality, and most drag troops had been disbanded by the end of the war (Bérubé, 1990).

The contemporary drag queen, often associated with the "gay bar" or the "club," can perhaps trace her origin back to the Molly Houses found in London in the 1700s (Baker, 1994, pp. 106-107) and directly to drag balls held in Europe and then the United States beginning in the late nineteenth century (Chauncey, 1994; Miller, 1995). Nevertheless, most female impersonation during the nineteenth century was undertaken in theatre settings in England and in burlesque and vaudeville shows in the United States (Ackroyd, 1979, p. 112). In fact, Baker (1994, p. 146) reports that "it was during the middle years of the nineteenth century that the word 'drag' was coined to describe the petticoats worn by men playing female parts" (see Senelick, 2000 and Rupp and Taylor, 2003 for other etymological explanations for "drag," "queens," and "drag queen").

Not surprisingly, from the earliest beginnings of the cinema and Hollywood, female impersonations would continue to play an important role in the emergence of these new "theatre" forms (Baker, 1994). While, again, little is know about the actual sexual orientations of female impersonators in the 1800s, self-identified heterosexual male actors have been the parties most likely to play women's roles in the movies and eventually on television. In contrast, the vast majority of female impersonators and drag queens today self-identify and live their daily lives as gay men, express no desire to undertake a transsexual operation, and predominantly perform in clubs and gay bars, often as a way to earn a living and/or to garner situational power (Schacht, 2002a).

As reflected in this brief history of female impersonators and drag queen, the reasons why men undertook playing female roles and the cultural meaning attached to their activities has varied considerably over history. They have both reflected and sustained men's images of what a women is, or should be, and other important cultural values of the given society, and in this sense, are very much symbols of the politics of the times. Carsten Balzer's article in this volume entitled, "The Beauty and the Beast: Reflections About the Socio-Historical and Subcultural Context of Drag Queens and 'Tunten' in Berlin," explores the ways in which what started out as an explicit form of gender protest by the tunten (what could be conceptualized as "radical fairies" in the United States), with the fall of the Berlin wall has been supplemented and, in some ways, contested by the arrival of the professional glamour drag queen. These changes in female impersonation in Berlin reflect much more than just changes in fashion sense; like a barometer of sorts, they also reflect and sustain the very real political changes that have taken place during the past 30 years with Western forms of capitalism ultimately "winning" the Cold War.

Similarly, the articles "Moffies, Artists, and Queens: Race and the Production of South African Gay Male Drag" by Amanda Lock Swarr and "Ad/Dressing the Nation: Drag and Authenticity in Post- Apartheid South Africa" by Jennifer Spruill both demonstrate how the acceptance and the types of drag performances have changed significantly since the end of apartheid in South Africa. Richard Niles' article, "Wigs, Laughter, and Subversion: Charles Busch and the Strategies of Drag Performance," explores the way that impersonating past accepted images of womanhood can be subversive to present images of womanhood. Moreover, all of the pieces in this volume capture a specific historical moment that, behaviorally speaking, may or may not have been possible in the past. What was once seen as a role of necessity to be undertaken only by professional actors has increasingly become a form of artistic expression associated with gay men that enact a multitude of performance styles (Schacht, 2002a). In short, by studying female impersonation much can be learned about the cultural values of the society in which they are found with drag queens very much being a sign of the times!

THE MYTH OF THE EFFEMINATE DRAG QUEEN: FEMALE IMPERSONATION AS VEILED MASCULINITY

As already noted, much of the early research on drag queens paints them as failed men and representatives of the stigma attached to all gay men (Newton, 1979; Perkins, 1996; Tewksbury, 1994). Underlying these observations is a theoretical outlook that a homophobic society so views gay men as effeminate, failed men that many capitulate to these stereotypes with drag queens perhaps being the most visible example. There is a seeming parsimony to viewing the hyper-feminine presentations of self by many female impersonators as indicative of the performers themselves being effeminate. From our extensive involvement in drag communities, however, and as suggested by several of the articles in this volume, we believe the relationship between the gender performed and gender self-identity is often far more complicated.

Masculinity is often conceptualized as a hegemonic way of being that is more about the "thou shalt nots" than the "thou shalls" with men being seen as operating in a very restrictive framework that forcibly prescribes–sometimes violently–what is acceptable behavior (Connell, 2000; Johnson, 1997; Kimmel and Messner, 2000; Schacht, 1996). Hegemonic masculinity is always conceived as inherently superior to the feminine and women, who in turn are framed as men's rightful subordinates. Thus, all "real" men are expected to always guard against appearing or acting in effeminate ways, lest they face the very real risk of also being seen and treated as the rightful subordinates of other men.

On the surface and in many male contexts this understanding of how male dominance ideologically works makes a great deal of sense. Yet such a model for explaining male dominance also suggests there are real limits to hegemonic masculinity, which would seem to be counterintuitive to it being an all powerful, encompassing cultural way of being. Christine Williams (1995) has documented how when men enter into traditionally female professions, such as nursing, elementary school teaching, librarianship, and social work, not only do they often continue to embrace and promote masculine values but they also experience a "glass elevator effect" whereby they are promoted more often and in greater numbers than their female coworkers. In other words, it would appear that men are not nearly as restricted from pursuing what are seen as ultimately female ways–vocations–of being in the world, and that when men do venture into the "effeminate" they still receive a "patriarchal dividend" (Connell, 2000).

Steven J. Hopkins' article, "'Let the Drag Race Begin': The Rewards of Becoming a Queen," demonstrates that there are often significant benefits, such as status and power, to becoming a drag queen, especially for those who are contextually successful. Moreover, as Verta Taylor and Leila J. Rupp report in their article, "Chicks with Dicks, Men in Dresses: What It Means to Be a Drag Queen," although many of the female impersonators they were ethnographically involved with have an effeminate and/or transgendered self-identity, doing drag nevertheless allowed them to become the center of attention, to take an in-your-face attitude, and to say and do things to both female and male audience members, especially self-identified straight men, that few would ever dare to do out of drag or outside the setting. Mary Kirk's article, "Kind of a Drag: Gender, Race, and Ambivalence in *The Birdcage* and *To Wong Foo, Thanks for Everything! Julie Newmar*," aptly highlights how some Hollywood drag queens, through the almost always larger than life lens of the movie director, have become superheroes (a province typically reserved for manly men) who are seemingly superior to not only women–often portrayed as in need of their rescue–but other forms of masculinity.

In our own experiences in drag settings we have consistently found female impersonators to be individuals who are held in the highest regard, often viewed with the utmost respect, with many wielding considerable contextual power over their minions found in the audience (Schacht, 2002a). The power of the drag queen is also illustrated in the first author's second article in this volume, "Beyond the Boundaries of the Classroom: Teaching About Gender and Sexuality at a Drag Show," where he has found that most straight men are quite intimidated by, many outright fearful of, female impersonators when attending a drag show at a gay bar (especially if it is their first time). Insomuch that exercising *power over* others is one of the most vitally important ethos of hegemonic masculinity, and lacking such power or being reluctant to use it is seen as being weak and feminine (Johnson, 1997, p. 85), many drag queens are far more "manly" than their appearance and attire would seem to suggest. Veiled beneath multiple layers of the feminine, female impersonators are frequently able to exercise considerable masculine power in the contexts in which they reside.

Race, class, gender, sexual orientation and other social statuses often have a direct bearing on what of type of masculinity is available to a given man to pursue (Connell, 2000; Kimmel and Messner, 2000). Gay men, especially effeminate appearing ones and drag queens, are largely blocked from pursuing masculinity in traditional settings but many continue to strongly self-identify as men. Like lower and working class men who often become innovators in the pursuit of masculinity (Messerschmidt, 1993), many female impersonators use their alternative drag persona as a means for doing masculinity. Images of the feminine are merely the real estate upon which many drag queens do status and power.

Perhaps more accurately reflecting just how hegemonic masculinity is in our society, we have often heard drag queens in numerous settings state that they "make better women than real women," just as apparently men make "better" nurses, elementary school teachers, and social workers than women. Through a sexist, ultimately misogynist cultural outlook combined with the real power that drag queens often contextually exercise, there would appear to be some "truth" in their assertion. Hegemonic masculinity is apparently so pervasive that in any activity a man might pursue, including those most associated with the feminine and women, he is by default seen as more competent and superior to a woman undertaking the same activity (e.g., women are cooks while men are chefs, women do crafts while men create art) and thus deserved of more status and power for his efforts. The only real restriction here, if it can be actually viewed as such, is that regardless of the gendered vocation/image adopted, the given man must periodically remind his co-workers/audience that he is a man. In this sense, actually being a drag queen in practice and contextual relation to others would often seem to be more about doing and experiencing masculinity than being effeminate.

FEMALE IMPERSONATION IN THE MATRICES OF RACE, CLASS, NATION, AND RELIGION

We live in a time where people increasingly have hyphenated identities, e.g., a middle-class, Catholic, Latino, twenty-something, gay male from Puerto Rico who is a drag queen living and performing in New York City. While most of our social statuses are seen as relatively fixed, how we identify with them and the ways in which they inform and influence our behavior are actually extremely fluid, varying considerably from setting to setting, throughout any given day, and over our lifetime

(West and Fenstermaker, 1995; West and Zimmerman, 1987). This is clearly demonstrated in several of the articles included in this volume.

Once again, the articles "Moffies, Artists, and Queens" by Amanda Lock Swarr and "Ad/Dressing the Nation" by Jennifer Spruill both demonstrate how drag can be used to create definitions of whiteness, blackness, and identities of authenticity in South Africa. More specifically, Swarr explores the ways in which urban drag produces and reifies that whiteness is not only inherently different but superior to Blackness while she finds those doing township drag have created their own unique, largely accepted identities–*moffies, skesana,* and *istabane*–within the sex-gender-sexuality systems of these localized contexts. Spruill shows us how a style of drag that features "traditional African" clothing is used to reify personal identities that embrace both being gay and what is increasingly seen as a more culturally authentic African way of being. In each of these articles the politics of identity are very reflective of the ongoing political changes in a post-apartheid South Africa.

Building on the limited but insightful literature on drag performers of color (Butler, 1993; Garber, 1992; hooks, 1992; Muñoz, 1999), Ragan Rhyne, in her article, "Racializing White Drag," astutely notes how whiteness largely remains an unmarked category of investigation. Then critically reviewing the movies *Polyester* and *Hairspray,* she explores the ways in which Divine's performance of femininity, basically "white trash," contests culturally idealized images of femininity; i.e., white, slender, heterosexual, and bourgeois. Just as the tunten and the drag queens in Carsten Balzer's "The Beauty and the Beast" represent very different political relationships to femininity, drag performances of working class versus upper class femininity strongly suggest very different politics of being and relating to others.

Three of the articles in this volume examine the ways in which religion can inform both drag identities and drag performances. Sandeep Bakshi's article, "A Comparative Analysis of Hijras and Drag Queens: The Subversive Possibilities and Limits of Parading Effeminacy and Negotiating Masculinity," demonstrates the ways in which hijras–female impersonators of sorts–are given cultural sanction to perform at religious ceremonies. "Balancing Acts: Drag Queens, Gender and Faith," by Constance R. Sullivan-Blum, analyzes the innovative and ultimately spiritually based ways in which gay drag queens who maintain Christian identities reconcile these seemingly contradictory states of being. Jeffrey Q. McCune's article, "Transformance: Reading the Gospel in Drag," explores the ironies of traditional gospel being undertaken by female impersonators, and how a "transformance" of space occurs whereby the "club space" also becomes a "church space" of sorts, a location that represents many of the complexities and paradoxes found between the Black church and the Black lgbtq community.

THE TRANSGRESSIVE LIMITS AND SUBVERSIVE POSSIBILITIES OF FEMALE IMPERSONATION

As clearly documented in many, if not all, of the pieces included in this volume, there are without question subversive aspects to many drag queens' performances. Yet, as we have also suggested in this introduction, and also reflected in several of these same articles, drag queens also undertake performances and hold personal identities that are often quite customary and supportive of preexisting inequalities in society. Accordingly, we think it would be helpful to offer a model that delineates what might have been conceived as culturally subversive versus the more benign transgressive or politics as usual.

While female impersonation, and all cross-dressing in general, is perhaps appropriately viewed as a transgendered form of behavior (Bolin, 1994, p. 465), it does not automatically follow that drag performers adopt a transgendered identity (most do not from our experience) or that their performances will actually be subversive to the existing gender order or other forms of inequality. Similarly, camp is seen as a form of gay sensibility and argot of sorts, born of oppression, that enables the drag performer to aesthetically highlight life's ironies in a theatrical, yet exaggerated, manner that is ultimately humorous in intent (Bergman, 1993; Meyer, 1994). As perhaps demonstrated in every article found in this volume, there is a certain transgressive campiness that underlies almost all drag performance, but again, it does not necessarily follow that all camp, or perhaps even most, is subversive in intent. Many camp performers take special delight in making fun of women and the feminine in a manner that reifies both women's subordination and men's superiority in society, and this is obviously anything but subversive (Schacht, 2002a).

Thus, we believe that any meaningful models of what is subversive must take into account an actor's explicit intent, the audiences for whom she/he performs, and dialectic between the two. Quite simply, drag performances that question and make light of the dominant structures of society, such as sexism, homophobia, racism, and classism, and the practices of oppression in society, such as exploitation, marginalization, cultural imperialism, powerlessness, and violence

(Young, 1988), can be framed as subversive in intent. Conversely, drag performances that reify and support these same structures and practices, even those that are transgressive in appearance and campy in attitude, would obviously not be subversive. The make-up of the given audience–largely gay, straight, or often a mixture of the two–also determines if the performance will be seen as subversive or merely transgressive at best. As all the papers in this volume demonstrate, what is and is not subversive is a complex interplay between the performer and audience where the mere intent to entertain can sometimes lead to subversive outcomes, while in other cases, seemingly subversive performances are in fact quite customary. Realistically, most drag performances are a combination of both subversive and status quo politics.

Amanda Lock Swarr's article, "Moffies, Artists, and Queens," clearly outlines the ways in which drag performances in white urban settings in South Africa often support stereotypical images of Blackness and subordination while drag performed by men of colour in the townships often directly subverts and questions these very same images. Mary Kirk, in her analysis of the movies *Too Wong Foo* and *The Birdcage*, finds both of these pictures to be subversive of institutionalized attitudes of heterosexism but reinforcing of others such as sexism and racism. In fact, based on our own extensive experiences in various drag settings, and as reflected in several of the papers in this volume, many drag queens seem quite successful in questioning and challenging notions of heterosexism, especially straight male privilege, but far less subversive when it comes to other oppressive inequalities, such as sexism, racism, and classism.

Perhaps key to understanding the subversive potential of the given drag performer are the identities that she/he brings to the stage. The majority of drag queens we have met over the years strongly self-identify as gay men, so it is perhaps not that surprising that their performances are often more sexist and masculine than subversive in intent when it comes to issues of gender. However, as the Taylor and Rupp article and the Balzer article both insightfully illustrate, when some performers embrace a transgendered identity that is neither explicitly male or female but rather their own complex genders, then the potential for their performances to subvert sexist ideals appears to increase significantly. Similarly, drag kings, often self-identifying as lesbian women, and men and women of color who are drag performers represent yet additional personal social identities with often very different subversive limits and possibilities (Butler, 1993; Halberstam, 1998; hooks, 1992; Muñoz, 1999; Schacht, 2002c; Volcano and Halberstam, 1999).

Like all social behaviors, there is nothing inherently status quo or subversive to drag performances. These outcomes are made real by the intent of the performers in concert with the audiences for which they perform. Contextually, whether subversive or not, most drag performances are often quite customary in that they explicitly play on the attitudes and normative expectations of the audience. Those who are most successful in their performances, to borrow from the argot of many drag settings, are viewed as "absolutely fabulous" and "flawless."

YOU'RE BORN NAKED AND THE REST IS DRAG

As the above RuPaul (1995, p. iii) quote used as a section title suggests, metaphorically speaking, we are all drag queens. We live in a hierarchical society where, dependent on the social statuses we have been seemingly ascribed, we are continuously expected to undertake performances that demonstrate our gender, race, class, sexual orientation, and so forth. Each status often carries with it a gender-race-class uniform of sorts that serves as a prop to further strengthen and make real the performance undertaken. People at the top of various hierarchal structures who most successfully perform their statuses are lavishly rewarded for their efforts and are often touted as "absolutely fabulous" and "flawless" role models for all (e.g., business leaders, politicians, and especially Hollywood actors and actresses). People at the bottom of our stratification system are often forced to perform the exploitive statuses they have typically been cast into at birth and given very few opportunities to undertake higher status performances. Of course, our society does allow for a limited amount of class mobility, further demonstrating the performed basis of status, but the fact remains that the stratification system ultimately makes metaphorical drag queens of us all (Schacht, 2000a).

The drag queen has become an institutionalized and accepted form of gendering in many subcultural contexts and, to a lesser extent, in our larger contemporary society. Drag queens (and their drag king brothers) demonstrate that oppressive status boundaries can be transgressed with relative ease, thus illuminating the ultimately performed basis of all inequalities. For those of us in search of constructing a less oppressive future, this accomplishment is certainly cause for hope and celebration. As argued in this introduction, however, while breaking a societal law can be appropriately viewed as transgressive it does automatically follow that the activity is subversive. In fact, much rule-breaking behavior is actually encouraged by dominant members of society both to further support the oppression of subordinates and to maintain the masters' lofty status (Reiman, 2000).

Truly subversive activities, on the other hand, are those that systematically attempt to overthrow or undermine existing political structures. Other social identities that the performer brings to the stage, such as gay male versus transgendered, combined with the contextual expectations of the audience, seem to play important roles in whether the drag queen is transgressive or subversive. While most drag queens today appear to be more focused on being transgressive, in both image and practice, they nevertheless do suggest many subversive possibilities for performing gender, race, sexuality and "equality drag."

NOTE

1. Some researchers have found it helpful to distinguish between the "female impersonator" and the "drag queen" in terms of whether they are trying to impersonate a specific female icon (e.g., Marilyn Monroe, Janet Jackson) or if they create their own drag personae and along other lines (Bullough and Bullough, 1993, p. 240; Fleisher, 1996, p. 14; Garber, 1992, p. 132). For the purposes of this introduction and in editing this volume, we have largely used these terms interchangeably, as this seems consistent with present usages of these expressions in most drag settings and by the public. Nevertheless, we do recognize that, especially historically speaking, there are contexts where one is preferred over the other and that the term "drag queen" did not come into widespread usage until very recently. Accordingly, wherever appropriate, we have attempted to write this introduction in a manner that reflects the conceptual differences that sometimes exist between the drag queen and female impersonator.

REFERENCES

Ackroyd, P. (1979). *Dressing up: Transvestism and drag: The history of an obsession.* New York: Simon and Schuster.

Baker, R. (1994). *Drag: A history of female impersonation in the performing arts.* New York: New York University Press.

Bergman, D. (Ed.). (1993). *Camp grounds: Style and homosexuality.* Amherst, MA: University of Massachusetts Press.

Bérubé, A. (1990). *Coming out under fire: The history of gay men and women in World War II.* New York: Free Press.

Bolin, A. (1994). Transcending and transgendering: Male-to-female transsexuals, dichotomy and Diversity. In G. Herdt (Ed.), *Third sex, third gender: Beyond sexual dimorphism in culture and history* (pp. 447-485). New York: Zone Books.

Brubach, H. (1998). *Girlfriend: Men, women, and drag.* New York: Random House.

Bulliet, C.L. (1928). *Venus Castina: Famous female impersonators, celestial and human.* New York: Covici, Friede Publishers.

Bullough, V.L. and Bullough, B. (1993). *Cross dressing, sex, and gender.* Philadelphia, PA: University of Pennsylvania Press.

Bullough, B., Bullough, V.L. and Ellias, J. (Eds.). (1997). *Gender blending.* Amherst, New York: Prometheus Books.

Butler, J. (1990). *Gender trouble: Feminism and the subversion of identity.* New York: Routledge.

Butler, J. (1993). Gender is burning: Questions of appropriation and subversion. *Bodies that matter: On the discursive limits of "sex"* (pp. 122-140). New York: Routledge.

Camerilla, M.A. (1994). *Ladies, please!* Toronto, Canada: Exile Editions Limited.

Chablis, L. (1996). *Hiding my candy: The autobiography of the grand empress of Savannah.* New York: Pocket Books.

Chauncey, G. (1994). *Gay New York: Gender, urban culture, and the making of the gay male world, 1890–1940.* New York: Basic Books.

Chermayeff, C., David, J., and Richardson, N. (1995). *Drag diaries.* San Francisco: Chronicle Books.

Connell, R.W. (2000). *The men and the boys.* Berkeley: University of California Press.

Duberman, M. (1994). *Stonewall.* New York: A Plume Book.

Ekins, R. and King, D. (1996). *Blending genders: Social aspects of cross-dressing and sex-changing.* New York: Routledge.

Epstein, J. and Straub, K. (1991). *Body guards: The cultural politics of gender ambiguity.* New York: Routledge.

Feinberg, L. (1996). *Transgender warriors: Making history from Joan of Arc to RuPaul.* Boston: Beacon Press.

Feinberg, L. (1998). *Trans liberation: Beyond pink or blue.* Boston: Beacon Press.

Fleisher, J. (1996). *The drag queens of New York: An illustrated field guide.* New York: Riverhead Books.

Garber, M. (1992). *Vested interests: Cross-dressing & cultural anxiety.* New York: Routledge.

Halberstam, J. (1998). *Female masculinity.* Durham: Duke University Press.

Hawkes, G.L. (1995). Dressing-up-cross-dressing and sexual dissonance. *Journal of Gender Studies*, 4, 261-270.

Herdt, G. (Ed.). (1994). *Third sex, third gender: Beyond sexual dimorphism in culture and history.* New York: Zone Books.

Hilbert, J. (1995). The politics of drag. In C.K. Creekmur and A. Doty (Eds.), *Out in culture: Gay, lesbian, and queer essays on popular culture* (pp. 463-469). Durham: Duke University Press.

Hirschfeld, M. (1991). *Transvestites: The erotic drive to cross-dress.* Translated by Michael A. Lombardi-Nash. Buffalo, NY: Prometheus Books.

hooks, b. (1992). Is Paris burning? *Black looks: Race and representation.* Boston: South End.

Johnson, A.G. (1997). *The gender knot: Unraveling our patriarchal legacy.* Philadelphia: Temple University Press.

Kimmel, M.S. and Messner, M.A. (Eds.). (2000). *Men's lives.* Boston: Allyn and Bacon.

Lorber, J. (1994). *Paradoxes of gender.* New Haven, CT: Yale University Press.

Messerschmidt, J.W. (1993). *Masculinities and crime: Critique and reconceptualization of theory.* Lanham, Maryland: Rowman & Littlefield.

Meyer, Moe. (1994). *Politics and poetics of camp.* New York: Routledge.

Miller, N. (1995). *Out of the past: Gays and lesbian history from 1868 to the present.* New York: Vintage Books.

Muñoz, J.E. (1999). *Disindentifications: Queers of color and the performance of politics.* Minneapolis: University of Minnesota Press.

Newton, E. (1979). *Mother camp: Female impersonators in America.* Chicago, IL: The University Chicago Press.

Perkins, R. (1996). The "Drag Queen Scene": Transsexuals in Kings Cross. In R. Ekins an D. Kings (Eds.), *Blending genders: Social aspects of cross-dressing and sex-changing* (pp. 53-62). New York: Routledge.

Reiman, J.H. (2000). *The rich get richer and the poor get prison: Ideology, class, and criminal justice* (6th Edition). Boston: Allyn and Bacon.

Richardson, B. (1994). *Guy to goddess: An intimate look at drag queens.* Vancouver, Canada: Whitecap Books.

RuPaul. (1995). *Letting it all hang out: An autobiography.* New York: Hyperion.

Rupp, L.J. and Taylor, V. (2003). *Drag queens at the 801 Cabaret.* Chicago: University of Chicago Press.

Schacht, S.P. (1996). Misogyny on and off the "pitch": The gendered world of male rugby players. *Gender & Society,* 10, 50-565.

Schacht, S.P. (1998). The multiple genders of the court: Issues of identity and performance in a drag setting. In S.P. Schacht and D.W. Ewing (Eds.), *Feminism and men: Reconstructing gender relations* (pp. 202-224). New York, NY: New York University Press.

Schacht, S.P. (2000b). Paris is burning: How society's stratification systems make drag queens of us all. *Race, Gender & Class,* 7, 147-166.

Schacht, S.P. (2000a). Gay female impersonators and the masculine construction of other. In P. Nardi (Ed.), *Gay masculinities* (pp. 247-268). Newbury Park, CA: Sage.

Schacht, S.P. (2002a). Four renditions of doing female drag: Feminine appearing conceptual variations of a masculine theme. In P. Gagné and R. Tewksbury (Eds.), "Gendered sexualities" in the series on *Advances in gender research* (pp. 157-180). Boston: Elsevier Science.

Schacht, S.P. (2002b). Turnabout: Gay drag queens and the masculine embodiment of the feminine. In N. Tuana et al. (Eds.), *Revealing male bodies* (pp. 155-177). Bloomington: Indiana University Press.

Schacht, S.P. (2002c). Lesbian drag kings and the feminine embodiment of the masculine. *Journal of Homosexuality,* 43(3/4).

Senelick, L. (2000). *The changing room: Sex, drag and theatre.* London: Routledge.

Tewksbury, R. (1994). Gender construction and the female impersonator: The process of transforming "he" to "she." *Deviant Behavior: An Interdisciplinary Journal,* 15, 27-43.

Thompson, C.J.S. (1974). *Mysteries of sex: Women who posed as men and men who impersonated women.* New York: Causeway Books.

Thompson, M. (1995). Children of paradise: A brief history of queens. In C.K. Creekmur and A. Doty (Eds.), *Out in culture: Gay, lesbian, and queer essays on popular culture* (pp. 447-462). Durham: Duke University Press.

Tyler, C. (1991). Boys will be girls: The politics of gay drag. In D. Fuss (Ed.), *Inside/out: Lesbian theories, gay theories* (pp. 32-70). New York: Routledge.

Volcano, D.L. and Halberstam, J.J. (1999). *The drag king book.* London: The Serpents Tail.

West, C. and Fenstermaker, S. (1995). Doing difference. *Gender & Society*, 9, 8-37.

West, C. and Zimmerman, D.H. (1987). Doing gender. *Gender & Society*, 1, 125-161.

Wheelwright, J. (1989). *Amazons and military maids: Women who dressed as men in pursuit of life, liberty and happiness.* London: Pandora.

Williams, C.L. (1995). *Still a man's world: Men who do "women's work."* Berkeley: University of California Press.

Young, I. (1988). The five faces of oppression. *The Philosophical Forum*, 19, 270-290.

A Lovely War:
Male to Female Cross-Dressing
and Canadian Military Entertainment
in World War II

Laurel Halladay, MA

University of Calgary

SUMMARY. This article explores the Canadian military entertainment units during World War II (WWII), specifically those formed by the Navy, Army and Air Force from talent found amongst their own personnel. These entertainment units toured extensively in Canada, the United Kingdom and Europe with the goal of increasing the morale of combat troops while encouraging the enlistment of Canada's domestic populations in the war effort generally and the armed forces specifically. By focusing on male to female cross-dressing in the performances of these entertainment units and their pre-WWII antecedents, it will become clear that the nature and importance of the representation of femininity within the virtually all-male milieu that existed near the battlefront changed

Laurel Halladay is a PhD candidate, Department of History, and a research associate, Center for Military and Strategic Studies, University of Calgary.

Correspondence may be addressed: Department of History, University of Calgary, 2500 University Dr. N.W., Calgary, AB T2N 1N4 Canada (E-mail: lmhallad@ucalgary.com).

[Haworth co-indexing entry note]: "A Lovely War: Male to Female Cross-Dressing and Canadian Military Entertainment in World War II." Halladay, Laurel. Co-published simultaneously in *Journal of Homosexuality* (Harrington Park Press, an imprint of The Haworth Press, Inc.) Vol. 46, No. 3/4, 2004, pp. 19-34; and: *The Drag Queen Anthology: The Absolutely Fabulous but Flawlessly Customary World of Female Impersonators* (ed: Steven P. Schacht, with Lisa Underwood) Harrington Park Press, an imprint of The Haworth Press, Inc., 2004, pp. 19-34. Single or multiple copies of this article are available for a fee from The Haworth Document Delivery Service [1-800-HAWORTH, 9:00 a.m. - 5:00 p.m. (EST). E-mail address: docdelivery@haworthpress.com].

over time in response to the demands of the audiences. Until the second half of WWII, soldier audiences were generally unwilling to form any ideological links between cross-dressing and homosexuality. Female impersonators were the key cast members in troop shows during the Great War, but eventually fell out of favor in the last years of WWII after women were recruited in large numbers into the Canadian military and thus its entertainment infrastructure. With women then on the military stage, men who persisted in female impersonation were decreasingly popular with audiences, ultimately under growing suspicion of being homosexuals and gradually removed from the productions. *[Article copies available for a fee from The Haworth Document Delivery Service: 1-800-HAWORTH. E-mail address: <docdelivery@haworthpress.com> Website: <http://www.HaworthPress.com> © 2004 by The Haworth Press, Inc. All rights reserved.]*

KEYWORDS. Canada, First World War, Second World War, entertainment, female impersonation, homosexuality, gender

THE NECESSITY OF FEMALE IMPERSONATION PRIOR TO WORLD WAR II[1]

Restricted access to female players within the garrison community and the long international tradition of employing men in feminine stage roles meant female impersonators of military background first appeared on the garrison stage over two hundred years prior to Canadian Confederation (Rewa, 1989). As both were employed as a means to assert civil stability, the parallel between garrison theatre and the manifestation of military theatrical amusements in the twentieth century is clear, though in later years these similarly developed entertainments strove to engineer the psychological equilibrium of populations affected by armed conflict rather than culture *per se*. Variety type entertainment for Canadian troops, thus already part of a long tradition, began during World War I with the Canadian Concert Parties, which were developed in response to the reluctance of the British Army to pay for the recreation of the Canadian Expeditionary Force (CEF). While staged troop entertainments were informally initiated by a number of talented infantrymen at the battalion or brigade level stationed in France prior to the Battle of the Somme in the summer of 1916, their success in raising morale meant that they were almost immediately officially assisted in the development of touring schedules, gathering supplies and arranging leave when necessary by Canadian military officials.

By far the most famous unit touring in France at this time was the Dumbells. Created in August of 1917, the Dumbells were a troupe of 16 men, the key personnel being members of the 3rd Division (O'Neill, 1983). As the popularity of the troupe increased, the players were released from other duties to be able to do typically twice daily shows of two and a half hours each in the rest areas behind the front but were always on call for service in the line. Having in more recent years been given long overdue credit for being the earliest form of a Canadian national theatre, the Dumbells and similar groups became a prototype for entertainment during the Second World War and set the standard for those troupes established in the first part of that conflict.

A stage rendition of anything outside the white/male/heterosexual normative was considered comedy by Canadian soldiers in WWI. The Dumbells act included characters in blackface and from historical events, mocked-up military officials and of course effeminate "campy" female impersonators (O'Neill, 1983). Both familiar with conditions at the front lines and the types of entertainment war-weary soldiers appreciated most, the Dumbells performed everything from the *H.M.S. Pinafore* to sketch comedy centered on the military life. Musical numbers included American and British hit songs like "Those Wild Wild Women Are Making a Wild Man of Me," and "divisions and battalions took great pride in these performers, particularly their female impersonators" (O'Neill, 1989, p. 60). While a small number of Canadian nurses were posted in battle zones on the continent, for better or worse, female impersonators became the primary representation of Canadian womanhood in the area and thus their presence allowed the CEF an opportunity, in the midst of chaos, to recreate a community comprised of both sexes.

From photographs and written accounts generated during the period, there seems to have been two types or styles of male to female cross-dressing in WWI military entertainment troupes. For versions of well-known British plays, for example, the drag was serious in tone, and flamboyant gestures, the use of obviously slapdash costumes, a lack of makeup, and apparent body hair were replaced by elaborate costumes and feminine preparation from head to toe. In such productions, performers conducted themselves demurely, took up little stage space and amplified what at the time could be said to be the most appealing "womanly" characteristics of the female persona. In more farcical pieces, female impersonators appropriately were very vocal, cried loudly and often, found every possible excuse to raise their skirts above their heads, and ran about the stage in a flustered pantomime of the hysterical female, the disguise in this case failing because it was obviously supposed to. The two styles, dramatic and comedic, were equally effective in raising a positive response from audience members, who, in addition to just being pleased with the availability of entertainment, had common conceptions of what constituted both the positive and negative features of womanhood. Cross-dressing of both types satisfied expectations both for the entire range of observable aspects of womanly behavior and of variety entertainment.

Men like Ross Hamilton, who was so appealing as Marjorie with his brunette hair and high-pitched voice that, apocryphally, a British officer had sent flowers and proposed marriage (Clark, 1997, p. 9), epitomized the ability to perform both versions of the Canadian WWI drag style. Frothy in frills and lace with painted-on cupid's bow lips, Hamilton fell just short of convincing the audience he was truly a woman and thus, as Clark has argued, became a physical representation of the sentiment Canadian soldiers held of being tricked, duped into participating in a war which promised a low probability of personal survival and contained only a faint memory of patriotic motivation. Marjorie adopted "the persona of the flower of Canadian womanhood the soldiers had been told they were going to war to preserve. She was 'poor Belgium' before the fiendish Hun had debased her" (p. 9). Reflecting the older theatrical traditions and contemporary popularity of the burlesque style, WWI entertainment near the front both respectfully imitated and mocked the object of its attention. As a component in the advent of irony that Eksteins (1989) and Fussell (1975) explore, the subtext here was that the whole war was a farce, the point of it all not quite a successful illusion, much like the rendition of femaleness presented by the impersonators. For most Canadian participants in the Great War, enlistment was an initiation into the only highly organized bureaucracy they had experienced in their lives—reversals and parodies on the military stage promised the possibility of escaping the rigid confines of conduct within that institution. Further, camaraderie could actually be said to have been strengthened by the community's acknowledgment that both the audience and the performers were dumbells for having let themselves be swayed by the ambiguously constructed calls to Empire that had landed them in a situation increasingly absent of any redeeming features and apparently without end.

In the happily despondent, head-shaking way it pointed out the in-joke of Canadian involvement in a European war, the historical record shows that female impersonators' mimicry in this period generated little or no condemnation from audience members who might be thought to have inflexible ideas about what constituted appropriate behavior for front line soldiers. One Canadian soldier spoke for many more when he said, "I think I never enjoyed anything more . . . the costumes of the men, especially those who took the part of ladies, were good and well made. . . . But the audience, composed of hundreds of strong, keen young men who had endured hard things. . . . Could any performer ask for a more sympathetic hearing?" (Scott in O'Neill, 1989, p. 59). Perhaps contrary to more modern expectations, drag performers were not the least bit threatening to the taken-for-granted heterosexual practices of their comrades and both contributed to and enjoyed the homosociability of the battlefield. This lack of tension between performers and audience, within the context of what historian Paul Fussell has called a protective "sublimated (i.e., 'chaste') form of temporary homosexuality" (1975, p. 272) among the "soldier boys" of WWII, had everything to do with the unique conditions of wartime.

Most obviously, if femininity is a quality that has meaning only in a context where comparisons are possible, the physical absence of a sustained female presence meant male audience members were relying on what invariably became aggrandized memories and conceptions of womanhood. In the way that distance, separation and time have of exaggerating human characteristics in our memories, cross-dressers merely reflected that aggrandizement on stage–both performers and audience members were on the same page in their thinking about women. Secondly, men engaging in combat were in the process of reaching the pinnacle of post-Victorian period definitions of masculinity by participating in an event that was, on one hand, defensive of Canadian and British values and family life, and on the other hand, adventurous and daring. Mike O'Brien has suggested that, "warfare has been seen as a quintessentially masculine activity. The quality of aggressiveness, bravery and loyalty, which 'make' a soldier, seem in many ways to define the very category of the 'masculine'" (1998, p. 115) and this was certainly the case in the first two decades of the century. Offstage as soldiers, impersonators were representative of this ideal masculine character and participated in the enterprise of war much the same as their audiences did. No doubt this was kept in mind by the spectators, who were then aware that the performers were actually on double duty a great deal of the time, and were thus less likely to express displeasure with this extra effort. Onstage, cross-dressers embodied the abnegation of this conception of the male gender, if only for a short time. Whether wrapped in the latest fashions or barely covered by makeshift burlap skirts, drag performers were certainly not the stuff of soldiers and thus were temporarily viewed as being unsuitable for combat duties, their womanly characteristics in effect discharging them from service. In this way, any negative audience interpretations stemming from the CEF-wide hysteria over shirkers and malingering was averted. Lastly, impersonators reinforced the maleness of the military and fostered the comradeship inherent in the all-male enterprise of war by substituting for real women whose presence would compromise the essential character and integrity of such a masculine endeavor. So while female impersonators were the very antithesis of masculinity while performing (Clark, 1997, p. 9), they were excused from any adverse repercussions this might have for them within this environment. They were soldiers and artists and garnered respect for both sets of duties–the only complaint audiences had was that this kind of entertainment was not available often enough.

Perhaps not surprisingly then, the available documents on military entertainment in this era are notably free of tensions arising from sexual orientation issues. Given the concern that military officials would develop in later years toward the "problem" of homosexuality, the absence of any speculation or finger-pointing in this era is remarkable and in some ways is evidence both of the unique relationship female impersonators had with their audiences and perhaps the existence of a more flexible cultural environment at that particular time and place, one created by the absolute necessity of group cohesion for survival. In any case, the beneficial impact of the Dumbells on the morale of Canadian troops was not forgotten and the connection between formally organized entertainment and morale had definitely been noted by the Canadian military.

CROSS-DRESSING ON THE MILITARY STAGE IN WWII

The basic structure of the Canadian concert party survived a period of military inactivity during the inter-war years and was quickly revived by members of the 1st Canadian Army in the spring of 1942. Repelled from the coast of France in 1940 and well aware of the terrible fate their comrades had met at Hong Kong, the quarter million Canadian troops based in the United Kingdom in the months preceding the invasion of Sicily desperately needed morale raising activities to improve what the Canadian Press had identified as *en masse* poor mental health (Morton, 1992, p. 209-210).[2] "Boredom, separation from families, inactivity and indefinite waiting" certainly increased the incidence of nervous disorders in this period (Copp and McAndrew, 1990, pp. 32-33). Four Canadian Concert Parties in the Army were formed on soldier initiative in England during this period and while left without official backing and with responsibility for finding their own equipment and transportation, represented an early, successful–though not entirely adequate–distraction for such a large number of personnel. Of these four shows, only the "Tin Hats" and the "Kit Bags" included drag performances. By the summer of 1942, the Canadian Army, Navy and Air Force established more formal entertainment plans and the renegade Concert Parties were reined in and subjected to orders from the highest levels of the Department of National Defense, a change in administration that coincided with the beginning of the end for female impersonation in the Canadian forces.

The Canadian Army Show and its several attached units, making up the greatest number of shows and employing the largest group of personnel in the Department of National Defense entertainment infrastructure, used impersonators most often of the three services. The satirical take on military and home front themes in these shows carried over into a satirization of the female gender, as well as slightly more respectful salutes to the effort put forward by women in their war work. The "Tin Hats" troupe had perhaps the most famous drag performers amongst its personnel, with Privates Johnny Heawood and Bill Dunstan as "Trilby" and "Trixie." These "girls," in drag for the entire show and all publicity shots (the normal practice after about 1944 was to employ the by-then rare female impersonator in one sketch for a short period of stage time but in other costumes and characterizations for the remainder of the performance), did songs like "Heaven Will Protect an Honest Girl" and "Ma, He's Makin' Eyes at Me" in over the top numbers that were musical, comedic and sometimes elegantly refined. Great effort went into the impersonators' costumes, wigs and makeup in an attempt to strengthen their impact in the show–even the hard to come by nylons were secured for these performers. Key to the role of impersonators and their complex relationship to the audience was the fact that they were, at that time, referred to as "feminine impersonators," and the concept of what was feminine had certainly changed since WWI. Contrasted with the frivolous Flapper girl of the inter-war period, the Second World War was the age of both the big studio movie star and the factory-working girl next door, and drag performers mastered both personas with surprising fluency. Magnifying feminine characteristics to the necessary point of caricature by cultivating huge hair, big eyes, massive breasts and incredibly high falsetto voices, female impersonators in this era generally carried themselves on stage with grace and poise. In short, the hysterical female of WWI was replaced by female characters that were portrayed as sexual prey and/or naive to the ways of the world they had been thrust into by war. However, military drag performers seldom imitated well-known women personalities but almost always impersonated average appearing young or middle-aged women with just a touch of glamour, as if they were about to be discovered by a Hollywood scout.

In contrast with the agenda of drag in the First World War to blatantly point out that troops had found themselves in a situation that was not what they had been led to believe, the undercurrent of drag performances in WWII seems to have mainly been a response to what was perceived as the rapid and violent alteration of gender roles in Canadian society. Soldiers were well aware and generally uneasy about the fact that while they were taking on the Germans, their wives, girlfriends, mothers and sisters were very ably taking on traditional male occupations and roles back at home. In a very real sense, female impersonators capitalized on this sea change and presented imitations of the female gender that were acceptable and concurrent with the standard gender stereotypes (Moore, 1994, p. 2)[3] and, in the process, gave voice to the hostility and anxiety felt by many men when faced with these so-called drastic changes in the standard gender pattern. For example, female characters whose actions on stage revealed them to be operating within permissible, traditional boundaries of womanhood were treated with some esteem while those who appeared to be enjoying newfound power were ridiculed and punished within the plot of the production. These kinds of cross-dressing performances were not gender-bending as such but gender-reinforcing because they presented stereotypes that magnified the penumbral paradigm of the audience and thus were of great comfort to soldiers.

FEMALE IMPERSONATION AND THE "TAINT" OF HOMOSEXUALITY

While undoubtedly there were homosexuals in the Canadian military and certainly within its entertainment units, direct references to the topic do not exist in the war diaries of these troupes. No mention is made of homosexuality nor to speculation on the sexual orientation of the shows' cast members, despite the frequent presence of other comments that basically amount to character assassination on other counts throughout all the shows' war files. The Canadian military seems to have been relatively more relaxed on this issue than the Americans who, as early as 1940, had policy in place that prevented homosexuals from serving in the military on the grounds that "their presence impairs the morale and discipline of the army and that homosexuality is a manifestation of a severe personality defect." In addition, it was supposed that homosexuals, if allowed to attain certain rank, would expose "normal" men to illicit seduction (Williams and Weinberg, 1971, pp. 24-25). Allan Bérubé's work on homosexuals in the WWII American military suggests that GI shows provided a "gay refuge," a climate in which "gay male GIs . . . could let their hair down to entertain their fellows." Of course, American officials found ways, mainly through the media, to construct a masculine, combative mystic for drag performers and, acknowledging the benefits to morale these characters created, managed to establish the means "to use drag (entertainments) for the duration while walking a fine line between its homosexual and heterosexual meanings" (Bérubé, 1990, p. 68). Regardless of this official interference and up until the end of the war, female impersonators remained very popular components of American military shows. One Australian male, part of the *50-50 Show* that teamed Australian military personnel with American soldiers to entertain the troops, commented that, "all the blokes loved them (the impersonators), especially the Americans . . . that was all good fun" (Heylen, 1989, p. 14).

Like all American initiatives of the period, this supervisory posture affected the other Allied militaries but for the purposes of this paper, whether or not particular female impersonators were homosexual is less important than the social construction of that possibility and how that affected their work. In the Canadian case, any conclusions concerning the actual practice of homosexual lifestyles by drag performers in entertainment units are purely speculative but, regardless, will have to be seen through the lens of the influential manpower issue that arose during World War II. Wishing to avoid a conscription crisis in the face of decreasing enlistment and high casualties (like that which occurred in the Great War), military officials were constantly aware and in some cases perhaps too eager to retain the services of those already enlisted. In other words, it appears that the Canadian military did not perceive itself as having the luxury of discharging those personnel suspected of practicing alternative sexual practices. Within this context, two possible avenues present themselves for further research. First, Canadian entertainment troupes did come in contact with homosexuals external to the group itself via their entry into the show business arena. While the

Americans discharged enlistees on the basis of fraternizing with known homosexuals, this does not seem to have been a cause for concern on the Canadian side. The Navy Show, for example, had a close association with Noel Coward and the married couple Lynn Fontanne and Alfred Lunt during their tour in the U.K. and Europe. While rumor had it that these people were practicing homosexuals, they were admired by cast members of "Meet the Navy" for their artistic reputation and the group's records show no hesitation in maintaining these creative alliances and in fact some pride in being able to publicly associate itself with such famous professionals.[4]

Secondly, especially toward the end of the war, several Canadian male entertainers were discharged for "psychological" reasons. While homosexuals, or those suspected of participating in homosexual acts, were deemed to have psychopathic personalities (Copp and McAndrew, 1990, p. 8) and thus were thought unfit for service, it is not clear whether some of the notable psychiatric discharges of male entertainers late in the war included homosexuals that had been "discovered," or if most simply involved cases of personnel that had broken down after years of exhausting rehearsal and performance far from family support. While the Americans immediately delved into sexual orientation issues as the source of any psychological problem, Canadian diagnoses seem to have been predisposed to exploring drug and alcohol abuse as the root cause of mental breakdown and thus the likelihood of text-based references to homosexuality is diminished. Definitive conclusions on homosexuality in the WWII Canadian military will have to await a national study that parallels Berube's.

There are surprisingly few incidences where female impersonators expressed some dissatisfaction with their role within the troupe. Those that did occur follow the general pattern of that which transpired in the RCAF "Swing Time" unit in the spring of 1944. Having been on tour in Canada for an extended period of time, "the unit (had) been living in one another's pockets for some time . . . it (was) getting a bit ragged." The morale of the group hit bottom while in Manitoba when most of the cast asked to be sent back to Ottawa and given other duties in a sort of troupe mutiny. Leading Aircraftman Bestall, the female impersonator in the unit, was one such person. Plagued by extremely poor dental health, a bad case of trench mouth and repeatedly failing to attend rehearsal, Bestall then "refused to do any more Women impersonation parts." While his refusal to carry out his assigned role may have had more to do with the less positive responses of audiences to impersonators, it backfired due to the ease with which other members of the group could pick up the drag duties. The officer in charge of the unit took over the drag roles while Bestall had a number of teeth extracted and in the process proved that "nobody is indispensable."[5]

While it is difficult in many cases to presume the reasons behind disciplinary troubles from the Department of National Defense (DND) archives for the period, those of female impersonators might be consequences of the cultural compulsion to project a masculine image offstage, a motivation that resulted in the most common problems of drinking and fighting, for example. While concrete evidence is lacking, it seems logical to surmise that the increased persecution of suspected homosexuals by Allied military psychiatric professionals created an uncomfortable environment for drag performers. Cross-dressing performers clearly had to toe the respectability line or risk being assigned to more dangerous and/or boring war work.

IN THE ARMY NOW:
FEMALE PERSONNEL AND THE END OF MILITARY DRAG

Not coincidentally, at the same time as Canadian troop entertainments were experiencing a period of growth due to the administrative consolidation of these units within DND command, the use of female impersonators largely fell out of favor after women were recruited into the military in an effort to free up men for service closer to or on the front. So while the manpower issue possibly protected homosexuals from dishonorable discharge from the military, it also eventually meant that all men in entertainment units were less likely to find themselves doing drag. Few Canadian military groups continued to rely on impersonators once women began to volunteer for the services,[6] though this change was not without its problems and concerns.

Virtually as soon as women began to enlist, a "moral panic" erupted that was, at its base, a result of the assumption that women involved in the military had somehow forfeited their morals by becoming less feminine and increasingly sexual (Pierson, 1986). Pierson concludes that while fundamental changes in gender roles were not visible (especially over the long term), "the great fear was that the war, by necessitating the mobilization of women on an unprecedented scale, might undermine the established male-dominant sex/gender system" (p. 20). With the appearance of women on the military stage, officials worried that sexual tension between female cast members and the audience would actually decrease morale, especially that of troops overseas who were presumably homesick and lonesome for their female intimates. This "moral panic" about female personnel in a way distracted officials from a similar panic concerning possible homosexuality among male enlistees. In any case, by way of their costumes and roles, women were employed rather blatantly for the then-allowable sexual titillation, despite claims to the opposite,[7] which may have increased sexual frustration for, but was a hit with, military audiences.

Female impersonation thus came to be associated with old-fashioned, amateur theatre while impatient Canadian soldiers grew to increasingly demand professional acts with real women in the feminine roles. When they did not receive them, unruly Canadian soldier audiences sometimes replaced the wolf whistles and catcalls they had given the impersonators in the past with booing and heckling. The attitude of the North Shore New Brunswick regiment, for example, was summed up by the "Tin Hats" war diarist: "from experience with nearly every formation in the Canadian Army, it should be recorded that this regiment provides the most inattentive and unmannerly audience with which we have been in contact."[8] Growing disillusionment with the female impersonator act coupled with poor morale, the availability of liquor and a performance on payday could make for a disorderly crowd.

WHEN THE CURTAIN FELL: CROSS-DRESSERS AFTER THE WAR

Needless to say, Canadian military entertainment units were the training ground for several female impersonators and drag performers who accumulated a great deal of experience and skill in developing stage productions during WWII. Like most other performers, impersonators made the transition from military to civilian life as soon as possible. They returned to their families (or began them), joined the regular work force and made use of the financial and educational assistance offered to veterans. Many employed the artistic skills they had gathered and the industry contacts they made during the war in the entertainment field in Canada, the United Kingdom and the United States. While several joined the Canadian Broadcasting Corporation in a variety of roles both in the radio and television mediums, many became key figures in local theatre, giving lessons and organizing community performances. Post-war expansion in the theatrical arts was propelled by the presence of these highly trained performers and allowed many to continue on in their show business careers, though work was limited for the female impersonation was decreasing demand often readily met by American and British talent. Although a select Canadian few went on to successful careers in drag, including Loren Lorenz who was a seasoned performer from the Royal Canadian Air Force revues and became the "first drag stripper in England" before taking what would become his long-running act to the Merchant Navy in 1950 (Senelick, 2000, p. 367), they were overwhelmed by post-war soldier shows like the British *Soldiers in Skirts, The Army Wore Skirts,* and *This Was the Army,* and the American *We Were in the Forces, Forces Showboat* and *Forces in Petticoats.* More often, big name performers like Milton Berle, Mickey Rooney and Bob Hope, those only tangentially associated with military personnel during the war, won what cross-dressing roles there were in the film and on stage, leaving veterans to find other avenues of performance and to pursue different career paths.

Cross-dressing in the Canadian military during WWII is important for what it reveals in terms of group dynamics, involving in this case a group that relied on masculine cohesion but demanded from their entertainment some appropriate theatrical representation of femininity, offered by female impersonators or eventually women themselves, as a salve to ease confusion, delusion and revulsion over the changes in gender roles wrought by war. It shows a pattern of communication between drag performers/impersonators and their audiences that speaks to a comradeship among personnel with radically divergent roles which made the Canadians such an efficient fighting force. This comradeship, perceived to be necessary for group survival, was devoid of any documentary evidence of bitterness or suspicion until the specter of homosexuality arose with the arrival of women in entertainment units and the closing of the relational gap. Up to that time, the dialogue between entertainer and audience reveals a sensitivity among all performers toward the needs of their audiences that resulted in, by all accounts, an extremely successful and useful social representation of femininity. Under the official approval of the military hierarchy and since well before the First World War, Canadian military cross-dressers were able to adapt their portrayals of femininity to suit the changing social needs of their audiences.

Many of the numerous histories of cross-dressing refer to Canadian military personnel as leaders in the field. The Dumbells especially are pointed to as the first effective translation of the popularity of minstrel, vaudeville and burlesque theatre forms to military audiences. To a great extent, the public performances of drag artists in the twentieth century found their primary inspiration from Canadian military units during

WWI and from there the style gained further refinement in WWII before being relegated almost exclusively to less mainstream communities. While Canadian female impersonators overall did not fair well in that field in the post-World War II cultural climate, it was not due to a lack of skill or show business connections. Rather it had more to do with changing expectations and assumptions on the part of audiences who increasingly associated cross-dressing with deviant sexual behavior and, in any case, no longer required either the commiseration that gender farce supplied or the onstage reinforcement of comfortable gender stereotypes. These messages were outdated and redundant after World War II and thus the Department of National Defense's eventual disapproval of drag performances ended a long run of successful and useful work increasing the morale of civilian and military wartime audiences.

NOTES

1. In order to clarify the methodology used in this paper, it should be noted that the World War I information relayed here is largely based on the small amount of secondary literature available. Although I have examined the primary documents relevant to this topic for the Great War period, they are not used directly in this paper. The discussion of World War II, however, is based on archival research, as no secondary sources exist on this field except my own early work (see Halladay, 2000, and Halladay, 2001). My conclusions for the WWII period thus result from watching hours of film footage, analyzing photographs, completing a preliminary round of oral interviews with non-impersonating entertainers of the period and exploring in great detail the documents kept by the groups themselves for the Department of National Defense. Lastly, there are some parameters in this study. Neglected in this examination of military cross-dressing is any reference to performances that occurred in Prisoner of War camps, either in WWI or II. Allied POW camps, largely supplied with material by the Young Men's Christian Association (YMCA), were heavily involved in theatrical productions and relied quite naturally on female impersonators in their shows.

2. For an examination of the situation on the home front during the same period, see R.H. Roy (1986).

3. F. Michael Moore (1994) states that "rather than blurring gender distinctions . . . performers concentrate on sharply delineated portrayals of the opposite sex in order to capture the essence of an 'ideal' man–or 'woman.'"

4. Letter from Noel Coward of London on March 3, 1945 to A/Lt. Cmdr. Stuart Robertson, SB Royal Canadian Naval Volunteer Reserves, CO Navy Show (National Archives of Canada, RG 24, Volume 3597, File 1210-11, Navy Show Promotion and Advertisement, Royal Canadian Navy).

5. F/O C.E.T. Ashdown, OC "Swing Time" unit, had earlier recommended a promotion for Bestall, which was revoked following this incident. Letter from Ashdown to S/L Gilchrist, RCAF Director of Music and Entertainment, at Air Force Headquarters on May 23, 1944 (National Archives of Canada, RG 24, Volume 3290, File HQ 250-14-8, volume 1, "Swing Time" Entertainment Unit, Royal Canadian Air Force).

6. In July 1941, the Royal Canadian Air Force admitted women into the RCAF Women's Division (RCAFWD) followed by the development of the Canadian Women's Army Corps (CWAC) in August of the same year. The Royal Canadian Navy was relatively late in accepting volunteers to the Women's Royal Canadian Naval Service (WRCNS or Wrens) in July of 1942. Nearly 50,000 women enlisted in the Canadian military and over 4,000 served overseas (Canadian War Museum publication, Catalogue No. NM 92-103/1987, National Museums of Canada, 1987, pg. 17). Indeed, not many changes to scripts were needed as the majority were written for both sexes.

7. There was a great deal of pressure from military officials not to allow women to perform in suggestive sketches and thus reinforce the commonly held idea that servicewomen lacked moral decorum (and as a consequence reduce recruitment) but in reality the shows with women always contained sketches that were essentially fashion shows and/or beauty pageants and had them presented to audiences purely for the crowd's visual pleasure. Of course, if men in drag were substituted for the real women in these sketches, it was classed as comedy and well within the realm of show material possibilities.

8. "Tin Hats" War Diary of December 29, 1942, Rottingdean, Sussex. National Archives of Canada, RG 24, Volume 16674, Serial 2636S, No. 1 Canadian Concert Party, the "Tin Hats" Canadian Army.

REFERENCES

Baker, R. (1994). *Drag: A history of female impersonation in the performing arts.* New York: New York University Press.

Bérubé, A. (1990). *Coming out under fire: The history of gay men and women in World War Two.* New York: The Free Press.

Clark, A. (1997). *Stand and deliver: Inside Canadian comedy.* Toronto: Doubleday Canada.

Copp, T. and McAndrew, B. (1990). *Battle exhaustion: Soldiers and psychiatrists in the Canadian Army, 1939-1945.* Montreal and Kingston: McGill-Queen's Press.

Eksteins, M. (1989). *Rites of spring: The great war and the birth of the modern age.* Toronto: Lester & Orpen Dennys.

Fussell, P. (1975). *The great war and modern memory.* New York: Oxford University Press.

Halladay, L. (2000). *"Ladies and gentlemen, soldiers and artists": Canadian military entertainers, 1939-1946.* MA Thesis, Department of History, University of Calgary.

Halladay, L. (2001). "Meet the Navy–and greet the Navy": The Royal Canadian Navy and broadway-style public relations, 1943. In C. Bullock and J. Dowding (Eds.), *Perspectives on war: Essays on security, society and the state* (pp. 31-42). Calgary, AB: The Society for Military and Strategic Studies.

Heylen, S. (1989). Interview with Ros Bowden. *Keith Murdoch Sound Archives,* Australian War Memorial.

Moore, M.F. (1994). *Drag! Male and female impersonators on stage, screen and television.* London: McFarland and Co. Publishers.

Morton, D. (1992). *A military history of Canada: From Champlain to the Gulf War.* Toronto: McClelland and Stewart.

O'Brien, M. (1998). Manhood and the militia myth: Masculinity, class and militarism in Ontario, 1902-1914. *Labour/Le Travail*, 42, 115-141.

O'Neill, P. (1983). The Canadian concert party in France. *Theatre Research in Canada*, 4/2, 192-207.

O'Neill, P. (1989). Entertaining the troops. *The Beaver*, October/November, 59-62.

Pierson, R.R. (1986). *"They're still women after all": The Second World War and Canadian womanhood.* Toronto: McClelland and Stewart.

Rewa, N. (1989). Garrison theatre. In Eugene Benson and L.W. Conolly (Eds.), *The Oxford companion to Canadian theatre* (pp. 223-224). Toronto: Oxford University Press.

Roy, R.H. (1986). Morale in the Canadian Army in Canada during the Second World War. *Canadian Defense Quarterly*, 16/2, 40-45.

Scott, C. (1934). *The great war as I saw it.* Vancouver, BC: Clark and Stuart.

Senelick, L. (2000). *The changing room: Sex, drag and the theatre.* New York: Routledge Press.

Slide, A. (1986). *The great pretenders: A history of female and male impersonation in the performing arts.* Lombard, Illinois: Wallace-Homestead Book Company.

Williams, C.J. and Weinberg, M.S. (1971). *Homosexuals and the military: A study of less than honorable discharge.* New York: Harper & Row Publishers.

Wigs, Laughter, and Subversion: Charles Busch and Strategies of Drag Performance

Richard Niles, PhD

Marymount Manhattan College

SUMMARY. This paper examines the strategies of drag performer/ playwright Charles Busch. His performance aesthetic is explored and shown to be subversive even though its initial impulse is to entertain. Basing my arguments on the work of Judith Butler, Elin Diamond, and others, I argue that drag queens like Busch can not only entertain but also make audiences question and criticize through drag's power to create a Brechtian alienation effect and historicize the subject. After showing how he can be viewed as a drag queen, I give a brief biography and discuss such contested terms as "camp" and "gay sensibility." I then focus

Richard Niles is Associate Professor of Theatre at Marymount Manhattan College, where he is Coordinator of the BFA Program in Acting and teaches acting, directing, and cultural studies.

Some material in this article appeared in *Ibsen News and Comment: The Journal of The Ibsen Society of America* (2000) and is reprinted with the kind permission of its editor, Joan Templeton. The author thanks Steven P. Schacht for his support and comments during the various revisions of the manuscript, and Court Prentice and Dean Macara of the 1807 House, Provincetown, who provided hospitality and friendship.

Correspondence may be addressed: Department of Theatre, Marymount Manhattan College, 221 East 71st Street, New York, NY 10021.

[Haworth co-indexing entry note]: "Wigs, Laughter, and Subversion: Charles Busch and Strategies of Drag Performance." Niles, Richard. Co-published simultaneously in *Journal of Homosexuality* (Harrington Park Press, an imprint of The Haworth Press, Inc.) Vol. 46, No. 3/4, 2004, pp. 35-53; and: *The Drag Queen Anthology: The Absolutely Fabulous but Flawlessly Customary World of Female Impersonators* (ed: Steven P. Schacht, with Lisa Underwood) Harrington Park Press, an imprint of The Haworth Press, Inc., 2004, pp. 35-53. Single or multiple copies of this article are available for a fee from The Haworth Document Delivery Service [1-800-HAWORTH, 9:00 a.m. - 5:00 p.m. (EST). E-mail address: docdelivery@haworthpress.com].

on Busch's staged reading of Ibsen's *Hedda Gabler* and *A Doll's House*, both done in one afternoon at Theatre for The New City (6 May 2000). By examining the performance of Busch and his fellow actors, I demonstrate how a contemporary relevancy is achieved by having the roles played by a female impersonator whose acting choices are filtered through a gay sensibility. The ongoing dialectic between spectator and performer creates a historicized moment in performance that underscores the gender dynamics in unexpected and stimulating ways. *[Article copies available for a fee from The Haworth Document Delivery Service: 1-800-HAWORTH. E-mail address: <docdelivery@ haworthpress.com> Website: <http://www.HaworthPress.com> © 2004 by The Haworth Press, Inc. All rights reserved.]*

KEYWORDS. Charles Busch, Theatre-in-Limbo, drag performance, drag queens, gender, sexuality, queer studies, Ibsen in performance, gay sensibility

When is a drag queen not a drag queen? The question begs to be addressed when discussing the work and career of Charles Busch. For almost two decades, he has written plays and performed drag roles in them, surrounded by professional actors, designers, and directors. His work is generally presented in legitimate theatres for commercial theatrical runs. At various times, he has described himself as an actor, an entertainer, a clown, a gender illusionist, and yes, a drag queen. The terms used to describe drag performers can cause frustration and confusion, especially since their interchangeability often seems arbitrary. In a colloquy about drag queens, we need to find a definition that is compatible with Busch's work and allows for his inclusion.

Julian Fleisher (1996) notes several characteristics that drag queens have in common: irony, glamour, and camp (more on this later). But Fleisher is almost apologetic when he adds Busch to his list. He comments that Busch's work, like that of his predecessor Charles Ludlam, "is theatre first, drag second. And depending on who is talking–queens or theatre people–the reaction to that notion can be quite strong" (p. 105). In fact, when talking about a professional actor, use of the term can be perceived as disparaging or a downright insult.

Steven P. Schacht (2002) is helpful in situating Busch's position in the drag queen typology. He offers a succinct overall definition: "individuals with an acknowledged penis, who have no desire to have it removed and replaced with female genitalia (such as transsexuals), that perform being women in front of an audience that all knows they are self-identified men, regardless of how compellingly female–'real'–they might otherwise appear" (p. 159). In his discussion of drag queen types, Schacht observes that the professional camp queen "utilize[s] exaggerated images of femininity as props to largely play the role of the stand-up comedian" (p. 171). They are the clowns of the drag queen world.

This is a fairly accurate description of Busch with some notable differences. First, Busch is not a stand-up comedian but usually performs in legitimate plays written by himself. Hence the confusion, noted above, about whether he should be considered a drag queen at all. Another element that makes him unique is that his drag, unlike that of other professional camp queens like Harvey Fierstein or Divine, is not based on grotesque physicality.[1] Busch has a slight build. When he is in drag, he does not present a visually off-putting appearance. Rather, he uses gestures, line deliveries, and physical stances to suggest female stars of Hollywood's golden era (1930-1950). His humor is not based on a body that is comically at odds with a glamorous image of femininity. Instead, his characterization is based on a collage of behavior that suggests a fascinating theatrical diva, foregrounding personality rather than the ability to create a character per se. In conclusion, while the fit is not perfect, there are enough traits that Busch has in common with drag queens to warrant his inclusion in their company.[2]

Many scholars and critics now feel that the ubiquitous presence of drag in mass culture has diluted its power to disturb. Lawrence Senelick (2000) notes that "most current drag is no more subversive than the black-face of minstrelsy, which accounts for its popularity" (p. 501). Senelick is also rather dismissive of Busch's work, calling it "a high spirited game of *Trivia*" (432). While he hardly addresses Busch the performer, Senelick faults him as a playwright for an excessive use of Hollywood film references and a corresponding lack of weightier aspects of high culture.[3] This is an oft-repeated criticism of Busch, which I believe is undeserved and will address later.

In this paper, I argue against Senelick's appraisal of Busch's work. I will show how Busch's drag performances still have the power to undermine ideological constructs and, moreover, make classic dramatic material (Ibsen, no less) resonate in unexpected ways that create unique contemporary relevance. I also disagree with Senelick's assessment of drag's present inability to destabilize ideological values. Even with drag's increasing presence in mass culture during the 1990s, it still has the power to subvert. By subversion, I mean the ability to foreground gender roles and relations, thereby undermining the received notion of gender's essentialism. Senelick is correct to observe that drag has lost its shock value with audiences that, during the past two decades, have become so relatively overexposed to cross-dressing on stage and in film. But drag's subversive effect need not be confrontational or abrasive in nature. Indeed, drag in American theatre has been and still is generally presented as sheer entertainment. But in addition to its ability to amuse, drag can isolate for the spectator specific gender related configurations found in particular historical contexts. While the subversive process I suggest is hardly radical in method or manner, it can be a highly effective way to reveal the process of gender expectations operating not only on the stage but also in the audience itself.

Butler (1993) calls drag subversive "to the extent that it reflects on the imitative structure by which hegemonic gender is itself produced and disputes heterosexuality's claim on naturalness and originality" (p. 125). Busch's drag can clearly be included in Butler's thesis. Busch's style, in fact, is not based on "real life" femininity but on movie star acting. One need only compare the behavior of Norma Shearer or Joan Crawford in their star vehicles of the 1930s with real life newsreels of women shot at the same time to observe the enormous discrepancy between these presentations of self. When Busch performs he is evoking behavior that is already an example of artifice.

Diamond (2001) applies the Brechtian alienation theory to drag performance in order to empower feminist performance (p. 79). By distancing the actress's identification with a male role, for example, and historicizing the theatrical subject in a specific context, Diamond suggests that the spectator can clearly see the ideological construct of gender in a particular time period. Diamond's Brechtian project can be applied to female impersonation, as well. This, of course, has great significance when performing Ibsen, whose work, though still germane, is so linked to a specific time period and culture.

Before examining how Busch employed this strategy in Ibsen's work, a brief biography follows for readers unfamiliar with him or his work. As of the writing of this article, Busch is probably best known for his play, *The Tale of the Allergist's Wife*, which featured neither drag nor Busch as performer in its two-year run on Broadway. Before *Tale of the Allergist's Wife* brought him to the attention of the commercial Broadway theatre, Busch's reputation was based on the plays he wrote to feature himself as a drag artist.

Busch was born in 1954 and grew up in Hartsdale, a suburb of New York City. After graduating the High School of Performing Arts in

Manhattan, he attended Northwestern University (1972-76) as a drama major. His thin frame and fey demeanor, combined with a lack of confidence in projecting masculinity on stage, made him difficult to cast. After returning to New York, he began to write plays and performance pieces in order to give himself roles. In 1984, Busch wrote *Vampire Lesbians of Sodom*, a one-act sketch comedy with a drag role for himself. For his own amusement, he and some friends performed it at the Limbo Lounge in Manhattan's East Village. Directed by Kenneth Elliott, a fellow graduate from Northwestern, *Vampire Lesbians* became a surprise hit.

Busch's timing was fortuitous. The East Village was becoming a dynamic artistic center where galleries, boutiques, and clubs were springing up in lofts and storefronts. Drag was a particularly popular form of theatrical expression, and performers such as John Kelly and Ethyl Eichelberger regularly played at various clubs. The self-referential style of drag queens performing at the Pyramid Club and Boy Bar with their constant allusions to mass culture, film, and television perfectly suited Busch's sensibility and taste. He formed his own company, Theatre-in-Limbo, and soon acquired a large and loyal gay following.

On June 19, 1985, *Vampire Lesbians* moved Off-Broadway to the Provincetown Playhouse, where it ran for a total of 17 previews and 2,024 performances, setting a new record for an Off-Broadway legitimate play. Busch continued to write a series of film genre parodies for his company. They included *Psycho Beach Party* (1987), a spoof of 1960s beach blanket pictures; *The Lady in Question* (1989), a parody of anti-Nazi films of the 1940s; and *Red Scare on Sunset* (1991), which concerned the communist witch-hunt in Hollywood during the McCarthy era.[4]

Like many of his colleagues in drag, Busch owed a significant debt to a drag artist and theatrical provocateur par excellence: Charles Ludlam. Founder of The Ridiculous Theatrical Company in 1967, Ludlam wrote, directed, and acted in a series of highly stylized productions that reveled in cheap theatrics and greatly exaggerated, camp performances. Drag, both male and female, was extensively used. Ludlam's work (*Camille, Bluebeard, Irma Vep,* and *The Artificial Jungle,* among others) brought drag to a new level of theatrical distinction, and his aesthetic of anti-naturalistic performance was a powerful influence and inspiration to Busch and his generation. Busch actually worked briefly in Ludlam's company. Ludlam also gave him the use of his theatre for Busch's first play in New York, *Hollywood Confidential* (1978). But

(l-r) Becky London, Charles Busch, Michael Belanger
in a scene from Charles Busch's new comedy *Psycho Beach Party* at the
Players Theatre, 115 Macdougal Street. *Psycho Beach Party* is the story of a
perky, teenage girl (circa 1960) with a problem. That problem leads to havoc
with her social life and turns beach parties into nightmares!
Photo: Adam Newman. Contact: Pete Sanders, Shirley Herz Associates (212)
221-8466

two divas in one company were one too many, and Busch soon left to
strike out on his own (Kaufman, 2002).

   As Busch began garnering critical notice, he was sometimes unfavor-
ably compared to Ludlam. Caveats were similar to Senelick's opinion,
which I find undeserved. Ludlam and Busch had very different agendas.
Ludlam wanted to create a new kind of theater, he saw himself as a revolutionary, and his plays were often steeped in references to various areas of cultural history. Sometimes this resulted in amateurish self-
indulgence and pretentiousness, more often in dazzling theatrical ex-
perimentation. Conversely, Busch saw himself as a clown with a man-
date to entertain. He was stirred by movies from the golden age of
Hollywood, not by the writings of Nietzsche. Sometimes he was obvious and puerile; but his clowning was frequently brilliant. To assume
that Busch and Ludlam are similar artists just because they both did
drag makes us consider their diverse talents and accomplishments as if

they were comparable. To place greater or lesser importance on innovation than on artistic expertise in a more conventional framework diminishes the very substantial contributions Busch and Ludlam have both made to theater. Why put them in competition with each other? Let them remain uniquely and irreplaceably themselves.

In the spring of 2000, Busch presented heavily edited versions of *Hedda Gabler* and *A Doll's House*, performing them as staged readings both in the same afternoon. Of course, he played "Hedda" and "Nora" himself.[5] It is this production that I will examine in depth. First, however, I would like to clarify some terminology that will be used in describing Busch's performance strategy. Doing so also helps to give a more detailed picture of Busch's audience and explains why it is able to appreciate his work as subversive.[6]

Reading the Samuel French acting edition of any of Busch's Theatre-in-Limbo scripts gives little idea of the humor and wit that infused the Off-Broadway production or explains the wildly enthusiastic audience response captured on several videotapes made at the time. Evidently, there were forces at work during the performance that could not be transmitted to the printed page. While this is problematic with any discussion of live theatre, it is particularly challenging when trying to describe or document drag performance because of the unique collaboration between audience and performer and the elusive factors of "camp" and "gay sensibility."[7] These two terms are hotly contested sites for queer theorists and their use can result in slippage and confusion.

From Theatre-in-Limbo's beginnings, critics and company members alike noted the cult audiences that filled the Limbo Lounge and loyally followed the company to Off-Broadway. These audiences, predominantly 20-40-year-old, white middle-class gays, account, in large part, for Busch's initial success. Clearly, there was a collective sensibility at work linking performer and spectator. By "sensibility," I mean the specific relationship that connects a cultural product (i.e., a play) with a particular audience (Grossberg, 1992, p. 54). We cannot, of course, assign distinctive cultural tendencies to the entire gay subculture, where communities differ significantly according to factors of economics, age, education, class, and race. No minority artist can speak for an entire community. But we can speak of the sensibility shared by Busch and his audience if we contain our discussion within a "specificity of experience" (Mercer, 1991, p. 205).

Although Busch emerged as a gay man during the post-Stonewall era of the early '70s, concealment was still often a function of daily life.

Certainly Busch and his peer group experienced less self-loathing and isolation than previous generations had suffered, but if the world-at-large was less hostile, it still held up heterosexuality as the norm. One tactic for dealing with this situation, which Busch shared with previous generations of gays and lesbians, was the strategy of camp. Babuscio (1977) argues that camp is a product of gay sensibility. Objects can be appropriated from mainstream popular culture and then reinscribed in ways that allow them to be used as a means of communication and empowerment within gay and lesbian communities.

Manipulated and coded by camp treatment, objects from heterosexual mainstream culture can "represent and respond" to the lives of gay men like Busch. Bronski (1984) elaborates on Babuscio's proposition, calling camp's function a way of reimagining "the real, hostile world into a new one which is controllable and safe . . . it exaggerates and therefore diffuses real threats . . . by exaggerating, stylizing, and remaking what is usually thought to be average or normal, camp creates a world in which the real becomes unreal, the threatening, unthreatening" (p. 42). Dyer (1986) gives a brief summary of camp's traits, which is also useful in exploring Busch's drag aesthetic: "Camp is a characteristically gay way of handling the values, images and products of the dominant culture through irony, exaggeration, trivialization, theatricalization, and an ambivalent making fun of and out of the serious and respectable" (p. 178). These basic features of camp can be seen in all of Busch's work in drag.

Busch's acting persona is an example of incongruous elements exaggerated for camp effect. Busch observes, "I've always played a duality. I guess I've always felt a duality in myself: elegance and vulgarity. There's humor in that. I've always found that fun on stage, as well. It's not enough for me to be the whore. I have to be the whore with pretensions or the great lady with a vulgar streak. It's the duality that I find interesting" (27 October 1992). This duality is often portrayed with such rapid transition that it breaks the bounds of naturalistic behavior. In Busch's zany world, the great lady and the pretentious social climber trying to transcend her lowly origins are veneers that eventually crack to reveal the characters' true essence. While this farcical exposure is a rich source of humor, it also has more thoughtful implications. The whore is more in touch with her sexual being than her pretentious social guise; the vulgar but down to earth woman is more able to deal with life's vicissitudes than the great lady. The character's fundamental nature is actually shown by presenting the audience with a constant parade of postures and deception that are abruptly abandoned in moments of high stress. A Busch performance is made up of equal parts of gender masquerade and character striptease. Sometimes this presentational technique gives the impression of probing far more deeply into a character's psyche than might be accomplished with a more naturalistic acting method.

All this talk of camp and gay sensibility does not mean that straight audiences cannot enjoy Busch's work. They can and do. In fact, Busch's popularity has been due, in part, to his ability to entertain without creating a "members only" atmosphere. The *New York Times* called him "New York's most beloved drag performer" (30 September 1993). But it is also true, as Román (1998) notes of Lypsinka (another drag performer whose act often refers to entertainers of previous generations), that "recognizing opera heroines, sopranos, lounge acts, and Hollywood icons is the litmus test for the ideal spectator" (p. 97). While knowledge of camp cultural references is not restricted to gays, a gay man is more likely to recognize and appreciate the irony of material in a particular context such as certain movie dialogue like *All About Eve* ("Fasten your seat belts, it's going to be a bumpy night!") and *Mommie Dearest* ("No wire hangers!"). It is easy to see why gay men in the generations prior to Stonewall would identify with characters trapped in conventions that stifled their "true natures" and rebelled against them. Bronski dubs this appeal "Hollywood Homo-sense" (p. 92). No wonder Busch finds himself attracted to Ibsen heroines who, likewise, find themselves in conflict with the conventions of their society, and why gay audiences can find aspects of their own lives analogous to the ones being presented on the stage.[8]

Busch's staged readings of Ibsen's *Hedda Gabler* and *A Doll's House* are a felicitous example of his style of drag performance, clearly exhibiting the requisites of camp described above. The two plays, each with a running time of one hour, were performed at the Theatre for The New City in New York City. Since it was a staged reading, production values were minimal. Most importantly, Busch was not creating a vehicle to showcase his unique talents, but acting the dialogue of a world-renowned playwright. I was a member of the audience. As I sat waiting for the show to begin, I knew it would be funny. I was unprepared, though, for the moments when the drag/camp performance produced images and subtextual narrative that were astonishing in their ability to illuminate some of the plays' underlying themes.

The whole event was designed to be viewed as a metatheatrical presentation, a highly self-reflexive homage to the grand style of 19th century dramatic traditions: personality privileged over characterization,

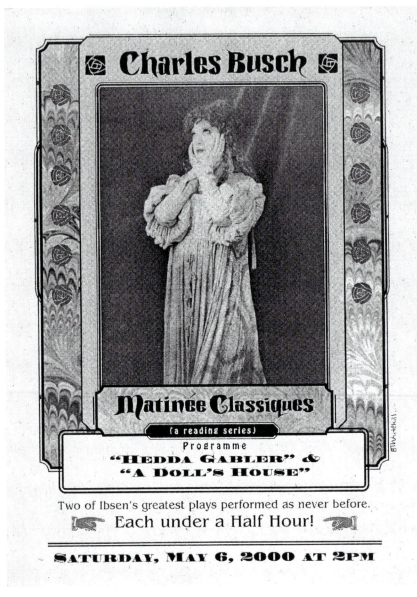

SATURDAY, MAY 6, 2000 AT 2PM

physically and vocally exaggerated behavior, and playing directly to the audience. The event was promoted as inaugurating a new series, "Matinée Classiques [sic]," even though Busch had no immediate plans to do any other dramatic masterpieces in this manner. The actors were billed on the playbill as "Mr." and "Miss," to emphasize the conceit that this was in the tradition of Anglo-American 19th century theatrical tradition. There was even a pianist providing musical score to accompany the dialogue as was often done in 19th century melodramas. The parodic conceit here (again on a metatheatrical level) was that Busch (as star of this faux company of 19th century actors) would be treating Ibsen's plays as mere vehicles for her self-aggrandizement; any alterations or adjustments would be made to the play, the star and her performance would remain inviolate. But the strategy also serves to historicize the characters themselves in the specific milieu of Ibsen's time. On this level, the performance not only can be seen as a critique of gender conventions of the period, but makes possible a broader correlation: that of the individual unwilling or unable to subscribe to social standards of the time.

The setting for this reading was formalized and neutral: black drapes surrounded the acting area. The only furniture was a bench and an easy chair. Production values were meager due to time constraints and budget. Costumes and wigs were the only design elements used to actually suggest the period. Patricia O'Connell, as "Hostess," opened each play offering prefatory comments, then sat in the easy chair to observe the action and deliver stage directions, all in her best *Masterpiece Theatre* manner. The actors (David Staller, Charlotte Maier, Peter Bartlett, Marcy McGuigan, and Carl Andress, who also directed) knew and/or had worked previously with Busch and were familiar with his technique of camp performance, enabling them to play comfortably within that style. The audience was comprised mainly of Busch fans who were well acquainted with camp's chief elements of irony, the contrast of genteel pretension with brash vulgarity, incongruity, and role-playing. They were not disappointed.

Busch's first appearance as Hedda was the ultimate diva's entrance. A veritable study in self-loathing, he contorted his face; his body suffered sudden spasms; his shoulders rose as if toward unseen threats hovering above him. As he swayed and lurched toward the piano where he finally rested, his walk recalled Bette Davis in her prime Warner Brothers days. Yet Busch's skill is such that this was no mere impersonation. Rather, he evoked the image of "star acting." As the performance proceeded, he growled like Tallulah Bankhead, fluttered and cocked his head like Norma Shearer, and spoke in a grandly patrician accent, devoid of regionalism, which he instantly dropped when he wanted to draw a laugh; again there was the contrast of pretension with vulgarity. The other actors also had fun with their characters. David Staller's Judge Brack was more than reminiscent of film star George Sanders, underlining his debonair and corrupt aspects to an absurd degree. Peter

Bartlett's ineffectual Tesman wrapped his lips and tongue around the French diphthong Œ when he tried to pronounce Lœvborg, bobbing his head anxiously and finally trailing off in despair. Occasionally the comedy stooped to the level of vaudeville, as when Busch played with General Gabler's pistols. The pianist launched into Cole Porter's "Don't Fence Me In" and Busch obliged by sauntering across the stage like a demented cowboy.

A Doll's House was even broader in its comic approach. At one point, Busch as Nora and Marcy McGuigan as Christine contemplated the mailbox with Krogstad's incriminating letter inside. Suddenly they transformed themselves into the Lucy and Ethel of I Love Lucy. They begin to imitate the physical and vocal mannerisms of Lucille Ball and Vivian Vance as they improvised a scene plotting a scheme to retrieve the letter. Although they quickly returned to Ibsen's lines, the moment was hysterically funny. It also revealed a very real link between Nora and Ball's Lucy character. Nora chafes under the constraints society places on her as a wife and mother. She is a true progenitor of Lucy, who desperately tries to transcend her restrictive lifestyle, even though the latter's situation is treated as farce. In fact, A Doll's House has been successfully staged set within the Eisenhower era of the 1950s.

Even from this brief description of the performance, it seems evident that Busch's goal was sheer entertainment. And yet, regardless of his initial motivation in putting on these pieces, I propose that placing the drag queen/performer before the spectator in Ibsen's work creates subversive elements and alienating effects that emphasize in visceral ways the role-playing and masquerade that Hedda and Nora must continually endure. In addition, having a gay man in drag play these characters emphasizes the dramatic condition of trapped, marginalized individuals, whether they are Ibsen's women of 19th century Norway or those who today find themselves in similar situations because of race, color, or sexual preference.

Ibsen's Hedda is trapped in a small town society into which she can never be assimilated. She is torn between her desire to express her genuine impulses and her fear of flouting convention and the consequent taint of scandal. Similarly, Busch's Hedda can never reveal his/her true identity, as a gay man. The gender impersonation was a potent metaphor for Hedda's deviance and isolation. It was an even stronger image for Nora's dilemma. Busch highlighted this when Nora confessed to Christine how she saved Torvald's life and noted, "it was almost like being a man." When Busch delivered the line, his voice dropped to a deep masculine register. This bit of business sharply reminded us of the ruse of impersonation, an action usually done at the end of a drag queen's act, when she takes off her wig.

Nora's attempts to manipulate the conventions of masculine ideology bear an uncanny similarity to Busch's attempt to do the same with gender roles. We suspend disbelief as we watch him because the story, even though well known, is still compelling. He uses our willingness to accept the drag impersonation as authentic in order to point to the intrinsic quality of masquerade in gender expectations. Nora's imitation of the "ideal wife" takes on an added desperation from the very first scene, because a man is portraying her. We know that eventually she/he will fail. In terms of the play's given circumstances, we see what Torvald doesn't, that his wife is not a woman at all, but living an absurd travesty for his benefit. Finally when Nora rejects the dictates of society and gives up the deception, Torvald reminds her of her duties as a wife and mother. She replies with passion, "I believe that before all else, I am a human being." This line has an eerie poignancy when uttered by a drag queen performing Nora.

We can even see Busch's Hedda and Nora as two variations on a single theme, a gay man trying to fit into an intolerant heterosexual community by pretending he is a woman, or on a more global level, any marginalized individual trying to function within the dominant culture. Hedda, faced with a sham existence, gives up and commits suicide, certainly the choice of many gay men in the past. Busch's Nora, however, more courageous and optimistic, rejects her home and family in search of a more compatible milieu in which she can express her true nature. We feel the inevitability of the character's departure and celebrate her decision, both on the literal level of the play and on a metatheatrical level created by the Brechtian device of gender masquerade.

Even Busch's acting persona conveys how Ibsen's suffocating environment affects the internal lives of these women. His delivery, particularly with Hedda, suggests the dual personality described earlier: a woman of great pretension desperately trying to maintain respectability and a tough, vulgar dame who "tells it like it is." Busch sustains the image of the grand diva until, at strategic moments, the effort of this subterfuge becomes too great. Then he drops it, seemingly reverting to his true character, a harsh, suspicious "broad" who knows the score, can take care of herself, and spits out lines with cynical self-assuredness. While this is a comic instance of the ultimate failure of pretense, it can also be read as a dramatization of the inner conflict between convention and freedom of expression that afflicts both Hedda and Nora. Through this performance of the two types of femininity favored by drag queens, the diva and the harlot, Busch continually reminds the spectator of the conflicted personality of these two heroines until it is resolved in the final moments of each play with a gunshot and a door slamming closed. Busch did not consciously choose this style of delivery for these particular plays, nor was he trying to create the added nuances I have mentioned above that drag brought to the material. However, the playtext, female impersonation, camp treatment of material, combined with the audience's sensibility, how they experienced and responded to the performance, make the production subtly different from the one the actors and director envisioned while they were in rehearsal.

I am not proposing that each and every member of the audience felt this way while witnessing the performance. Yes, there were many moments of raucous laughter. But there were also more than a few points at which the audience fell suddenly silent, involved in a strangely affecting and unexpected way, some of which I have noted above. These reactions made me feel that I was not alone in experiencing something more than a drag parody of a classic 19th century play. My point here is that the audience/actor collaboration that is so necessary for successful communication in camp and drag performance brings unexpected layers of meaning, whether or not this has been a performance or directorial choice. Whether Busch had meant to be subversive or not, the act of drag, as Butler asserts, undermines the production of hegemonic gender in the eyes of the spectator. Drawing on Butler's claim that gender is produced through a repetition of stylized acts, Meyer (1994) declares queer identity is performative as well, and defines camp as "the total body of performative practices and strategies" used to enact and make visible that identity (p. 5). Since a queer identity implies a political stance that actively resists assimilation, camp, as a queer practice, is political in nature, as well. To be political is to belong to a faction within the social order, and thus, hostile to factions that do not share similar aims. Hence, queer identity, camp, and drag are political and/or subversive toward social norms of gender and sexuality.

I earlier noted Senelick's statement that drag currently lacks as much subversion as minstrelsy once did, hence its popularity. I argue that minstrelsy, if performed today, can be quite subversive, if one factors in the audience's sensitivity to race relations and its responses to how race is being portrayed on the stage.[9] Similarly, drag can also be subversive by making the audience aware of the process of marginalization as it watches a historical moment sculpted and emphasized with the broad strokes of camp performance. This is particularly true if the audience comes equipped with an appreciative knowledge of and previous exposure to camp, gay sensibility, and the source material on which the performance text is based.

In conclusion, I believe that even though Busch himself produces theatre without a political agenda, audiences (particularly those who are queer) can view his performance as activist in nature. I do not agree with Senelick that drag has become so overexposed in recent years that it has become passé. Nor do I believe it has been absorbed and disseminated by mass culture to such an extent that it is now declawed and defanged. If used with skill and imagination, drag still has the power to disconcert us, and as Diamond proposes, to historicize the subject by "making strange" the ordinary and conventional. Busch has been able to successfully exploit this by endowing two of Ibsen's greatest female creations with features that spark with a contemporary immediacy. As long as the heterosexual ideal maintains its privileged status, I believe that we can still use drag to chip away at values that inhibit our ability to express our natures and our desires. In this daunting but crucial ongoing project, the drag queen remains a welcome participant. And there is a place in the legitimate theatre for her, as well. Charles Busch has demonstrated that through his successful career on the commercial stage. And if he can entertain and make us laugh, while making us question and reevaluate, so much the better.

NOTES

1. Harvey Fierstein is author of *Torch Song Trilogy* and is currently appearing on Broadway in the musical *Hairspray* in a drag role. Although he wears padding for the role, his natural physique is hardly svelte. The movie version of *Hairspray,* directed by John Waters, starred the late Glenn Milstead in his drag persona of Divine. Milstead was an extremely heavyset man. This coupled with his highly exaggerated makeup made his drag characters unsettling and bizarre.

2. In my own discussions with Schacht, subsequent to the publication of his article, he suggests that Busch is a combination of female illusionist and camp queen and, in fact, deserves a category of his own.

3. Senelick includes a disturbing amount of misinformation in his strongly opinionated view of Busch. He states that Busch rose from the clubs rather than the legitimate stage. Busch, as I note, studied theatre for 4 years as an undergraduate at Northwestern University and played his one-man show (out of drag) for 6 years in many legitimate houses prior to his tenure at the Limbo Lounge. In addition, Senelick gets key plot elements of the plays wrong. In *Times Square Angel*, Irish O'Flanagan was a nightclub singer, not a reporter. Chicklet, in *Psycho Beach Party*, does not go berserk when someone says "fish," which Senelick calls an "old chestnut of gay misogyny," but at the word "red," hardly misogynistic in tone or meaning. Actresses, not drag artists, played "Bettina Barnes" and "Berdine" in *Psycho Beach Party*, while "Marvel Ann,"

whom he does not mention, was indeed played by a man. There is bound to be some misinformation in a work as massive and ambitious as the one Senelick attempts. However, so many mistakes in the brief amount of space given to Busch is troubling given the high academic standards generally maintained in the work.

4. Although these productions received critical approval, none achieved the run of *Vampire Lesbians of Sodom*, in part because the play's title was so provocative that tourists were intrigued. Low running costs and a steady stream of out-of-towners kept the show alive.

5. All of the above productions played in New York, other than *Die, Mommy, Die*, which premiered in Los Angeles and never moved to New York.

6. I was present in the audience for *Hedda Gabler/A Doll's House* for its only performance, 6 May 2000 at Theatre for The New City, New York City. My comments are based on notes taken at that time and subsequent viewings of the videotape made of that performance.

7. I subscribe to the conventional distinction now made between "gay" and "queer." Queer is a term embracing all who do not fit the social norms of gender and sexuality. Gay refers specifically to homosexual men.

8. Busch is not the first actor to have played Hedda Gabler. Charles Ludlam, founder of the Ridiculous Theatrical Company, essayed the role in Pittsburgh for the American Ibsen Theatre. That production attempted a legitimate interpretation, albeit with a male in the title role.

9. In *Bamboozled* (2000), filmmaker Spike Lee has an unscrupulous black television producer create a modern version of a minstrel show that turns out to be a tremendous hit. The film's satirical premise and its treatment of minstrelsy demonstrate that the minstrel show has acquired subversive qualities that allow it to interrogate racial stereotypes in unexpected and exhilarating ways.

SOURCES CITED

Babuscio, J. (1991). The cinema of camp. In *Gay roots: Twenty years of gay sunshine* (pp. 431-449). San Francisco: Gay Sunshine Press.

Bronski, M. (1984). *Culture clash: The making of gay sensibility*. Boston: South End Press.

Busch, C. (10 February 1990-2 June 2000). Series of interviews by author. Tape recording. New York City.

Busch, C. (6 May 2000). *Hedda Gabler/A Doll's House*. Theatre for The New City, New York City.

Busch, C. (6 May 2000). *Hedda Gabler/A Doll's House*. Videocassette. Property of author. New York City.

Butler, J. (1993). *Bodies that matter*. New York: Routledge.

Diamond, E. (2001). Brechtian theory/feminist theory: Towards a gestic feminist criticism. In C. Counsell and L. Wolf (Eds.), *Performance analysis*. New York: Routledge.

Dyer, R. (1986). *Heavenly bodies: Film stars and society*. New York: St. Martins Press.

Fleisher, J. (1996). *The drag queens of New York*. New York: Riverhead Books.

Grossberg, L. (1992). Is there a fan in the house?: The affective sensibility of fandom. In L. Lewis (Ed.), *The adoring audience: Fan culture and popular media* (pp. 50-65). London: Routledge.

Kaufman, D. (2002). *Ridiculous!: The theatrical life and times of Charles Ludlam.* New York: Applause Theatre and Cinema Books.

Mercer, K. (1991). Skin head sex thing: Racial difference and the homoerotic imaginary. In Bad Object-Choices (Eds.), *How do I look?: Queer film and video.* Seattle: Bay Press.

Meyer, M. (Ed.). (1994). *The politics and poetics of camp.* London: Routledge.

Román, D. (1998). *Acts of intervention: Performance, gay culture, and AIDS.* Bloomington: Indiana University Press.

Schacht, S. P. (2002). Four renditions of doing female drag: Feminine appearing conceptual variations of a masculine theme. *Gendered Sexualities,* (6), 157-180.

Senelick, L. (2000). *The changing room.* London: Routledge.

The Beauty and the Beast:
Reflections About the Socio-Historical and Subcultural Context of Drag Queens and "Tunten" in Berlin

Carsten Balzer, MA

Free University Berlin, Germany

SUMMARY. In this article, I focus on two different faces found in Berlin's gay subculture: the Tunten and the drag queens. Both are com-

Carsten Balzer (a.k.a. Carla LaGata) is an anthropologist, currently writing her dissertation on transgender communities in Rio de Janeiro, New York and Berlin. She has conducted fieldwork in the Brazilian Amazon and the urban centers of Rio de Janeiro, New York and Berlin and published a book and several articles in Brazil, Germany and the United States.

Author note: I would like to acknowledge my friends, especially Chou-Chou de Briquette and Thomas G. Kirsch in Berlin and Flawless Sabrina and Curtis B. Carmen in New York for their support and discussion as well as to thank Steven Schacht, David Keys and S. J. Hopkins for comments on an earlier and extended version of this article. Furthermore, I thank the organizational team of "Wigstöckel–transgender united" and all my informants in Berlin and New York for welcoming me so heartily. I am also very grateful to the NaFöG-Foundation of the Free University Berlin for financing my fieldwork in Berlin and the German Academic Exchange Service (DAAD) for financing the fieldwork in New York City.

Correspondence may be addressed: Free University Berlin, Institute for Latin American Studies, Rüdesheimerstr. 54-56, 14197 Berlin, Germany (E-mail: mana@zedat.fu-berlin.de).

[Haworth co-indexing entry note]: "The Beauty and the Beast: Reflections About the Socio-Historical and Subcultural Context of Drag Queens and 'Tunten' in Berlin." Balzer, Carsten. Co-published simultaneously in *Journal of Homosexuality* (Harrington Park Press, an imprint of The Haworth Press, Inc.) Vol. 46, No. 3/4, 2004, pp. 55-71; and: *The Drag Queen Anthology: The Absolutely Fabulous but Flawlessly Customary World of Female Impersonators* (ed: Steven P. Schacht, with Lisa Underwood) Harrington Park Press, an imprint of The Haworth Press, Inc., 2004, pp. 55-71. Single or multiple copies of this article are available for a fee from The Haworth Document Delivery Service [1-800-HAWORTH, 9:00 a.m. - 5:00 p.m. (EST). E-mail address: docdelivery@haworthpress.com].

monly seen as "male homosexual transvestites," although many such individuals today prefer to identify themselves somewhere within a diverse transgender spectrum rather than as transvestites. Tunten and drag queens differ in their gender performativity, their self-image and their chosen role models as well as in the niches in which they have been able to establish themselves in German mainstream society. Based on ethnographic data, I argue against the widespread reductionist view that the differences between Tunten and drag queens lie primarily in style, behavior, talent and success. Nor can these differences be easily explained away as a result of subculture globalization. Instead, I show that there is a simultaneous coexistence of both a subculturally established, "traditional" local transgender culture and a more recently adopted and partly imported, new local transgender culture. The coexistence of these two urban transgender cultures also indicates the paradigm shift in German gay and youth cultures of the last decades. Thus, I will emphasize the importance of the socio-historical and subcultural processes in studying transgender cultures in Western societies. *[Article copies available for a fee from The Haworth Document Delivery Service: 1-800-HAWORTH. E-mail address: <docdelivery@haworthpress.com> Website: <http://www.HaworthPress.com> © 2004 by The Haworth Press, Inc. All rights reserved.]*

KEYWORDS. Tunten, drag queens, transvestites, transgender, gay culture in transition, internationalization of gay identities, autochthony, cultural globalization

INTRODUCTION

In certain parts of Berlin such as the former West Berlin neighborhoods of Kreuzberg and Schöneberg, one may see on a sunny summer afternoon seemingly exotic people; people known as "female impersonators" from theater, cabaret and mass media are about on the town, in the street, going shopping, sitting in street cafés or coming out of the subway. Here, what dominant society construes as exotic turns into subculturally performed and lived normality. This normality, however, is not free of society's intolerance against gender variant people. It is more a result of the fierce fights for acceptance and respect that these people started 30 years ago. If you asked these people–who are still referred to within German psycho-medical discourse as "male homosexual transvestites"–about their self-identification, most of them would call themselves "Tunte" and some of them would answer "drag queen." Most of them also refuse to consider themselves transvestites and prefer the imported term "transgender."

At first sight this use of a German name "Tunte" or an English one "drag queen" seems to be a question of "local" versus "international" terminology for the very same people and thus could be explained by the current trend of using English labels in other languages. However, if one gets to know these people closely and observe them and their gender performativity (Butler, 1990) on stage, at parties and in daily life, if one talks to them about the two categories, you quickly realize the essential differences between the two. The differences abound: in their gender performativity; in their self-images and role models; and in the niches in which they have been able to establish themselves in German mainstream society.

Based on ethnographical data collected over the last two years, I will demonstrate that drag queens and Tunten are indeed two different transgender subcultures, which–on a societal and historical level–are simultaneously connected with and detached from each other. This apparent contradiction can be explained when examining two different areas of change from a historical and ethnological perspective: first, the changes in gay subculture, and second, the societal changes that have taken place in Berlin since the reunification of Germany.

TRANSGENDER, GENDER DIVERSITY AND (SUB)CULTURAL GLOBALIZATION IN AN ETHNOLOGICAL PERSPECTIVE

Transgender became a trendy label in the last decade of the 20th century, a label that is now used with different meanings within different western societies. In order to avoid the false connection that is often made between gender identity and sexual identity, the label transgendered is sometimes used by people who are otherwise known as "transsexuals." It also serves as an umbrella term for different forms of gender variant people and is used yet differently again by others within the emerging international transgender movement and some western academic discourse as a language tool to illustrate their unease with gender-dichotomous names (Bolin, 1994; Dallas, 1998; Valentine, 2000). In Germany, and especially in Berlin, this imported term "transgender" is used by different groups ranging from those traditionally referred to as transsexuals and (heterosexual) transvestites to Tunten, drag queens and drag kings or self-defined androgynous people. A dozen of these transgender groups are united in a network: the Transgender Network Berlin. Following this emic discourse and using transgender as an umbrella term, it seems therefore appropriate to speak of transgender subcultures or transgender cultures in the case of drag queens and Tunten in Berlin.

With the emerging transgender discourse grew a new scholarly interest in the gender diversity of nonwestern societies. Researchers have shown that gender variant or transgender persons as individuals, as social groups or as their own gender (category) are a widespread phenomenon in our world (see Bleibtreu-Ehrenberg, 1984; Herdt, 1994a; Balzer, 2001). In focusing on the emic perspective of indigenous cultures, anthropologists redefined phenomena such as the "berdache," no longer using such ethnocentric terms as "indigenous transvestitism" or "indigenous homosexuality" and moving on to discuss the concept of a third and, in some cases, a fourth gender, pointing out the gender diversity of such cultures (Roscoe, 1998). While the gender ambivalence of a third gender in those societies is often recognized with respect and honor and can lead to an important role and function for the entire society (Herdt, 1994b; Nanda, 1994; Mageo, 1996; Roscoe, 1998), transgender people in western (and westernized) societies are still primarily explained by psychological and medical discourses and are marginalized in the broader society (Lindemann, 1993; Bolin, 1994; Kulick, 1998; Valentine, 2000).[1]

Gender identities, as cultural entities, are not fixed, but rather flexible and influenced by cultural changes. These changes can be cultural changes within the society or influences from the outside. The best-known influences in ethnographic scholarship are found in colonialism and missionary work (Herdt, 1994b). In Thailand, for example, the influence of the western gay movement has had its impact on the local transgender culture in urban contexts. The local third gender "kathoey," which still exists in rural contexts, is now referred to as lady boy and tom boy in urban contexts (Jackson and Sullivan, 1999). Some "kathoeys" in Bangkok also call themselves drag queens (Brummelhuis, 1999, p. 123) and thus seem to be influenced by concepts of western gay culture.

In Samoa, where the local third gender "fa'affafine" is associated with the traditional Samoan theater, recent researchers report that in urban settings young "fa'affafine" now call themselves drag queens and perform in trendy Discotheques (Mageo, 1996, p. 601). The increase of drag queens as an identifiable and identified set of individuals in urban centers in the last decade has also been found in South America (e.g.,

Argentina, Brazil, Columbia), Asia (e.g., Japan, South Korea, Thailand) and some European countries.[2] Against the backdrop of the international media spotlight and the commercialization of drag queens in the mid-1990s, this might appear to stem from the processes of cultural globalization described as Westernization, Americanization or "McWorld Culture" (Berger, 1997, p. 26) or more specifically as "internationalization of postmodern gay identities" (Altman, 1996, p. 77) or "globalization of sexual identities" and "McDonaldizing of sexual minorities" (Bell and Binnie, 2000, pp. 5 &116). Some scholars, however, argue that such general theories often lack detailed ethnographic information and a deeper knowledge of the local contexts and thus are underestimating the local (Cvetkovich and Kellner, 1997; Roberts, 2001).

While doing fieldwork on transgender subcultures in Rio de Janeiro (Brazil) I observed the coexistence of the local "traditional" transgender subculture of "travestis"/"transformistas" and the recently emerged, western-influenced transgender subculture of drag queens. I had already noticed a very similar kind of coexistence between the Tunten and drag queens during my fieldwork on transgender subcultures in Berlin. With the latter example, I will present more in-depth detailed ethnographic information in a local context in order to demonstrate a form of local transgender autochthony as part of a global transgender diversity.

From the dozens of transgender people I came to know closely during my two years of fieldwork in Berlin, I selected eight drag queens and eight Tunten,[3] whom I interviewed in detail about being a drag queen or being a Tunte. This ethnographical data is supplemented by participant observation in both the local community and in the interviewees' daily lives, by many informal talks as well as the analysis of historical documents (videos, flyers, underground publications, etc.) and current publications (gay magazines, weekly magazines, tabloid newspapers).

In considering the coexistence of these two transgender subcultures as a social phenomenon from an ethnological perspective–similar to the examples mentioned above (e.g., Herdt, 1994a; Mageo, 1996; Roscoe, 1998; Kulick, 1998; Valentine, 2000)–I concentrate on the emic perspective, meaning the self-images of these people. Thus, I emphasize the societal and subcultural aspects, instead of individual- and family-based aspects, and the social interaction in daily life, instead of solely stage performances and performing. Consequently, I include in my analysis the context of cultural changes (within Berlin society) and influences from outside (media popularity and success of New York drag queens).

THE BEAUTY AND THE BEAST

Drag queens and Tunten are self-chosen labels for people who are often otherwise referred to as "male homosexual transvestites." At first glance, the protagonists of the two groups might look like Beauty and the Beast. In Berlin's gay community, they are often distinguished further as "Glamour Queens" and "Trash Tunten" (Trümmer-Tunten) because of their different gender performativity and appearance (Van Blond, 1999). Tunten, who tend to dress in a somewhat trashy and sometimes in a theatrical or *grotesque* way, use their gender performativity as a means of political protest/statement and to distinguish themselves from the German mainstream female impersonation (travesty). They see their gender performativity as an expression of their inner femaleness as well as a criticism of a certain mainstream model of femininity. What Tunten want and fight for in drag is acceptance and respect from the mainstream for their different way of life and for alternative lifestyles. Tunten have resignified a label used outside of the community as a slur term associated with "soft men," "feminine men" or "men in women's clothes" to a *nom de guerre* in a political sense.

Mireille,[4] a forty-year-old Tunten activist and artist who was socialized as a Tunte in the 1980s, explains:

> Tunte was an abusive term formerly used by the heterosexuals, but we appropriated this term and transformed it in an offensive way for our own political purposes as leftist gay people.

Yvonne, a twenty-five-year-old Tunte who came out in the late 1990s, confirms this political attitude for the younger Tunten generation by saying that:

> A Tunte is not simply wearing drag: it's the political attitude and activity that makes you a Tunte.

This political attitude is primarily seen in the context of gay activism against discrimination and for acceptance of gay people and their lifestyles. Tunten are also engaged in social work in the areas of AIDS prevention and care. A few remain, like many in the 1980s, activists in the leftist counterculture. The Berlin Tunten may be compared best with the New York-East Village drag queens of the 1980s, where Drag was described as a fierce and wild thing (Fleisher, 1996, p. 40) and such contemporary New York drag queens has Flloyd, Lavinia or Hattie Hathaway would fit perfectly into the Berlin Tunten scene. Tunten can also be categorized as what Steven Schacht (2002) termed "professional camp queens" (p. 171), with the added difference of a specific political attitude and subcultural context.

Most drag queens, on the other hand, tend to look more for applause, confirmation and money when they perform at parties and on stage. They want to be integrated in the media mainstream–preferably as celebrated superstars or as admired divas. Due to these goals, beauty and perfection in their appearance and their gender performativity as well as a certain noble attitude have become an important factor for them. Explains Sunny, a 23-year-old German drag queen, "being a Diva means that you're allowed to be arrogant, because you know that you are better than the masses!" Whitney, an American drag queen who came to Berlin in the late 1990s, talks about the process of becoming a drag queen: "You become a drag queen when you start to do your makeup better." Berlin drag queens dress generally in a more glamorous way, look like the success-oriented and commercialized American drag queens of the 1990s, such as the US drag icon RuPaul, and could be compared with those Steven Schacht (2002) has termed "professional glamour queens" (p. 169).

While some of the drag queens look down upon Tunten for their look and their societally critical performances, many Tunten saw in the newly emerging drag queen scene the same essence of illusion and conformity against which they had revolted in the 1980s, when they dissociated themselves from the German travesty performers. This distinction becomes even clearer in drag shows. Drag queens generally impersonate on stage famous international superstars like Marilyn Monroe, Kylie Minogue, Madonna or Marlene Dietrich, but they do so exclusively for entertainment value. Tunten, on the other hand, portray on stage the woman next door: the cashier girl in the supermarket, the dumb daughter of a right-wing politician, the old woman in the restroom, and often just themselves. Thus, they combine an intrinsic (self-)parody with a twofold societal criticism, a criticism of the heterosexual and male dominated majority and its clichés and of the genre travesty itself.

Members of both groups, however, state, that their drag is not simply "female impersonation," but moreover an expression of their female side and partly their gender identity. Only a few individuals of both groups reported that they once took female hormones or are still taking female hormones or are thinking about taking female hormones in the future. While the majority of the Tunten are called by their female names in daily life within their community, very rarely was this observed among the Berlin drag queens. Another main difference can be observed in the self-organization in the niches they occupy in mainstream society: while Tunten tend to organize collectively within their community (e.g., in ensembles, and political groups) drag queens tend to be loners trying to start solo careers in the mainstream business.

As I will further demonstrate, the different appearance and gender performativity of drag queens and Tunten onstage and offstage–the conforming and entertaining perfection of the "Beauty" in contrast to the rebellious and critical *grotesqueness* of the "Beast"–is not merely a matter of talent and physical appearance, but of different lifestyles and attitudes existing in the contemporary gay scene of new metropolitan Berlin. Considering the academic debate of whether transgender and drag are subversive (Butler, 1990; Schacht, 2002), drag queens in Berlin might appear as "gender conservatives" and Tunten as "gender anarchists" based on these lifestyles and attitudes. In a socio-historic and subcultural perspective, these significant differences go even further. For a better understanding of these different lifestyles and attitudes, it is necessary to bring into focus the beginnings of the self-organization and emergence of the Tunten-culture in West Berlin in the 1970s and 1980s, which laid the foundation for the drag queen vogue of the new and changing Berlin of the 1990s.[5]

THE HOMOSEXUAL CAMPAIGN WEST BERLIN AND THE CHILDREN OF THE REVOLUTION

From the late 1960s to the early 1990s, West Berlin gained a reputation as a fertile ground for all kinds of alternative subcultures, underground and counterculture movements. The student revolt of the late 1960s that started in West Berlin became famous as the "Out-of-Parliament-Opposition" and as the 1968 Generation throughout all of West Germany. The recent German gay movement dates back to the rebel years of the student revolt in West Berlin as well.

In 1971 fifty young gay men, many of whom were students, founded the Homosexual Campaign West Berlin/Homosexuelle Aktion West-Berlin (HAW) in the social climate of the student revolt and the Out-of-Parliament-Opposition. One year later, the HAW counted 160 members and established the first gay center in West Berlin. When in 1973 gay men from Italy and France marched in drag to a gay demonstration in West Berlin, the so-called "Tunten-Streit" (Tunten-Debate) arose in the HAW. In heated political discussions, it was discussed whether drag, such a "scandalous appearance," could be considered emancipating or not. The conservative part of the HAW separated and joined a more moderate gay group, whereas those who stayed followed the idea of a "feminist revolution" and started to use drag as a political means. In the late 1970s, the HAW blossomed into a dozen gay projects (e.g., gay bookstores, gay magazines, gay bars, gay publishing house) and their center was called the SchwuZ: Schwulen-Zentrum or gay men's center) (Frings & Kraushaar, 1982, pp. 329). In the early 1980s gay men who defined themselves as Tunten dominated the SchwuZ and so it soon became the home of the emerging Tunten-culture. As Mireille, who came out as a Tunte in SchwuZ in the early 1980s, explains, "The SchwuZ was a germ-cell for the Tunten-culture during the 1980s. Many young Tunten came out in SchwuZ and learned from the elders how to become a Tunte."

Whereas the HAW-Tunten of the 1970s used drag mainly at demonstrations and for political reasons, the SchwuZ-Tunten of the 1980s followed that young tradition, but they also added elements of fun and performance to their politics. The SchwuZ-Tunten organized themselves not only in loose political groups, but also in artistic ensembles, which combined politics with having fun and performance with (self-)parody and societal reflection. The performances of the Tunten-Ensemble "Bermudaas" in 1983 and 1984, for example, were a criticism of the mainstream Travesty-Shows, the performed illusion for a well-paying heterosexual audience (Bermudaas, 1985). Elfriede, a fifty-year-old Tunte and former member of the "Bermudaas," summarizes the fundamental criticism that Tunten direct towards travesty performers, saying that pulling off the wig on stage after the show is simply a "mortal sin" for a Tunte. She adds that for Tunten in the 1980s, you were a kind of misfit if you wore nylons *without* runs. The "Bermudaas," who usually performed for free, also talked about political issues and social problems (like AIDS) in their shows. The SchwuZ-Tunten had connections to the counterculture movement as well and some of them lived in a squatted house, which became well known as the "Tunten-Haus" (Tunten-House) (Bashore, 1990).

As a result and a means of their political tradition and activities–which claimed "the personal is the political"–drag was not only presented in nightlife and on stage by the performing artists, but also during the day and by nonperformers. Thus, the subculturally constructed gender identity of Tunten was also based on a political attitude. This attitude was rooted not only in a political gay activism, but also in the counterculture movement of the left.

The West Berlin Tunten-culture of the 1980s had its heyday in the late 1980s, when a Tunten-Ensemble called "Ladies Neid" (Ladies Envy) performed with 30 Tunten on stage. At that time the SchwuZ-Tunten organized AIDS benefit concerts, founded the first mobile AIDS-homecare service and the first gay and lesbian artists' agency. At that time, the SchwuZ-Tunten saw their community as a family.[6]

A NEW BERLIN IN THE 1990s:
THE REMAINS OF THE TUNTEN CULTURE MEET
THE DRAG QUEEN HYPE

After the fall of the Berlin Wall in November 1989 and the ensuing euphoria in the very first years after the reunification of Germany, the public opinion about foreigners and other minorities who were not "good Germans" changed. In the beginning of the 1990s, the Tunten community was, like other minorities and alternative subcultures in Berlin, confronted with an increase in discrimination and violence as well as the other major changes in the city. This was due not only to the patriotic *zeitgeist*, but also to other societal changes that took place in "New Berlin." All of a sudden, West Berlin was not an isolated island anymore, and together with East Berlin, was about to become the new capital of Germany. In the years after the reunification, the hunger for freedom and for consumption on the part of the East Berliners coincided with both a migration of young people from all parts of Germany, the fun-and-consumption-oriented young people, the "1989 Generation" as they were later named, as well as the move of wealthy West German businessmen to Berlin. Thus, the "New Berlin" became not only the symbol of the reunification and the end of the Cold War, but also a fertile ground for investors, businesspeople and young "party people." Sociologists diagnosed a significant paradigm shift in the German youth culture from the more collective and political "1968 Generation" to the heterogeneous, individualistic and more fun-and-consumption-oriented "1989 Generation" that emerged in the "New Berlin" (Leggewie, 1995).

The best example for the significant and fast societal change shifting West Berlin from the island of alternative and political subcultures to the new metropolitan Berlin was the "Love Parade." While in the summer of 1989, a hundred people were partying in the streets of West Berlin as a demonstration for peace and happiness (thus inventing the "Love Parade"), in the mid-1990s this fast-growing and already copyrighted commercial event became Berlin's main tourist attraction, drawing more than a million people from all of the European countries and from other parts of the world. At the same time, similar developments could be observed in Berlin's gay scene. Christopher Street Day, Berlin's annual parade commemorating the Stonewall riots in New York in 1969, changed from a political demonstration in the 1980s to a partly commercialized Gay Parade along the same lines as the (heterosexually dominated) "Love Parade" in the 1990s.[7] Thus, in the mid-1990s, interconnected developments were identifiable: an increasing of acceptance of gay people by the broader society and at the same time an increased tendency to conform to the "heterosexual society" by major parts of the gay community (Hinzpeter, 1997, p. 160).

Moreover, the new patriotic *zeitgeist* mixed with the desire for consumption and commerce led to a marginalization of the alternative and political subcultures and of the Tunten culture of the former West Berlin. The response of the gay community can be seen as a reflection of the shifts that have taken place in the society as a whole. When the gay community started to adopt and to influence the new lifestyle of the party scene in Berlin, the Tunten culture, which once played an important role in the gay movement, was marginalized in the gay subculture. In the middle of these changes, drag queens appeared on the Berlin gay scene and symbolically would be become the new vogue.

Despite the fact that there had been only a few people with the attitudes and gender performativity of contemporary German drag queens before, the name "drag queen" as a self-selected label became popular among German drag queens in the mid-1990s. Angelique, a forty-year-old drag queen, who had always been an outsider among the SchwuZ-Tunten of the late 1980s because of her glamorous style and manner (and thus always refused to see herself as a Tunte), did not start to call herself a drag queen until the mid-1990s, when popular drag queen movies, the success of the self-proclaimed "supermodel of the world" RuPaul (RuPaul, 1995) and the media coverage about New York drag queens supported and influenced the new Berlin drag queens.

Both as a result of the gay activism and the fights for respect and visibility by Tunten during the 1980s and due to their own perfection in appearance and performance, drag queens were accepted right from the start on the "New Berlin" party scene, into which they fit better than

Tunten ever did. Soon they were appearing on the cover of gay magazines and the first real Berlin drag queen star, Biggy van Blond, got her own locally broadcast TV talk show and her own column in a nationwide tabloid newspaper. Unlike the Berlin Tunten, the Berlin drag queens had had no collective organizational framework. They knew each other from parties and events, but worked mostly in solo shows and performances or as waitresses in the Techno- and House-music scene. With this fast success, many of them separated themselves from the still existent remains of the Tunten culture, and as a further reflection of the broader society, the competition among them was high and the solidarity low. Explains the drag queen Angelique, who attended the New York Wigstock festival in 1994 and who had the idea to organize a Berlin Wigstock called "Wigstöckel,"[8]

> In the mid-1990s everybody knew each other from seeing and purposely ignoring one another and the community was very splintered. It was an unbearable condition.

TRANSGENDER UNITED:
DRAG QUEENS AND TUNTEN DIVIDED

The first Wigstöckel took place in 1996 under the theme "Drag Queens United." The event was organized with the intention to overcome the differences between the individuals of the scattered Tunten and drag queen scenes and to gather the different drag performers in a single show. Thus, more than 400 people in drag attended the first "Wigstöckel." Because of internal disputes in the organizational team of Wigstöckel in the earliest stages and the development of a more political character for Wigstöckel, some of the Berlin drag queens, like Angelique, withdrew from the organization as well as from participating in the show.[9] Today, the Wigstöckel cast is a team of Tunten, drag kings, cross-dressers and transsexual people, who all perform under the heading "Wigstöckel Transgender United."

Wigstöckel was only one attempt to reunite the splintered scene. Another attempt was the Tunten-Ensemble "Café Transler": a political performance group in the tradition of the 1980s Tunten-culture. "Café Transler" started "open stage" nights, which served as a means to support young drag performers during their first steps on stage. This opportunity was and still is used by Tunten as well as by young drag queens (and recently also by drag kings). Supported and promoted by Café

Transler and its open stage, in the late 1990s three young Tunten joined and created a new Trash-Tunten-Ensemble: the "Albrecht Diseusen" (AlDis). The AlDis gained a reputation for reviving an almost extinct tradition of Tunten-Trash as performed by the Bermudaas in the early 1980s. The members of both Café Transler and the AlDis are politically active within the gay community. This activism is reflected in their shows in a form of societal criticism. In performing as supermarket cashier girls on stage, the AlDis also follow the 1980s Tunten tradition using a *grotesque* and unglamorous form of drag to demonstrate their nonconformity and to parody female impersonation.

At the same time, in the late 1990s, some of the Berlin drag queens who had withdrawn from Wigstöckel founded for their own purposes "Superstar Management," an agency that promotes drag queens and so-called club kids for model agencies and mainstream party events and as solo performers. With their contrary motifs, the drag queen agency Superstar Management and the Tunten-Ensemble AlDis displayed once again the significant differences in Berlin between the Beauty and the Beast, the drag queens and Tunten.

URBAN TRANSGENDER CULTURES IN CONTEXT: THE BEAUTY AND THE BEAST REVISED

As I have shown, the emergence of a drag queen culture in Berlin reflects not only a change in the lifestyle in large parts of the gay scene, but also the dramatic changes that took place in the city during the consolidation of Berlin as the metropolitan capital of a reunified Germany; i.e., the transition from being the center of West Germany's counterculture movement to becoming the center of Germany's Techno and Party movement. While Tunten in the past and still today organize themselves in the socially and politically active parts of the gay subculture, the drag queens not only conquered the gay party scene as solo performers, but also achieved access to parts of the mainstream business (advertisement, TV, heterosexual club scene). Apart from the first Wigstöckel festivals and the agency Superstar Management, drag queens made no efforts to organize themselves and preferred to start solo careers. For most of the Tunten their gender performativity not only is an expression of their inner femaleness, but also serves as a way of making a socially critical political statement.

In contrast, for most of the drag queens, their gender performativity is (beyond being an expression of their inner femaleness) a successful means to make their names as performers. As Wigstöckel became better known as a political transgender event, the drag queens withdrew and established themselves in a more well-defined "market," one more specifically made for drag queens, which was a recent development. As I previously noted, the Berlin drag queen of today has a strong focus on appearance and performance, largely conforms to societal expectations, and also a certain noble attitude. This noble attitude–which is sometimes also expressed in a form of arrogance towards both Tunten and people in general–stands in direct contrast to the egalitarian attitude of the Tunten.

The Berlin drag queens have been influenced by the media hype about New York drag queens right from the start. Here it is very important to understand that the media most promote drag queens like RuPaul, self-proclaimed supermodel of the world, and not drag queens like her longtime friend, the shocking performer Flloyd. Moreover, the immense diversity of contemporary New York drag queens is often forgotten due to the limiting stereotypes of the media (Fleisher, 1996, p. 39). Politically active and nonconforming drag queens are not part of the mainstream hype, nor do they serve as a role model for the Berlin drag queens. This is due less to a lack of knowledge than to a conscious selection. The new vogue of drag queens in Berlin coincides nicely with the current German *zeitgeist*, which also helped to shape the way that certain international drag queens are selected as role models. Hence, the rich internal diversity of a drag queen community like the one in New York is contrasted by the present drag queen-Tunten antagonism in the transgender subculture of Berlin.

The antagonism of Tunten and drag queens in Berlin is best revealed in the polarity of an ensemble like the AlDis and an agency like Superstar Management, both groups that were founded by young gay people who came out in the 1990s. They can be seen as representatives not only of two faces of the contemporary gay community, but also of two different and coexisting urban transgender subcultures. The Tunten still belong to and carry on certain "old" traditions of the counterculture movement of 1980s West Berlin. They are keeping alive a tradition that emerged in a very specific socio-historic and also subcultural context. Insofar the contemporary Berlin Tunten culture can be seen as a "traditional" local transgender subculture.

On the other hand, the Berlin drag queens are not simply copying the drag queen scene of New York. They correspond well with the new German youth culture as well as to the changes in the contemporary Berlin gay scene and thus they pick out their international role models like RuPaul in a very selective way. The new drag queen vogue of Berlin must be seen, like the Tunten culture, in the socio-historical context in which it emerged and thus represents a new local transgender subculture. In the same way drag queens in Berlin are not simply an imported trend from the U.S., but a reflection of a significant change in German youth and gay culture, the contemporary Tunten-culture of Berlin is a reflection of a now only marginally existing German youth and gay culture that dates back to the 1970s and 1980s.

This example of two different and coexisting transgender subcultures–like the case of "travestis" and drag queens in Rio de Janeiro and other ethnographical exemplifications sketched out early on–demonstrates the importance of emphasizing the socio-historical and subcultural contexts of urban transgender cultures in order to understand their different self-images, gender performances, and cultures. The simultaneous coexistence of two transgender subcultures, the Tunten and the drag queens in Berlin, exemplifies a local urban transgender autochthony, which is also part of global transgender diversity. As such, it is only partly influenced by and is not primarily the simple results of developments of subculture globalization, which are discussed in terms of internationalization of gay identities.

NOTES

1. That some transgender persons in western and westernized societies have become famous as performers, singers and/or models (e.g., RuPaul, Romy Haag, Roberta Close) is due to their talent, beauty and/or ability to fulfill certain expectations of a mainstream audience and not to their gender identity.

2. As I learned from Asian and Latin-American drag queens I met in Berlin, Rio de Janeiro and New York. See also Brubach & O'Brien, 1999.

3. They are between 23 and 50 years old and mostly of German descent, but also of Afro- and Latin-American and Asian descent.

4. Mireille is, like all other informant names used in this article, a pseudonym created by me and not the self-chosen female Tunten name under which Mireille is known in Berlin. I use this method to provide more anonymity, because in the Berlin transgender subculture some people like Mireille have their artist names written in their ID cards and even use them to sign checks, tenancy agreements, etc.

5. Transgender people existed also in East Berlin and East Germany, but apart from outsiders like the well-known Charlotte von Mahlsdorf, they lived mostly clandestinely and there was no self-organization and subculture as in the West (Brubach & O'Brien, 1999, p. 25).

6. In 1988, the photographer Jürgen Baldiga published a photo book with portraits of 26 Berlin Tunten, which was seen by the protagonists as their family album (Baldiga, 1988).

7. In 1996, the Christopher Street Day Parade was celebrated by 50,000 people partying in the street and sponsored by the tobacco industry (Hinzpeter, 1997, p. 140).

8. "Stöckel" is the German term for high heels.

9. For example, at Wigstöckel 2002 the Gaysha-Boys from Kyoto (Japan) and Sherry Vine from New York City were the only self-identified drag queens performing.

REFERENCES

Altman, D. (1996). Rupture or continuity. The internationalization of gay identities. *Social Text*, 48, 77-94.

Baldiga, J. (1988). *Tunten queens tantes*. Oberkaufungen: Vis-aVis.

Balzer, C. (2001). *Vielfalt der Geschlechter im interkulturellen Vergleich*. Paper presented at the Annual German Transgender Conference in Berlin, Germany.

Bashore, J. (1990). *The battle of tuntenhaus*. Documentary (BRD/USA).

Bell, D. and Binnie, J. (2000). *The sexual citizen. Queer politics and beyond*. Cambridge: Polity.

Berger, Peter L. (1997). The four faces of global culture. *National Interest*, 49, Fall 97, 23-30.

Bermudaas (1985). *Gesamtdeutsche nudeln*. Videotape.

Bleibtreu-Ehrenberg, G. (1984). *Der weibmann. Kultischer geschlechtswechsel im schamanismus*. Frankfurt: Fischer Taschenbuch Verlag.

Bolin, A. (1994). Transcending and transgendering: Male-to-female transsexuals, dichotomy and diversity. In Herdt, G. (Ed.), *Third sex /third gender: Beyond sexual dimorphism in culture and history* (pp. 419-446). New York: Zone Books.

Brubach, H. and O'Brien, M. J. (1999). *Girlfriend. Men, women and drag*. New York: Random House.

Brummelhuis, H. ten. (1999). Transformations of transgender: The case of the Thai kathoey. In Jackson, P.A. & Sullivan, G. (Eds.), *Lady boys, tom boys, rent boys: Male and female homosexualities in contemporary Thailand* (pp. 121-139). New York: Haworth Press.

Butler, J. (1990). *Gender trouble: Feminism and the subversion of identity*. New York: Routledge.

Cvetkovich, A. and Kellner, D. (1997). Introduction: Thinking global and local. In Cvetkovich, A. and Kellner, D. (Eds.), *Articulating the global and the local. Globalization and cultural studies* (pp. 1-30). Boulder: Westview Press.

Dallas, D. (Ed.). (1998). *Current concepts in transgender identity*. New York: Garland Publishing.

Fleisher, J. (1996). *The drag queens of New York. An illustrated field guide*. New York: Riverhead Books.

Frings, M. and Kraushaar, E. (1982). *Männer: Liebe*. Franfurt/Main: Rowohlt.

Herdt, G. (Ed.). (1994a). *Third sex/third gender: Beyond sexual dimorphism in culture and history*. New York: Zone Books.

Herdt, G. (1994b). Introduction: Third sexes and third genders. In Herdt, G. (Ed.), *Third sex/third gender: Beyond sexual dimorphism in culture and history* (pp. 21-81). New York: Zone Books.

Hinzpeter, W. (1997). *Schöne schwule welt. Der schlussverkauf einer bewegung.* Berlin: Querverlag.

Jackson, P. A. and Sullivan, G. (1999). A panoply of roles: Sexual and gender diversity in contemporary Thailand. In Jackson, P.A. & Sullivan, G. (Eds.), *Lady boys, tom boys, rent boys: Male and female homosexualities in contemporary Thailand* (pp. 1-27). New York: Haworth Press.

Kulick, D. (1998). *Travesti: Sex, gender and culture among Brazilian transgendered prostitutes.* University of Chicago Press.

Leggewie, C. (1995). *Die 89er: Portrait einer generation.* Hamburg: Hoffmann & Campe.

Lindemann, G. (1993). *Das paradoxe geschlecht: Transsexualität im spannungsfeld von körper, leib und gefühl.* Frankfurt: Fischer Taschenbuch Verlag.

Mageo, J-M. (1996). Samoa, on the wilde side: Male transvestism, Oscar Wilde, and liminality in making gender. *Ethos* 24(4), 588-627.

Nanda, S. (1994). Hijras: An alternative sex and gender role in India. In Herdt, G. (Ed.), *Third sex/third gender: Beyond sexual dimorphism in culture and history* (pp. 373-418). New York: Zone Books.

Roberts, M. (2001). Notes on the global underground: Subcultural elites, conspicuous cosmopolitanism. Paper presented at the Globalization, Identity & the Arts Conference, University of Manitoba.

Roscoe, W. (1998). *Changing ones: Third and fourth genders in Native North America.* New York: St. Martin's Griffin.

RuPaul. (1995). *Letting it all hang out. An autobiography.* New York: Hyperion.

Schacht, S. (2002). Four renditions of doing female drag: Feminine appearing conceptual variations of a masculine theme. *Gendered Sexualities*, 6, 157-180.

Valentine, David. (2000). *"I know what I am": The category "transgender" in the construction of contemporary American conceptions of gender and sexuality*, PhD Dissertation, New York University.

Van Blond, Biggy (1999). *Vive la différence!: Von Glamourqueens und trümmertunten.* In: 1. Berliner tuntenbuch, Berlin (unpublished manuscript).

Moffies, Artists, and Queens:
Race and the Production
of South African Gay Male Drag

Amanda Lock Swarr, MA

University of Minnesota

SUMMARY. This article draws on seventeen months of ethnographic fieldwork in South Africa to explore the experiences of urban and township drag performers. I show that two distinct sex-gender-sexuality systems have emerged based in the sociopolitical history of South Africa, and I argue that urban drag produces race oppositionally and examine how township femininity creates raced forms of gender, sex, and sexual-

Amanda Lock Swarr is a PhD candidate in Feminist Studies at the University of Minnesota. She is completing her dissertation, "Exploring the Boundaries of Sex, Gender, and Race: Transgendered Subjectivities in Contemporary South Africa."

Author note: Support for this research came from the MacArthur Program, University of Minnesota Graduate School, and Center for Advanced Feminist Studies. Thanks especially to: Midi, Theresa, Mario, Faezel, Virgil, Nazma, Brooke, Cindy, Kevin, Rieyadh, Kieron, Clive, Walter, Olivia, Preston, Bernard, Scarlet, Barbie, Pieter, Dawie, Juan, Emuel, Michael, and Martin. I am grateful for generous advice from Lisa Disch, Amy Kaminsky, Premesh Lalu, Richa Nagar, Graeme Reid, Steven P. Schacht, and Joel Wainwright. Finally, the contributions of my research collaborator and partner Susan Bullington were invaluable to completion of this article.

Correspondence may be addressed: Department of Women's Studies, University of Minnesota, 425 Ford Hall, Minneapolis, MN 55455.

[Haworth co-indexing entry note]: "Moffies, Artists, and Queens: Race and the Production of South African Gay Male Drag." Swarr, Amanda Lock. Co-published simultaneously in *Journal of Homosexuality* (Harrington Park Press, an imprint of The Haworth Press, Inc.) Vol. 46, No. 3/4, 2004, pp. 73-89; and: *The Drag Queen Anthology: The Absolutely Fabulous but Flawlessly Customary World of Female Impersonators* (ed: Steven P. Schacht, with Lisa Underwood) Harrington Park Press, an imprint of The Haworth Press, Inc., 2004, pp. 73-89. Single or multiple copies of this article are available for a fee from The Haworth Document Delivery Service [1-800-HAWORTH, 9:00 a.m. - 5:00 p.m. (EST). E-mail address: docdelivery@haworthpress.com].

ity. Contemporary South African drag foregrounds the performativity and constitution of race and gender. My analysis attempts to challenge definitions of "drag" and "audience," suggesting the necessity for an integrated reconceptualization of drag studies. *[Article copies available for a fee from The Haworth Document Delivery Service: 1-800-HAWORTH. E-mail address: <docdelivery@haworthpress.com> Website: <http://www.HaworthPress.com> © 2004 by The Haworth Press, Inc. All rights reserved.]*

KEYWORDS. South Africa, drag, race, gay, gender, sex, sexuality

Drag performances take complex forms in contemporary South Africa. Drag is performed widely in elite white clubs, gay township *shebeens*, and as part of mainstream community celebrations. When apartheid ended in 1994, South African gays and lesbians were the first in the world to obtain constitutional protection based on sexual orientation. Yet they continue to live in a society fraught with enormous social, economic, and political contradictions. Understanding the disparities inherent in this context is fundamental to understanding South African drag and allows us to see not only how social differences influence drag, but also how drag produces race and gender.

This article is based on seventeen months of fieldwork conducted in South Africa in 1997 and 1999-2000 and draws on interviews and participant observation to highlight the words and experiences of South African drag performers. In particular, I consider historical and contemporary drag in the urban centers and surrounding townships of Cape Town, Johannesburg, and Pretoria from the perspectives of its participants.[1] There are three parts to my argument. I postulate that two distinct sex-gender-sexuality systems have emerged in South Africa that shape and are shaped by historical manifestations of drag. I argue that urban and township drag produce whiteness and femininity through raced and classed juxtapositions. Finally, I contend that an examination of South African drag not only illustrates the ways that drag produces gender and race, but may affect how we understand "audience" and "drag."

Gendered and raced categories of identity and analysis are inseparable and are produced by specific historical practices. Contemporary theorists and activists have increasingly imagined ways to avoid the false separation of race, gender, class, and sexuality to conceptualize interstices referred to as, for example, borderlands (Anzaldúa, 1987) or intersectionality (Crenshaw, 1993).[2] Analyses of gender performances that pose race and class as supplementary are always incomplete, as there is no generic "woman" or "man" represented in drag. It is impossible to generalize about drag without exploring the various ways that each drag performance articulates the simultaneity of social categories.[3] Here, I draw on the work of scholars who dwell in the contradictions of race and gender (McClintock, 1995; Stoler, 1991), considering individuals who both adopt and confront dominant ideals by combining contingent social identities.

Though gender and race may seem to be fixed, their meanings are never fully consistent and must constantly be reworked and negotiated. My use of articulation as a method for conceptualizing intersectionalities works alongside Butler's notion of *performativity*. Performativity allows us to avoid oversimplifying race and gender as natural or as socially constructed. It also gives space for staged "performances" while moving beyond this definition. Iterative performativity, "regularized and constrained repetition of norms" (Butler, 1993, p. 95), is a process that creates the effect of fixity over time. Performativity is not simply about individuals' practices and will; through citationality–the invocation of norms and conventions–norms are reiterated which "preceed, constrain, and exceed the performer" (p. 234). In sum, race and gender are imitations for which there are no originals (Butler, 1991). They come into being and constantly change through repeated performances and everyday practices.

At the same time, categories such as white/Black or man/woman may be critical to individuals' self-perceptions and have political relevance. The simultaneous instability of identity categories and their self-descriptive use present methodological difficulties. For instance, I rely on the racial designators of apartheid–"white," "Coloured," and "Black"–since these are ways that South Africans describe themselves, while recognizing the assumptions underlying such categories.[4] Similarly, terms like "transgender" and "cross-dresser" imply that there are only two sexes/genders, and "drag" indicates a rupture between gendered appearance and sex that essentializes anatomy. I necessarily employ the same words and ideas undercut by my own research and consciously work within this paradox.

This article also assumes that gender and race operate oppositionally. Heterosexuality is conceptualized at the borders of queerness (Chauncey, 1994), femininity and femaleness operate in opposition to masculinity and maleness (Kessler and McKenna, 1978), and Blackness functions as the negative antithesis of whiteness (Said, 1978).

None of these categories is monolithic; however, they function socially as oppositions, and examining their relationality reveals how drag is produced by and produces a range of social factors. Here, I contribute to discussions of this oppositional simultaneity by analyzing the constitution of whiteness/Blackness, masculinity/femininity, and heterosexuality/homosexuality and the cracks within these dichotomies.

RACING SOUTH AFRICAN DRAG

Although since the end of apartheid South Africans have created a nation based on rhetoric of freedom from oppression, the legacy of apartheid and forms of racial and economic division it ruthlessly enforced are still central components of South Africans' daily lives. Those who perform in drag are no exception. Gay men of all races in South Africa drag, but drag venues, forms, and opportunities are shaped by race and class. Performances by white gay men occur in urban bars and clubs in front of largely white audiences. As part of troupes, they do not receive tips but are paid by venue owners and are part of choreographed shows. While some urban troupes include Black and Coloured performers, most Black and Coloured gays drag primarily in pageants and competitions for titles, and unlike most white gay men, many also drag publicly in their daily lives.

Differences among drag performances are rooted in the racialized sex-gender-sexuality systems within which South Africans operate. Distinguishing among sex (male or female bodies), gender (masculinity and femininity), and sexuality (sexual practices and orientation) is critical to understanding these systems. White South African drag performers function within a self-policed gender-sex-sexuality system that links sex and gender. Generally, most white gay men who identify as gay are masculine. Indeed, while playing with gender in social settings is accepted, transgender identities are looked down upon within white gay communities. White South African drag parallels this construction. For most South African urban whites, drag is an aestheticized form of self-expression confined to bars and clubs—it is a bounded spectacle, not an everyday practice, performed by "drag artists."

Drag is an integral part of urban white gay communities but does not necessarily reflect the gender of the person who is dragging. Within these communities, same-sex desire usually indicates homosexual identity; males who have sex with other males label themselves "gay." But in Coloured and Black township communities, masculine males who have sex with feminine males are often considered "straight." In order to be a Black or Coloured "gay" man in the townships, one must have both same-sex desire and feminine gender. Most gay men in the townships have relationships with "straight" men, and such relationships are central to many township gay experiences. Thus, in township sex-gender-sexuality ideologies, gender is disconnected from sex and instead coupled with sexuality.[5]

In recent years, as Reid (1999) and Donham (1998) have pointed out, white and northern definitions of "gayness" have influenced how urban Black and Coloured gay men identify themselves. Among educated gay men, especially those who are upwardly mobile and move out of the townships, increasing numbers of Black and Coloured masculine men identify as gay. However, according to the approximately 150 informants I spoke with during my research in the Western Cape and Gauteng, these men are the exception to township ideologies. In fact, feminine gay men in the townships fall outside of the man/woman binary into their own categories as *moffies* (in Coloured townships) and *skesana* and *istabane* (in some Black townships).[6] In South Africa's townships, drag performances are not simply personal expressions; they have implications for relationships and community visibility. Dragging in pageants and to attract masculine males' attention is an important way that township "drag queens" affirm their feminine genders.

These two sex-gender-sexuality systems and the ways they are articulated today cannot be separated from the specific national and regional histories of South Africa. South Africa is well-known for its brutal and contradictory system of legalized racial segregation, but like most colonial states, the apartheid regime also legitimated itself by affirming gender subversion or gender rigidity to maintain repressive authority. Slippages in the treatment of gender and sexuality affected the development of drag in South Africa.

Historically, drag has not simply been an aesthetic practice for Black and Coloured gays. In the Coloured townships outside of Cape Town, *moffies* dragged in their jobs and in sport (Gevisser, 1994). The annual Coon Carnival has also been a site for drag performances by *moffies* since at least the 1930s.[7] Although some historians have claimed that *moffies* reversed or subverted gender and sexuality through their roles in the Coon Carnival (Jeppie, 1990; Chetty, 1994), the *moffie* might alternately be seen as a crucial part of the sex-gender-sexuality system unique to Coloured township culture.

As apartheid undermined the Coon Carnival by restricting the movement of Coloureds through the 1966 Group Areas Act and similar legislation, troupe captains increasingly viewed *moffies* as symbolic of autonomy and freedom (Martin, 1994, p. 16). However, despite Coons' defiant attitudes, apartheid officials simultaneously manipulated the Coon Carnival to demonstrate the supposed inferiority and "primitiveness" of Coloureds (pp. 127, 130). The perceived outrageousness of Coons, who sing and dance in satin costumes with painted faces, and *moffies* was a source of entertainment for whites, and often a source of embarrassment for aspirant Coloureds (Jeppie, 1990).

Drag among Black South Africans was also accepted by apartheid officials when it served the interests of the state and capital. Historically, same-sex relationships between Black men have been common, though not always indicating "homosexual" identities. For instance, gendered "mine marriages" among Black men who lived in the compounds of South Africa's diamond and gold mines benefited "husbands" as a source of sex, companionship, and domestic service. "Wives" participated, according to Philemon, a Tsonga miner, "for the sake of security, for the acquisition of property, and for the fun itself" (Wa Sibuye, 1993, p. 62). Under colonialism and apartheid, these same-sex relationships included both a feminine and masculine partner and were accepted among miners. The feminine partner, who was usually younger, would often drag to attract partners, receive protection and privileges, or establish roles in the relationship (Moodie, 1989; Murray and Roscoe, 1998).

Miners' same-sex relationships were common enough to be acknowledged, and indeed encouraged, by the state. Homosexuality and drag on the mines provided an outlet for Black male sexuality, as men were confined to compounds, and provided domestic service for the miners, which kept them from demanding to bring their wives to the mines and hence necessitating higher wages (Elder, 1995). Consequently, Black same-sex sexuality and, by association, drag, was supported by the apartheid government to the extent that it facilitated control over Black labor.

Like with Black and Coloured drag, the South African state attempted to use white drag to reinforce its own power. For example, drag performer Matthew Krouse describes how drag shows in the South African Defense Force during 1984 were sometimes organized by the military, which paid for costumes and wigs. Shows were attended by "a couple of thousand soldiers" (1994, p. 216) and intentionally posited male homosexuality as abnormal by linking it to femininity. Drag performers were objectified by the largely straight audience; in Krouse's words, "During the performance there was an enormous din of catcalls and mocking masturbatory behavior" (p. 216). These shows reinforced the inferiority of drag artists and the masculinity of their straight audiences in ways he found degrading. Krouse writes, "I can only imagine that the upper echelons of the camp must have felt a tremendous sense of strength on those nights [of drag performances]" (p. 218), as they reaffirmed the state's control over white drag's subversive potential.

Apartheid was a system fraught with raced and gendered contradictions, however, and the South African state also struggled to restrict drag and enforce heterosexuality among all races through laws and police violence (Retief, 1994). For instance, although access to private spaces and the privileges of whiteness often protected upper class white homosexuals from detection, policing of white males' gender and sexuality was especially vigorous under apartheid (Elder, 1995). Uncontrolled threats posed by drag and homosexuality were not accepted under Afrikaner nationalism, since supposedly normative gender and sexuality were essential components of the racial categories of apartheid (McClintock, 1995).

Beginning in the 1960s, Parliament enacted a variety of laws intended to suppress "homosexual" behaviors, including the Prohibition of Disguises Act 16 of 1969 that criminalized males dressing in feminine clothing. Gay men of all races were increasingly charged with "masquerading as women in public" (Cameron, 1994); drag, as a public marker of disruption to apartheid conceptions of sex, gender, and sexuality, was outlawed when outside of the control of the state. Not surprisingly, drag still flourished in spaces like private parties and gay bars, but it was driven further underground by restrictive legislation. Today, drag is still characterized by contradiction, but white drag continues to be largely confined to urban gay bars and clubs, while Black and Coloured men incorporate drag into their daily lives.

URBAN WHITENESS AND DRAG

In June 1997, Lili Slapstilli, a member of the drag troupe "Mince," was favorably reviewed in the mainstream *Cape Times* newspaper as "one of the most convincing impersonations of Tina Turner on the market" (Devenish, 1997). Slapstilli gyrated to a live recording of "Proud Mary," her mime perfectly matching the difficult lyrics, and, as the tempo of the song increased, she danced flawlessly like Turner in concert.[8] Slapstilli herself does not try to perfectly mimic the women she impersonates, stating, "At 6'2" there's no way I'll look exactly like them."[9] However, the fissure in Slapstilli's authenticity came not through her height, her skill, or her costume, but through her race. Lili Slapstilli is white. How is it that she could be considered to be an "authentic" Tina Turner?

Despite outward differences between Slapstilli and Tina Turner, white South African performers enjoy great autonomy and are perceived as authentic in their performances of Blackness. In some ways, Slapstilli's authenticity as Tina Turner might be interpreted as undermining racial expectations and revealing the fiction of race; Slapstilli's clothes, miming, and mannerisms superseded phenotypical differences in the eyes of the audience and reviewers. Impersonations of Eartha Kitt, Millie Jackson, Jennifer Holiday, and Aretha Franklin by white drag performers in South Africa's urban clubs and bars garner similar praise. However, this is not because whiteness is unimportant to white audiences; instead, drag produces whiteness as an unmarked category, a space in which to create characters, while Black and Coloured performers are largely restricted to impersonating women of color.

Whiteness in South Africa is anxiously policed, as the new post-apartheid "non-racialism" threatens this category that still retains enormous legal, social, and economic privileges. In South Africa, as elsewhere, whiteness hinges on an implicit comparison to "non-white," a catch-all category that elides difference. Race is an unstable complex of social meanings (Omi and Winant, 1994). The embodiment of race is similar to the embodiment of gender and sex; both are without significant biological basis but articulated through repeated nebulous practices, beliefs, and behaviors.

Race is also predicated on the hierarchical conception that whiteness is not only fundamentally different from but also superior to Blackness. Although South African racial articulations include categories beyond Black and white, the apartheid regime nevertheless conceived of itself in term of whiteness, with other categories implicitly falling into the inferior "non-white." Drag is one means through which the instability of whiteness is fixed and its meaning is produced.[10]

Drag among South African urban white gay men is socially accepted if confined to commercial performances, and gay male drag is found in almost all gay-owned bars and clubs in Cape Town and Pretoria. Some urban drag may be glamorous, while other performances are comedic. Comic performances are one site for producing racial juxtapositions, explored through interviews with Warren.[11] Warren not only is the owner of a prominent urban gay bar but also hires all of the performers, choreographs all of their numbers, and even chooses their costumes, stage names, and musical pieces. When describing how he envisions performers' roles, Warren states that Coloured and Black performers must be comic in order to entertain a white crowd. In urban drag, white audiences are comfortable seeing Black and Coloured performers in the roles of entertaining and silly clowns. It is important to note, however, that Warren's comments are undermined by the sensual acts of the few Coloured and Black members of his drag troupe. Their performances reinforce the contradictions of racial production, as well as the autonomy of the artists themselves. Black sexuality is simultaneously desired while repressed as immoral. Given white fears of this sexuality, glamorous and sensual performances by Black and Coloured artists are potentially both titillating and disruptive to white audiences.

White drag artists also differentiate among and complicate forms of whiteness. One such performer is Sonja Koekemoer, who during 1996-1997 performed as a *boeremeisie*, literally "farm girl," a favorite trope of Afrikaans drag artists in Cape Town and Pretoria. The *boeremeisie* embodied on stage is an example of unsuccessful femininity. Koekemoer as a *boeremeisie* wore bright, clashing colors and garish styles as well as giant plastic flowers or bright ribbons in her teased blonde hair. She moved awkwardly and used props such as bedroom slippers to emphasize her working class values. Koekemoer's drag included silver and blue makeup with sparkles contrasted with her intentionally hairy arms, and she mimed in Afrikaans to traditional songs in an overdramatized, tragic style. Her performances were immensely popular; she was featured in mainstream newspapers in Cape Town and was the headline performer in a national drag tour. Koekemoer's parody articulates contemporary ambivalence about the place of Afrikaner culture in post-apartheid South Africa. Upwardly mobile Afrikaners, in particular, often distance themselves from their working class, rural roots. However, Koekemoer also reflects white gay men's increasing rejection of traditional South African values in favor of an emerging international gay sensibility.

Racial tension is often produced by drag performances. For instance, when Brenda, a Coloured drag artist, performs comically to the "Click Song (Qongqothwane)" by Miriam Makeba, a legendary Black South African singer, she reinforces the white/Black dichotomy and stereotypes of Black inferiority. Brenda's traditional African costume and padded buttocks, exaggerated miming and ridicule of the clicks of the Xhosa language, and overtly sexualized dancing during which she intentionally opens her legs to expose her crotch leave her largely white audiences in stitches. Further, Brenda's performances occur in the context of Cape Town's Coloured/Black racial tensions exacerbated by divisive labor policies and voting privileges afforded to Coloureds under apartheid. As a Coloured performer stereotyping a Black woman, her performances affirm the Coloured/Black distinction and her superiority in South Africa's racial hierarchy as a Coloured person. But Brenda's tenuous position and her strict supervision by a white bar owner in this urban context also allows for the reinscription of the overarching white/Black binary.

Drag is an important way that gay whiteness is constituted in South Africa. The sex-gender-sexuality system under which urban white gay men operate values masculine gender identities, and many middle-class white gays are concerned with respectability and social approval. Despite the acceptance of drag in commercial performances, transgender identities are often rejected and ridiculed. For example, Jan, a white middle-class gay man from an urban area, believes that drag artists are "backwards," especially those who cross-dress in their daily lives. He sees them as "unresolved" psychologically and claims that in the gay and lesbian movement, "we don't want court jesters." Jan's comments are commonplace among white gays, and in South Africa such sentiments have distinctly racial overtones. Jan is disdainful of white drag artists' performances, but he is far more condemnatory of Black and Coloured drag queens with transgendered identities. Here, he implicitly establishes his own gender and race as superior and normative, while drag queens are seen as inferior and inappropriate.

Warren's comments are similarly instructive for understanding how drag produces racial differences in urban contexts. In interviews, he distinguishes between "drag artists" who perform in his bar and "common drag queens." This comparison is loaded with racial and classed meanings and simultaneously constructs hierarchies of race, gender, and sexuality. White drag is considered superior in this context because it is a conscious performance, an upper class theatric art form (thus the preferred term, "drag artist") that is economically valuable. Such drag may not explicitly challenge the sex-gender-sexuality system within which it operates, as most performers are not transgendered–they drag as actors, as characters in a play. Black and Coloured drag queens' drag, in comparison, is part of their identities. Gendered differences between forms of drag allow some white gays to make judgements that subtly establish their racial and economic superiority.

FEMININITY AND TOWNSHIP DRAG

The interrelationships among gender, sex, and sexuality have presented gender theorists with theoretical puzzles. Within this complex, inattention to race and location and the invisibility of queers of color, particularly in the developing world, have been increasingly addressed (Hammonds, 1994; Constantine-Simms, 2000). I explore this conundrum through an examination of Coloured and Black township drag, as it enables the binary construction of masculinity and femininity as opposites while simultaneously constituting "gayness" as its own gender category. I consider three components of this articulation in these township contexts: drag pageants, drag and sexual relationships, and the vulnerabilities drag facilitates.

Black and Coloured drag illustrates the performativity of femininity. Drag pageants follow formats of beauty contests, featuring various dress competitions and interviews. Participants sometimes pay to enter, instead of being paid as in urban drag, though pageant winners may obtain cash and prizes. They enter competitions as individuals and answer questions based on their opinions, not as "artists" in a show. For example, the Miss GLOW 1999 pageant final (Gays and Lesbians of the Witswaterstrand) was held in a gay *shebeen* (township bar) in Sebokeng and attended by gay and straight members of Black township communities surrounding Johannesburg. The seven finalists showcased both casual and evening dress, and each answered two questions on topics ranging from trivia about local gay icons to their own positions on coming out. Participants did not wear false breasts or wigs to make their bodies appear female, but performed femininity through their dress, makeup, and movements.

In the eyes of the audience and judges, contestants embody a particular form of Black and Coloured township drag in which juxtapositions between male bodies and feminine performances are the norm. In his discussion of the 1993 funeral of Linda Ngcobo, a well-known Black gay activist, journalist Mark Gevisser describes some mourners wearing "that peculiar androgyny of township drag borne of scant resources and much imagination, nodding at gender–inversion with no more than a frilly shirt, a pair of garish earrings, a touch of rouge, a pair of low-heeled pumps, a third-hand wig" (1994, pp. 14-15). In township contexts, the raced and classed ways that femininity is articulated, while perhaps slight or even indecipherable to outsiders, provide signposts to indicate the parameters of the performance to those who can read them. This form of drag produces gender, as Gevisser says, of "scant resources and much imagination." "Imagination" is the key word here. It suggests how drag queens and their audiences (per)form something not entirely real–gender–and in so doing make it "real" by sustaining the collective illusion of gender fixity.

Drag queens prepare their physical bodies with their audiences, especially masculine men, in mind. To prepare for the Miss Gay Universe 2000 pageant, Nasreen, a self-defined Coloured drag queen, describes having her eyebrows shaped and growing her hair, in addition to making her own gowns. She helps audiences forget that she has a male body and performs an exoticized femininity considered beautiful. Nasreen believes that "passing" as a woman and being sexually desired while dragging are great affirmations of her femininity. Dragging also provides her with family and community approval. She describes how a neighbor told her mother: "You know, I saw your son, but I didn't know he was your son. I thought he was a real lady." Her success as a woman leads her family to be, in Nasreen's words, "not proud, but supportive." While Nasreen fits sex-gender-sexuality ideologies of her township community as a *moffie*, she would rather be a woman and drags to pass. Township drag produces contradictions within sex and gender. Township gender and sexuality systems are inclusive of *moffies*, *istabane*, and *skesanas*, but the man/woman binary retains significant social relevance. Drag queens like Nasreen articulate gender and sex in ways that can fit the category of "woman," while they simultaneously crack its coherence.

Drag is also an important component of Black and Coloured drag queens' sexual relationships, and these relationships actively produce gay femininity through contrast with its supposed opposite, the "real man." Relationships with masculine men re-inscribe gender binaries and thus affirm drag queens' femininity. The more masculine their partner is, the more feminine they are by association. Many drag queens, like Rashid and Kenneth, go solely to "straight" bars because they are only interested in "real men" as partners. Their sexual relationships, which are frequently characterized in townships as "butch/femme," render same-sex sexuality culturally intelligible within their communities. They make it easy for families to understand gay relationships because they pair masculinity and femininity. Further, butch/femme roles, articulated publicly through drag, clarify sexual expectations in relationships. Nasreen explains this popular sentiment among both Coloured and Black drag queens:

> [Butch/femme relationships are] very, very, very good . . . you'll see it's like boyfriend and girlfriend, the one is passive and the one active. You know which one is the girl and which one is the boy . . . I enjoy being a drag queen, because I know who I am.

Sexual roles and drag are important in constructing credible femininity and masculinity for both partners, and the binaries within which they function secure these identities. Gender and sex are not simply produced through drag performance, but through sex acts themselves in which partners articulate their respective genders.

Although embodying a convincing femininity is a goal of most drag queens and the ability to "pass" is idealized, passing also leads to one of the ambiguities of township drag. That drag queens are also *moffies*, *skesana*, or *istabane*–categories neither entirely man or woman–makes individuals constantly unsure whether or not they are passing as women, which can be quite dangerous. Brandy, a Coloured drag queen who was extremely successful in drag competitions in the Western Cape in her youth, describes the difficulties she faced:

> I was even shot for my beauty. I didn't know that this man was stalking me all the time in Mitchell's Plain at a night club, and eventually the man found out I was gay and the man shot me right here in this spot.

The dangers that Brandy and other drag queens confront may seem contradictory considering the social acceptance of gays in many townships. Farid suggests that "people adore gays" in Coloured townships, but this approval is not uniform, especially because of the violent gangs that dominate South Africa's townships. Farid explains that, despite the tolerance of many community members, drag queens are targeted by *tsotsis* or *skollies* (gangsters) to be terrorized and even murdered. He states, "That's why I basically had to stop [dragging] because it just got too dangerous for me . . . I just felt that this was not the life for me." Drag has contradictory draws and consequences for Black and Coloured South Africans, as drag queens are frequently raped and murdered. They produce femininity through pageants and relationships, but their sex-gender expressions put them at risk for violent attacks.

RECONSIDERING "AUDIENCE" AND "DRAG"

Analyzing the complexity of South African drag allows us to reconsider "audience" and "drag" as concepts. As Butler has pointed out, drag offers one means of examining the performativity of gender and race; the specificity of drag performances simply calls attention to this quality. The differences between performativity and performance have been explored at length (Lloyd, 1999), but in township gay vernacular, "performance" has another meaning. To perform is to try to gain attention, to act outrageously, to cause a scene. For example, a *moffie* who gets drunk and acts flamboyantly in a public place may be accused of "performing," the essence of which is drama. When a drag queen "performs" in this sense, the streets are her stage.

In most scholarship, gay male drag is defined as that which is performed in front of an audience cognizant of performers' male bodies. The role of "audience," and especially the collusion between audience and performer in maintaining or disrupting the linkage between sex and gender, has been critical to scholarship analyzing drag (Baker, 1994). However, the classed assumptions that drag necessitates a paying audience have often been overlooked.[12] Few Black and Coloured South Africans have the opportunity to drag on stage, as white performers do. The audience to drag queens' performances are community members and township streets are their stages, thus calling into question the racial, class, national, and cultural assumptions that underlie perceptions of "audience."

South African township drag also blurs and races the distinctions among "drag" and "cross-dressing." South African "drag" is not simply about maintaining illusion or "crossing" from one gender to another; such assumptions re-inscribe gender and sex binaries. Township drag relies on transgenderism, as drag queens articulate gender expressions that match, instead of contradicting, their genders. The differentiation between drag queens and drag artists, which often has roots in racist and pathologizing ideologies, are called into question. Just as South African drag illuminates the performativity of race and gender, it raises possibilities about what kinds of performances can be redefined as "drag."

In South Africa, urban drag artists are paid to drag in gay bars and clubs, while township drag queens perform for community recognition in competitions and their daily lives. As both of these forms of drag emerge from the racially segregated history of South African apartheid, they reflect the sex-gender-sexuality systems of their communities. But drag does not merely mirror the societies in which it occurs. Rather, drag produces race and gender through artists and queens' performances. By analyzing some of the complexities of South African drag, we can not only ascertain the motivations of individual performers, but also begin to better understand the contexts in which their performances are created and understand the processes by which social differences are articulated and produced.

NOTES

1. Under apartheid, Black and Coloured people who came to urban areas to work were forced to settle in townships known for their poor infrastructure.

2. Central to this study are the ways that scholars including Butler (1993) and Muñoz (1999) have reconceptualized the relationships among queerness and race in contemporary drag.

3. I borrow from Stuart Hall's understanding of articulation as "the form of connection that can make a unity of two different elements, under certain conditions . . . a linkage which is not necessary, determined, absolute and essential for all time" (Slack, 1992, p. 115).

4. Historically "white" has referred to those of English or Afrikaans descent in South Africa. The origins of "Coloured" are in the Population Registration Act of 1950 which designated seven subgroups as Coloured: Cape Coloured, Cape Malay, Griqua, Indian, Chinese, Other Asiatic, and Other Coloured. "Black" or "African" encompasses nations indigenous to South Africa, or is used as an overarching term in opposition to "white."

5. See Kulick (1998) and Lancaster (1992) for similar discussions of gender and homosexuality in South America.

6. Within Afrikaans etymology, the term *moffie* may be derogatory or a self-chosen identification and connotes an effeminate gay man. *Skesanas* are feminine gay men "who play the passive, receptive (femme or bottom) role in homosexual sex" (McLean and Ngcobo, 1994, p. 185). *Istabane* is a derogatory term in Black township vernacular referring to gays or lesbians. Both *moffie* and *istabane* connote not only homosexuality, but intersexuality. I explore the etymology and implications of the concept *istabane* elsewhere.

7. Despite its racist origins, "Coon" has been reclaimed by the carnival's participants (Martin, 1999, p. 4).

8. "Miming" is how South African drag performers describe "lip synching" to the words of pre-recorded songs.

9. "Impersonation" indicates drag intended to imitate a particular female singer.

10. I work here within the growing body of scholarship that explores the relationships between drag and race (Schacht, 2000).

11. Pseudonyms protect narrators' anonymity, except when analyzing performances reviewed in newspapers.

12. Exceptions to this trend include Newton (1972) and Muñoz (1999).

REFERENCES

Anzaldúa, G. (1987). *Borderlands/la frontera: The new mestiza.* San Francisco: Aunt Lute Press.

Baker, R. (1994). *Drag: A history of female impersonation in the performing arts.* London: Cassell.

Butler, J. (1993). *Bodies that matter: On the discursive limits of "sex."* New York: Routledge.

Butler, J. (1991). Imitation and gender subordination. In D. Fuss, (Ed.), *Inside/out: Lesbian theories, gay theories* (pp. 13-31). New York: Routledge.

Cameron, E. (1994). 'Unapprehended felons': Gays and lesbians and the law in South Africa. In M. Gevisser and E. Cameron (Eds.), *Defiant desire: Gay and lesbian lives in South Africa* (pp. 89-111). Johannesburg: Ravan.

Chauncey, G. (1994). *Gay New York: Gender, urban culture, and the making of the gay male world, 1980-1940.* New York: Basic.

Chetty, D. R. (1994). A drag at madame costello's: Cape moffie life and the popular press in the 1950s and 1960s. In M. Gevisser and E. Cameron (Eds.), *Defiant desire: Gay and lesbian lives in South Africa* (pp. 115-127). Johannesburg: Ravan.

Constantine-Simms, D. (Ed.). (2000). *The greatest taboo: Homosexuality in black communities.* Los Angeles: Alyson.

Crenshaw, K. W. (1993). Beyond racism and misogyny: Black feminism and 2 live crew. In M. J. Matsuda et al. (Eds.), *Words that wound: Critical race theory, assaultive speech, and the first amendment* (pp. 111-132). Boulder: Westview.

Devenish, M. (1997). High-kicking class act is on the cards from the start. *Cape Times* (Cape Town), 5 June.

Donham, D. L. (1998). Freeing South Africa: The 'modernization' of male-male sexuality in Soweto. *Cultural Anthropology* 13, 3-21.

Elder, G. (1995). Of moffies, kaffirs, and perverts: Male homosexuality and the discourse of moral order in the apartheid state. In D. Bell and G. Valentine (Eds.), *Mapping desire: Geographies of sexualities* (pp. 56-65). New York: Routledge.

Gevisser, M. (1994). A different fight for freedom: A history of South African lesbian and gay organization from the 1950s to the 1990s. In M. Gevisser and E. Cameron (Eds.), *Defiant desire: Gay and lesbian lives in South Africa* (pp. 14-86). Johannesburg: Ravan.

Hammonds, E. (1994). "Black (w)holes and the geometry of black female sexuality." *Differences: A Journal of Feminist Cultural Studies, 6,* 126-145.

Jeppie, S. (1990). "Popular culture and carnival in Cape Town: the 1940s and 1950s." In S. Jeppie and C. Soudien (Eds.), *The struggle for district six: Past and present* (pp. 67-87). Cape Town: Buchu.

Kessler, S., and W. McKenna. (1978). *Gender: An ethnomethodological approach.* New York: John Wiley and Sons.

Krouse, M. (1994). "The artista sisters–September 1984: An account of army drag." In M. Gevisser and E. Cameron (Eds.), *Defiant desire: Gay and lesbian lives in South Africa* (pp. 209-218). Johannesburg: Ravan.

Kulick, D. (1998). *Travesti: Sex, gender and culture among Brazilian transgendered prostitutes.* Chicago: University of Chicago.

Lancaster, R. (1992). *Life is hard: Machismo, danger, and the intimacy of power in Nicaragua.* Berkeley: University of California.

Lloyd, M. (1999). "Performativity, parody, politics." In V. Bell (Ed.), *Performativity and belonging* (pp. 195-213). London: SAGE.

Martin, D. (1999). *Coon carnival: New year in Cape Town, past and present.* Cape Town: David Philip.

McClintock, A. (1995). *Imperial leather: Race, gender, and sexuality in the colonial contest.* New York: Routledge.

McLean, H., and L. Ngcobo. (1994). "Abangibhamayo bathi ngimnandi (Those who fuck me say I'm tasty): Gay sexuality in reef townships." In M. Gevisser and E. Cameron (Eds.), *Defiant desire: Gay and lesbian lives in South Africa* (pp. 158-185). Johannesburg: Ravan.

Moodie, T. D. (1989). "Migrancy and male sexuality on the South African gold mines." In M. Duberman, M. Vicinus, and G. Chauncey, Jr. (Eds.), *Hidden from history: Reclaiming the gay and lesbian past*. New York: Meridian.

Muñoz, J. E. (1999). *Disidentifications: Queers of color and the performance of politics*. Minneapolis: University of Minnesota.

Murray, S., and W. Roscoe. (1998). *Boy-wives and female husbands: Studies in African homosexualities*. New York: Palgrave.

Newton, E. (1972). *Mother camp: Female impersonators in America*. Chicago: University of Chicago.

Omi, M., and H. Winant. (1994). *Racial formation in the United States: From the 1960s to the 1990s*. New York: Routledge.

Reid, G. C. (1999). "Above the skyline: Integrating African, Christian and gay and lesbian identities in a South African church community." Master's thesis, University of the Witswaterstrand.

Retief, G. (1994). "Keeping sodom out of the laager: State repression of homosexuality in apartheid South Africa." In M. Gevisser and E. Cameron (Eds.), *Defiant desire: Gay and lesbian lives in South Africa* (pp. 99-111). Johannesburg: Ravan.

Said, E. W. (1978). *Orientalism*. New York: Vintage.

Schacht, S. P. (2002). "Four Renditions of Doing Female Drag: Feminine Appearing Conceptual Variations of a Masculine Theme." In P. Gagne and R. Tewksbury (Eds.), "Gendered Sexualities" in the on *Advances in Gender Research* (pp. 157-180). Boston: Elsevier Science.

Slack, J. D. (1996). "The theory and method of articulation in cultural studies." In D. Morley and K. Chen (Eds.), *Stuart Hall: Critical dialogues in cultural studies* (pp. 112-127). London: Routledge.

Stoler, A. L. (1991). "Carnal knowledge and imperial power: Gender, race, and morality in colonial Asia." In M. di Leonardo (Ed.), *Gender at the crossroads of knowledge: Feminist anthropology in the postmodern era* (pp. 51-101). Berkeley: University of California.

Wa Sibuye, M. (1993). "Tinkoncana etimayinini: The wives of the mines." In M. Krouse (Ed.), *Invisible ghetto: Lesbian and gay writing from South Africa* (pp. 52-64). London: Gay Men's Press.

Ad/Dressing the Nation: Drag and Authenticity in Post-Apartheid South Africa

Jennifer Spruill, JD, MA

University of Chicago

SUMMARY. This paper examines a style of drag in South Africa that features "traditional African" clothing. In a region in which homosexuality is denigrated as a colonial, European import and "unAfrican," the meaning of "traditional drag" is deeply inflected by the question of cultural authenticity. This dragging practice fits within a distinctly post-colonial production of tradition and its self-conscious display–in the form of attire–of a decidedly "gay" one. Traditional drag also responds to ongoing politics within and between lesbian and gay communities about racial "representivity" and "transformation." The paper focuses on displays of

Jennifer Spruill is a PhD candidate in the Anthropology Department at the University of Chicago and a 2000-2002 doctoral fellow at the American Bar Foundation.

An earlier version of this paper was presented at the American Anthropological Association Meetings in San Francisco, CA, November 2000.

The author thanks John Comaroff and Elizabeth Povinelli for their helpful comments on a previous draft of this paper.

Correspondence may be addressed: Department of Anthropology, University of Chicago, 1126 East 59th Street, Chicago, IL 60637 (E-mail: spru@midway.uchicago.edu).

[Haworth co-indexing entry note]: "Ad/Dressing the Nation: Drag and Authenticity in Post-Apartheid South Africa." Spruill, Jennifer. Co-published simultaneously in *Journal of Homosexuality* (Harrington Park Press, an imprint of The Haworth Press, Inc.) Vol. 46, No. 3/4, 2004, pp. 91-111; and: *The Drag Queen Anthology: The Absolutely Fabulous but Flawlessly Customary World of Female Impersonators* (ed: Steven P. Schacht, with Lisa Underwood) Harrington Park Press, an imprint of The Haworth Press, Inc., 2004, pp. 91-111. Single or multiple copies of this article are available for a fee from The Haworth Document Delivery Service [1-800-HAWORTH, 9:00 a.m. - 5:00 p.m. (EST). E-mail address: docdelivery@haworthpress.com].

traditional drag at Johannesburg's Gay and Lesbian Pride Parade but also explores the complex politics of publicity and address suggested by varying contexts in which traditional dress and drag are mobilized. *[Article copies available for a fee from The Haworth Document Delivery Service: 1-800-HAWORTH. E-mail address: <docdelivery@haworthpress.com> Website: <http://www.HaworthPress.com> © 2004 by The Haworth Press, Inc. All rights reserved.]*

KEYWORDS. Drag, South Africa, Pride Parade, clothing, sexual identity, "African" identity, gay, homosexuality

Please be careful. We must remember that the whole country is watching us, so we must be very careful how we present ourselves. (Gevisser, 1995, p. 281)

This caution interrupted several "particularly edgy black transvestites" (Gevisser, 1995, p. 281) over the loudspeaker after they had taken the stage to dance in Pieter Roos Park following Johannesburg's Third Annual Gay Pride March ("Pride") in 1992. The vulnerability in this warning spoke to the times: the sense of exposure for a gay institution only recently asserted in the "public eye," the consciousness of mainstream suspicion of gender nonconformity, and the awareness of a nation in transition barely beginning to find definition. This occurred against a backdrop of unexpected and fragile hope among South African gays and lesbians awakened when the African National Congress included "sexual orientation" in the equality clause of its draft constitution. All of this would be profoundly transformed just five years later when a new style of drag appeared at Johannesburg's Pride. Drag in "traditional African" attire enlists the politics and publicity of Pride to address a nation newly engaged with its "African heritage" and also addresses gay and lesbian communities struggling with the dilemmas of identity, democracy, and history. This paper draws on field research,[1] media reports and interviews to explore the meanings, implications and broader social context surrounding this form of drag.[2]

PRIDE'S TRADITION

South Africa's first Gay Pride March in 1990 initiated a critical and contested exception to the more usually semi-public existence of lesbian and gay life in South Africa. As Herrell (1992) says of Chicago's Pride Parade, the march was a strategic response to the "invisibility and oppression of lesbians and gays" in society (p. 226). By organizing the Pride March, The Gay and Lesbian Organization of the Witwatersrand ("GLOW") sought to "incorporate the gay and lesbian struggle in the mass democratic movement" in the early days of the post-apartheid transition, thus attesting to the "persistence of street performance in times of social flux" (Cohen-Cruz, 1998a, p. 6). Despite the now notorious and "paradoxical" provision of brown paper bags "for the shy ones,"[3] this first Pride certainly had the quality of an "ominous gust of an enormous closet door opening" (Berlant and Freeman, 1993, p. 210) on the streets of Johannesburg.

Pride has become the most reliably mass-mediated realization of a gay and lesbian counterpublic, attracting coverage from newspapers, magazines, television and radio. Throughout, Pride has sustained the use of the street as a "site in which symbols and identity are forged, negotiated, and contested" (Cohen-Cruz, 1998a, p. 1) as the political and social transition to democracy proceeds. Like protest marches and political funerals in apartheid South Africa (see Cohen-Cruz, 1998b), Pride has proven to be a ritual occasion in which the street becomes "an arena [not only] for the display [but for the] creation of power" (Cohen-Cruz, 1998a, p. 4). However, the tension within Pride's dual nature as a "space of withdrawal [and] basis for agitation directed toward wider publics" (Fraser, 1993, p. 124) is acute:

> The march is unique in South Africa, in that it is simultaneously angry and carnivalesque; both deeply earnest in its call for lesbian and gay rights and wildly subversive in its challenge to heterosexual stereotyping . . . On the one hand [it] fits into and invokes the tradition of human rights protest marches in South Africa . . . On the other hand, it draws its style and indeed its name from the carnivalesque tradition of the pride march, initiated in North America after the Stonewall uprising. (Gevisser, 1995, p. 278)

This tension is embedded in the very structure of Pride, not only in the change in title from a "march" to a "parade," but in the chronology of the event itself as Pride participants anxious to get on to the music and other entertainment listen impatiently to the political speeches by community leaders that customarily follow Pride.

As a subaltern counterpublic, Pride "contest[s] the exclusionary norms of the [dominant] public and elaborate[s] . . . alternative norms of public speech" (Fraser, 1993, p. 116). Communicative *nonspeech* acts also constitute Pride (Herrell, 1992, p. 227), and indeed clothing is an "index" (Herrell, 1992, p. 227) at which Pride's purposes both diverge and converge. Whereas the colorful characters in sequins and feather boas often featured in the media capture the frivolity of Pride, others have very different politics in mind. For example, an individual at Pride 1997 literally wrapped in the South African flag addressed Minister of Justice Dullah Omar following his opposition to a court petition to overturn the "sodomy" laws in 1997. His sign read, "Dear Mr. Dullah Omar, decriminalize gay sex now or forever hold your piece."

DRAG AT PRIDE

Drag, "one of the gay world's most notorious indexes" (Herrell, 1992, p. 231), features centrally in "the conflict of gay abandon and gay respectability" (Gevisser and Reid, 1995, p. 281). Indeed, the "strangely dual character" of Pride in South Africa might be "illustrated . . . by the incongruity of comrades and drag queens" (Gevisser and Reid, 1995, p. 278). In fact "there was much argument about the participation of drag queens [in the first Pride March]–some felt they would draw the focus of news reports away from the *moffies*[4] who were trying to demonstrate how 'normal' they were."[5] And indeed, among the multiple modes of dress and address Pride encompasses, drag is imagined as the most tantalizing of Pride's cultural forms and expression sought out for media attention. Gevisser and Reid (1995) wrote,

> The drag queen issue has raged after each march: do we represent a public face that is clean and acceptable, even if it means ostracizing those members of our own community in the very ways we have been ostracized by a homophobic world? Or do we embrace and celebrate our diversity, even if it means playing into stereotypes and allowing the media to sensationalize the march and ignore its very real, substantive issues? (p. 281)

Debates about the political values and dangers of drag, about whether it captures Pride's capacities as an opportunity for creative expression, for restrained politics–or for their collaboration–reflect what Herrell (1992) says is Pride's unique discourse about defining "the gay community" and how it should present itself in the face of stigma (pp. 229, 242-243). Today, however, "no one raises any objection to [drag queens'] right to participate . . . There are more drags than ever at the parade."[6]

While critics of drag worry about its trivializing and diversionary impact on Pride's political messages, some drag is pointedly political. The theme of Pride, 1998, was "Recognize Our Relationships," which was adopted directly from the most recent campaign of the National Coalition for Gay and Lesbian Equality aimed at gaining legal and social recognition of same-sex partnerships. As the *Mail and Guardian*[7] reported, "There were more brides than usual at the gay pride march this year."[8] Several of those brides carried signs saying "fight for the right to marry," "legalize gay marriage" and "5 funerals, no weddings." Not far behind, though, was a letter to *Exit* (Southern Africa's oldest and most widely distributed "gay" newspaper, with a primarily white suburban readership) asking:

> Was it necessary for them to wear drag? Does this exhibitionist advertising help the cause of gay marriage? Doesn't this . . . do the campaign for homosexual unions more harm than good? Surely, one partner taking on the role of a bride plays right into the hands of the anti-gay lobby? Maybe they have given our cause some publicity, but I would rather have it enshrined in law than sensationalized in the Metro section of the *Sunday Times*.[9]

"TRADITIONAL" ATTIRE

A strikingly politicized dragging practice at Johannesburg Pride Parades that ambitiously seeks to define gay and lesbian identities and communities features a display of "traditional African" attire. These drag artists draw on a variety of clothing styles. One marcher wore a Xhosa outfit in orange cotton with black braid trim and accompanying head wrap (see Figure 1). Another displayed the distinctive headpiece worn by Zulu women (see Figure 2). Yet two more donned the Herero "long dress"–here in magenta and indigo print (see Figures 3-4). These examples from the 1997 and 1998 Pride Parades reference politics that have emerged since the first Pride marches that are now played out at Pride and in South African society at large.

Clothing that invokes "Africa" is gaining new familiarity in post-apartheid South Africa. As the first democratic election approached in 1994, "African" styles of dress began to find new appeal among South Africa's emerging Black elite (Klopper, 2000, p. 217). And while "Afri-

FIGURE 1

can attire" may be "burdened by a history of sectarian 'ethnic' concerns that many of South Africa's new leaders are reluctant to endorse" (Klopper, 1998, p. 133), a number of parliamentarians and other state officials have appeared at the opening of parliament and other state functions wearing it. Klopper (2000) observes that it is the "Victorian-inspired Xhosa-style garments" of more affordable orange or white cotton cloth with black trim that are "gradually assuming the status, albeit unofficially, of a national costume" (p. 221). While often worn by South African diplomats and politicians, Xhosa fashions are also produced by small businesses for a Xhosa-speaking market for whom it is a symbol of "ethnic pride and identity" (Klopper, 2000, p. 222).

These uses of "traditional" clothing underscore South Africans' exploration of post-apartheid identities and their "increasingly complex understanding of themselves as Africans" (Klopper, 2000, p. 216; see also Klopper, 1998). However, the designation of "African" and the politics of who claims it are highly unstable in post-apartheid South Africa. President Thabo Mbeki sought to consolidate the idea of "African" through his appeal to a broadly shared African heritage and his entreaty to the "African Renaissance." And like Mbeki's "pan" African vision, contemporary "African" styles reach beyond local references to mine a variety of sources throughout Africa and beyond.[10]

FIGURE 2

FIGURE 3

FIGURE 4

These examples are only the latest in a historical trajectory through which "African tradition," and its self-conscious display in the form of attire, were produced through the colonial encounter (Comaroff and Comaroff, 1997, pp. 258, 267) and further reified through the apartheid era. To be sure, local clothing styles were "a repeated invocation of the very process of articulation that encompassed local identities, reified them, and redefined them in Eurocentric terms" (Comaroff and Comaroff, 1997, p. 262).

The process through which "traditional" clothing has become increasingly ethnicized in Southern Africa, particularly its use in performance and ritual, is fraught with the contradictions of colonialism; this includes the initial transformations in pre-colonial clothing from skins and leather to cloth in the colonial era (Comaroff and Comaroff, 1997, p. 261; Hendrickson, 1994, p. 33), the subsequent use of this dress in anti-colonial struggles and political nationalism in post-colonial states (Kuper, 1973, p. 358), and new deployments of traditional clothing in post-colonial politics of "ethnicity."

Hendrickson's (1994) examination of "traditional" Herero attire in Southern Africa places the emergence of the Herero long dress in a broad social context as a product of nineteenth century "intercultural" relations not only with Europeans but with Africans as well (p. 45; see also Comaroff and Comaroff, 1997, pp. 261, 268). And she describes the Herero long dress as not mere imitation or mimicry of European dress, noting that it was often "worn in ways [that] contradicted European usage" (Hendrickson, 1994, p. 51). Similarly, the Comaroffs (1997) report that nineteenth century Tswana parodied the gender of European styles (p. 235). Traditional drag might in many ways be said to contradict the gendered premises of "traditional" clothing–but it may also be read as reinforcing them. Women's dress in Southern Africa has become particularly associated with notions of tradition and cultural identity, while Western clothing has become associated with men, as Hendrickson (1996) and James (1996) explore in the Herero and Sotho cases. The Comaroffs (1997) show that while Tswana men and their clothing became absorbed by the demands and constraints of the colonial, migrant labour economy in "modern" urban centres, women, the rural domains to which they would be largely limited, and their dress were re-made as bearers of "tradition" (p. 258).

DRAG AND THE POLITICS OF TRADITION

By invoking tradition through dress, traditional drag artists do more than fashion themselves as "Africans." Traditional drag is directed at political and cultural struggles prompted by new mobilizations of ethnic nationalism in South Africa that sexualize South African identity and "ethnicity." Indeed, in many national settings homosexuality is excluded from the nation by reference to a heterosexualized national membership (see Alexander, 1994; Essig, 1999; Hayes, 2000; Thadani, 1996). In South Africa some ethno-nationalist discourses in South Africa construe homosexuality as "unAfrican," a white, colonial defilement introduced to "African" culture and undeserving of legal "equality" in post-apartheid South Africa. This rhetoric conflates racial, cultural, and national identities and its construal of homosexuality as a Western import is intensified by the increasing globalization of gay and lesbian identities (see Hoad, 1999; see also Manalansan, 2002). The heterosexualization of post-apartheid citizenship and Africanness itself, in South Africa and elsewhere in Africa, is well documented replete with its many ironies.[11] Some proponents of this idea have responded directly to Pride. The author of a 1997 letter to the *Mail and Guardian* counterposes South African "heritage" and homosexuality:

> After last week's gay and lesbian parade . . . one is forced to ask who exactly these marchers were marching for–themselves or South Africans at large . . . There is a difference between engaging in a cultural event for the purpose of reviving heritage, and showing off to the public–like the gays and lesbians were doing. In South Africa our heritage does not include homosexuality, or nudity. We should be careful to separate an invention of Western lies and our heritage. Homosexuality, in the form it is today, is a facet of Western freedom . . . What we witnessed last Saturday is the beginning of greater things to come: . . . the decadence of another African norm.[12]

Though Johannesburg's Pride has been criticized as overly representative of white gay communities, the idea of homosexuality as "unAfrican" does not go unremarked by those individuals who are confronted with it in their everyday lives by family, neighbors, political leadership and the media[13]–indeed, a number of those families have taken gay relatives to *sangomas*, or "traditional healers," for "traditional cures" for their homosexuality. In 1996 some signs at Pride read: "Black Lesbians Are Here to Stay," "Gay Proud and African," and "Black, Proud Lesbian." And in 1998 GLOW's float featured members in "gender appropriate" Zulu dress on the back of a truck surrounded by balloons (see Figure 5). Here, GLOW used "traditional" clothing to interpose sexual identity in ongoing mobilizations of Zulu ethnicity and its symbols (see Mathieson and Attwell, 1998).

Through the productive dimension of bodily adornment, traditional drag insists on an African homosexuality by embodying African "gayness." Themba,[14] a Pride participant, said,

> Black people are very proud of their traditions or culture and it has been said by the black elites that being gay it's not African. Traditional clothing says . . . Hey we are black gay Africans and proud . . . It becomes an eye opener to some of the black people who seriously believe that there are no black gay people, especially those who come from the villages.[15]

And as the ethnonationalist thesis is also phrased in ethnicized terms, as one employee of the National Coalition for Gay and Lesbian Equality encountered when he was told that homosexuality is not Xhosa, so Themba said of traditional clothing at Pride: "they wear their traditional clothing to make a statement and to prove a point . . . We don't care–this is our tradition and we are gay though we are what ever, Xhosas or Zulu." In an "ethnic" register traditional drag "asserts sameness where

FIGURE 5

difference is perceived," another distinctive characteristic of Pride parades, according to Herrell (1992, p. 245).

Therefore, traditional drag artists also follow in a different history of traditional clothing, that is, its use in political struggles. In South Africa, the African National Congress used African dress as "a symbol of resistance and validation" (Klopper, 2000, p. 229, n. 6) during its fight against the apartheid state in the 1960s (see also Procter and Klopper, 1993). Recall that Nelson Mandela wore a Xhosa *kaross*[16] and beadwork to court during the Rivonia trial to "emphasize the symbolism that [he] was a black African walking into a white man's court . . . literally carrying on [his] back the history, culture, and heritage of [his] people" (Mandela, 1994, pp. 282-283). Klopper (2000) also reports calls to "boycott 'white' clothes" during the Soweto Uprising of 1976 (p. 228).

The assertion of African identity by traditional drag artists addresses multiple audiences and engages complex politics of address. And indeed, the role of the audience as an interpretive community "has been consistently under-explored in the discussion of culture and its production in South Africa" (Gunner, 1994, pp. 2-3). This is important where a performance is engaged in a political struggle and with "making culture from below" (Gunner, 1994, p. 2)–and when the onlookers to a procession, along with organizers and participants, are involved in defining the event and its references (Herrell, 1992, p. 229). Of traditional drag Themba adds, "Another thing, whites have taken over every thing . . . the first gay parade was organized by Simon Nkoli and other black people, meaning there were few whites at the time. But now whites just organize every thing–black people they have a very small voice in the whole matter, so they wear their traditional clothing to make a statement and to prove a point."[17]

Indeed, while many white gay men stayed away from earlier marches because they were "too closely linked to anti-apartheid liberation movements" (Gevisser, 1995, p. 279), this has changed since the (primarily white) Pride Committee took over. By 1996, although Pride was rescheduled to coincide with Heritage Day to signal Pride's inclusion in the inheritance of the new nation, GLOW began to voice its dissatisfaction with the Pride Committee's "sidelining of the black brothers and sisters who had initiated the event in pre-election 1990."[18] Pride in 1996 also heard the first rumors of moving Pride from the once grey[19] and still gay areas of Hillbrow and Yeoville to affluent Sandton or Rosebank, "away from its roots and even further from Soweto."[20] And before his death in 1998 Simon Nkoli, a prominent South African gay rights activist, said it was "far too soon and far too easy to be calling the event 'truly African.'"[21] "African" dress at Pride, then, seeks to define "an increasingly diverse post-liberation community."[22]

DRAG AS TRADITION

Prior to Pride in 1997 and 1998, traditional drag was also invoked in a 1996 pageant staged by the Hope and Unity Metropolitan Community Church ("HUMCC"), a "gay church" in Hillbrow, Johannesburg. HUMCC held an "historic" "Mr. and Miss HUMCC" contest in which members of the church in Johannesburg and a church in Durban competed for the titles. For the organizers, the novelty of the contest lay in the facts that both men and women would compete on the same stage, and more controversially, the pageant was not a drag contest (Reid, 1999, p. 120). To the contrary, the church leader, Rev. Thandekiso, went to great lengths to construct a contest based on "men being men and women being women"–contestants for Mister HUMCC were to be male, Miss HUMCC female (Reid, 1999, p. 120).[23] The goal was to appoint "ambassadors" to represent the church who, by subverting "effeminate" stereotypes about gay men, could show that gay men "are men and are proud about it" (Reid, 1999, pp. 125, 138, 142). However, this drew great resistance from participating church members who insisted on the "naturalness" of their "queenish" manner (Reid, 1999, p. 140). Once cajoled into competing, the contestants underwent instruction from a model and a choreographer in "gender appropriate" movement, gesture, posture, and speech so that they would not look like "gay men in drag" (Reid, 1999, pp. 121, 127).

However, during the process of recruiting contestants, Rev. Thandekiso acknowledged the history and import of drag for the church members. He said, "When you drag it is beautiful. It is called our heritage. You know gay people do it so well" (Reid, 1999, p. 143, n. 9). The contest itself was restructured to incorporate the "tradition" of drag– and critically it did so with "traditional" clothing. In a preliminary segment that was not judged, the contestants were introduced wearing traditional clothing:

> This part of the pageant was originally conceived of as the drag component of the competition that was not for points, but merely for "fun." The 15 contestants took the stage dancing a "traditional dance." The compere [in drag] commented on the performance: "Aren't they beautiful in their tradition? Isn't Africa beautiful?"

The traditional wear consisted of anything ranging from a Swazi outfit to a South African flag tied around the waist, to the designer clothes of the new Africanesque boutiques of the Small Street Mall [in Johannesburg]. (Reid, 1999, p. 131)

By including this "traditional drag" segment, the HUMCC competition construed drag as the bearer of gay and African tradition and of the "natural" order of the gay gender cosmos.

Drag's place in South African gay history and society is indeed vibrant and varied[24] and includes other examples of African dress. Some of the earliest accounts from same-sex mining compounds dating to the 1910s describe highly ritualized marriage ceremonies and relationships between senior men and younger boys ("wives") in which "mine wives were expected to 'look feminine,'" for example, by wearing bras sewn from pieces of cloth and "imitation breasts" (Moodie, 1989, p. 417; see also Harries, 1990, p. 329). And in 1950s Mkhumbane, a workers settlement near Durban, Louw (2001), describes one Khumalo who, "using the tradition of Zulu dancing . . . organized the *isikhesana*[25] into dressing up as Zulu maidens so they could openly celebrate their sexuality" (p. 289). Marriage ceremonies in the "homosexual community" in Mkhumbane were styled after "traditional Zulu weddings," including "customary" attire (Louw, 2001, p. 290).

Cross-dressing is still pivotal to gay culture in the townships around Johannesburg (see Miller, 1993; Donham, 1998). Perhaps most common is "that peculiar androgyny of township drag borne of scant resources and much imagination, nodding at gender inversion with no more than a frilly shirt, a pair of garish earrings, a touch of rouge, a pair of low-heeled pumps, a third hand wig" (Gevisser, 1995, pp. 14-15). And of course drag contests remain enormously popular. Introduced in 1989, the Miss GLOW competitions, "the country's premiere black drag pageant,"[26] have made "drag shows . . . the central bonding point of gay township life, and it is the annual Miss Glow finals . . . rather than the annual Pride March, that is the highlight of the black gay calendar on the Reef" (Gevisser, 1995, p. 68).

CONCLUSION:
TRADITION AS DRAG

Through the publicity of Pride, traditional drag instigates conversations both within and beyond an increasingly complex gay "community" presumed by Pride. It addresses an audience of African onlookers and media consumers to challenge the idea that homosexuality is "unAfrican" and does so through a medium broadly in use to define post-apartheid African identities. Traditional drag also uses Pride's capacities to create community to emphasize the presence of Black gays to white Pride participants and organizers. In short, traditional drag artists affirm the existence of Black, African gays in post-apartheid South Africa. This would appear to confirm Donham's (1998) assertion that, "The overlapping of the national and gay questions [in South Africa] means that gay identity reverberates . . . with a proud, new national identity" (p. 16). However, this analysis of traditional drag reveals that gay and national identities in South Africa are in fact highly unstable, and their articulation uneasy.

At the core of traditional drag is a claim to sexual and cultural authenticity with the goal of appropriating the representational power of the ethnonationalist ideology. This claim to authenticity differentiates this form of drag in critical ways from those classically portrayed in the literature on drag and gender. Traditional drag certainly concerns gender identity, not least because it responds to the post-colonial desire to re-masculate "the African man" that underpins the ethnonationalist perspective (see Gevisser, 1995). However, it may be less a performance about gender (see Morris, 1995, p. 583) than it is about the authentic coincidence of sexual and cultural identities. Many "feminine" gay men who may have once identified as "women" are increasingly identifying as "gay" (see Donham, 1998), incorporating their gender identity into a sexual identity more often asserted following the inclusion of "sexual orientation" in South Africa's constitutional equality clause and with the increasing globalization of "gay" identities.[27] Traditional drag signals sexual identity and productively re-imagines it simultaneously with "African tradition." Here, unmistakably, "the order of sexual difference is not prior to that of race or class in the constitution of the subject" (Butler, 1993, p. 130).

The display of gender and race in traditional drag is distinct from the "realness" contestants sought, for example, in *Paris Is Burning* (Butler, 1993, p. 129). Traditional drag artists do not seek to surpass their racial designation (or its denial) through a highly gendered performance. Therefore, traditional drag does not require "belief" that the performers appear "as women" and like everyday township androgyny, it is not susceptible to being "read." Muñoz (1999) also describes drag that resists nationalism and racial stereotypes without reference to "realness," but through parody. However, traditional drag is not about parody either. It lacks the familiar gender excess in more "traditional" drag and it lacks the usual "wink" of camp (Dynes, 1990; see also Davy, 1994). Neither does traditional drag fetishize (Tyler, 1991, p. 57) the distance between "gay" and "African" or shuttle it to create a "hybrid" identity (Muñoz, 1999, p. 32). Instead, traditional drag seeks to erase that distance and suggest that a gay African does not present the incongruous contrast that others describe as elemental to parodic irony (Tyler, 1991). Therefore, the "politics of parody" (Morris, 1995, p. 582) that have dominated the theorization of drag do not provide the purchase here that they might on other forms of drag.[28]

Despite its assertion to authenticity, traditional drag is not without its own ironies. Traditional drag artists seek to counteract the idea that gay Africans have forfeited their African identity by virtue of their sexual identity. The use of *women's* clothing to signal tradition exploits the association of women with tradition, thus affirming an ideal not only associated with gender inequality but one that emerged through the colonial encounter. While seeking to secure a new idea of "Africanness," traditional drag employs and exposes the instability inherent in the notion. Therefore, traditional drag reveals traditional clothing, and indeed "tradition" itself, as a form of drag in that, as Butler (1991) says of gender, it produces its own original through its very repetition (p. 21). Indeed, the idea of "African tradition" is itself a legacy of the colonial project (see Mamdani, 1996), which enlisted the clothing now used to assert a post-colonial African culture to "reform" African styles and re-make "the native." Thus, like the forms of drag that Butler and Muñoz examine, traditional drag reinforces hegemonic norms while also undermining them.

Hoad (1999) is skeptical about whether same-sex sexuality will ever be "insertable as authentically African tradition" (p. 569)–and with many political activists, he instead resituates the question of gay and lesbian rights within the new South African "culture of equality." Traditional drag artists want more. Like nineteenth century Africans who appropriated European clothing styles, traditional drag artists do not simply conform to dominant norms; neither is "mere imitation." Traditional drag artists use the capacity of dress to *effect* states of being (Donham, 1998, pp. 3-4) in order to "conjure new social identities and senses of self" (Comaroff and Comaroff, 1997, p. 235). And like Tswana styles of the early 1900s, traditional drag in part creates the "times of radical change" (Comaroff and Comaroff, 1997, p. 261) through which it emerged. These drag artists are indeed "careful" of how they present themselves in the hope that the whole country is watching.

NOTES

1. Twenty months of participant observation in lesbian and gay communities and organizations primarily in Johannesburg.

2. I focus here on drag that invokes indigenous African "tradition." Other forms of drag seen at Johannesburg's Pride reference, for example, Afrikaner and Indian "traditions" and offer fruitful material for analysis, but are beyond the scope of the present paper.

3. "Marching from Fear to Fun," *Mail and Guardian*, 19 September, 1999.

4. Derogatory slang for male homosexual, now often "re-appropriated" by gay men.

5. "Marching from Fear to Fun," *Mail and Guardian*, 19 September, 1999.

6. "Marching from Fear to Fun," *Mail and Guardian*, 19 September, 1999.

7. An historically "liberal" weekly first published in the mid-1980s.

8. "The fight for gay civil rights gets under way," *Mail and Guardian*, 2 October, 1998.

9. *Exit*, Issue 104, 1998, p. 2.

10. These styles also extend to the use of "New South Africa" flags as clothing (Klopper, 2000, pp. 221, 228; Klopper, 1998, p. 134).

11. See, for example Antonio (1997), Epprecht (1998), Hoad (1998), and Holmes (1995).

12. *Mail and Guardian*, 3 October, 1997, p. 22.

13. For a fuller discussion of these responses see Spruill (2000).

14. A pseudonym. I use pseudonyms against the wishes of virtually all of my informants in order to comply with the requirements placed on my project by the Institutional Review Board of the University of Chicago.

15. Interview, 16 July, 2000, Johannesburg.

16. Cloak made of skins.

17. Interview 16 July, 2000, Johannesburg.

18. "A Matter of Pride," *Mail and Guardian*, Sept. 26, 1997, p. 23.

19. Urban areas designated "white" under apartheid into which black South Africans first moved.

20. "A Matter of Pride," *Mail and Guardian*, Sept. 26, 1997, p. 23.

21. "A Matter of Pride," *Mail and Guardian*, Sept. 26, 1997, p. 23.

22. "A Matter of Pride," *Mail and Guardian*, Sept. 26, 1997, p. 23.

23. There was one female contestant. Lesbians' resistance to wearing dresses and swim suits was perhaps even greater than the men's resistance to the contest (Reid, 1999, p.123).

24. Regarding the tradition of drag in Cape Town see Chetty (1995) and "The History of Drag in the Fairest Cape," *Cape Times*, 3 November, 1999.

25. Described by Louw (2001) as "men who adopt a female homosexual gender" (p. 289).

26. "A Glow in the Dark in Sebokeng," *Mail and Guardian*, 8 October, 1999.

27. Historically, the gender/sexuality system reflected in township gay relationships included *skesanas*, partners who assume a feminine social role, and *injongas* who adopt a male social role. While in the past only *skesanas* were considered "gay" (and often identified as "women"), with the growth of the gay and lesbian movement in South Africa a new conceptualization of gay identity has emerged, one in which both *skesanas* and *injongas* more often identify as both gay and male (see Donham, 1998 and Reid, 1999).

28. Kennedy and Davis (1993) and Halberstam (1998) suggest that parody is disso-
nant with the use of drag to appropriate hegemonic power, as in the case of the butch
desire to "usurp [male] prerogatives in order to assert women's sexual autonomy"
(Kennedy and Davis, 1993, p. 383). Muñoz, criticizing Davy's (1994) conclusion that
camp is "counterproductive for lesbians," seeks to resuscitate women's use of camp
and its capacity to usurp multiple forms of power (1999, pp. 130-131).

REFERENCES

Alexander, J. (1994). Not just (any)body can be a citizen: The politics of law, sexuality,
and postcoloniality in Trinidad and Tobago and the Bahamas. *Feminist Review*, 48,
5-23.

Antonio, E. (1997). Homosexuality and African culture. In P. Germond and S. de
Gruchy (Eds.), *Aliens in the household of God* (pp. 295-315). Cape Town: David.

Berlant, Philip L. and Freeman, E. (1993). Queer nationality. In M. Warner (Ed.), *Fear
of a queer planet: Queer politics and social theory* (pp. 193-229). Minneapolis:
University of Minnesota Press.

Berlant, L. and Warner, M. (2000). Sex in public. In L. Berlant (Ed.), *Intimacy*
(pp. 311-330). Chicago: University of Chicago Press.

Butler, J. (1991). Imitation and gender insubordination. In D. Fuss (Ed.), *Inside/out:
Lesbian theories, gay theories* (pp. 13-31). New York: Routledge.

Butler, J. (1993). *Bodies that matter: On the discursive limits of 'sex.'* New York:
Routledge.

Chetty, D. (1995). A drag and Madame Costello's: Cape moffie life and the popular
press in the 1950's and 1960's. In M. Gevisser and E. Cameron (Eds.), *Defiant desire: Gay and lesbian lives in South Africa* (pp. 115-127). New York: Routledge.

Cohen-Cruz, J. (1998a). General introduction. In J. Cohen-Cruz (Ed.), *Radical street
performance: An international anthology* (pp. 1-6). New York: Routledge.

Cohen-Cruz, J. (1998b). Notes toward an unwritten history of anti-apartheid street performance. In J. Cohen-Cruz (Ed.), *Radical street performance: An international
anthology* (pp. 282-288). New York: Routledge.

Comaroff, J.L. and J. Comaroff (1997). *Of revelation and revolution: The dialectics of
modernity on a South African frontier* (Volume Two). Chicago: University of Chicago Press.

Davy, K. (1994). Fe/male impersonation: The discourse of Camp. In M. Meyer (Ed.),
The politics and poetics of camp (pp. 130-148). New York: Routledge.

Donham, D. (1998). Freeing South Africa: The 'modernization' of male-male sexuality in Soweto. *Cultural Anthropology*, 13(1), 3-21.

Dynes, W. (1990). Camp. In W. Dynes (Ed.), *Encyclopedia of homosexuality*
(pp. 189-190). New York: Garland Press.

Epprecht, M. (1998). The 'unsaying' of indigenous homosexualities in Zimbabwe:
Mapping a blindspot in an African masculinity. *Journal of Southern African
Studies*, 24(4), 631-651.

Essig, L. (1999). *Queer in Russia: A story of sex, self, and the other.* Durham: Duke
University Press.

Fraser, N. (1993). Rethinking the public sphere: A contribution to the critique of actually existing democracy. In. C. Calhoun (Ed.), *Habermas and the public sphere* (pp. 109-142). Boston: Massachusetts Institute of Technology.

Gevisser, M. (1995). A different fight for freedom: A history of South African lesbian and gay organization from the 1950's to the 1990's. In M. Gevisser and E. Cameron (Eds.), *Defiant desire: Gay and lesbian lives in South Africa* (pp. 14-88). New York: Routledge.

Gevisser, M. and Reid, G. (1995). Pride or protest?: Drag queens, comrades, and the lesbian and gay pride march. In M. Gevisser and E. Cameron (Eds.), *Defiant desire: Gay and lesbian lives in South Africa* (pp. 278-83). New York: Routledge.

Gunner, L. (1994). Introduction: The struggle for space. In L. Gunner (Ed.), *Politics and performance: Theatre, poetry and song in Southern Africa* (pp. 1-10). Johannesburg: Witwatersrand University Press.

Harries, P. (1990). Symbols and sexuality: Culture and identity on the early Witwatersrand gold mines. *Gender and History*, 2(3), 318-336.

Hayes, J. (2000). *Queer nations: Marginal sexualities in the Maghreb*. Chicago: University of Chicago Press.

Hendrickson, H. (1994). The "long" dress and the construction of herero identities in Southern Africa. *African Studies*, 53(2), 25-54.

Hendrickson, H. (1996). Bodies and flags: The representation of herero identity in colonial Namibia. In H. Hendrickson (Ed.), *Clothing and difference: Embodying colonial and post-colonial identities* (pp. 213-244). Durham: Duke University Press.

Herrell, R. (1992). The symbolic strategies of Chicago's gay and lesbian pride day parade. In G. Herdt (Ed.), *Gay culture in America: Essays from the field* (pp. 225-252). Boston: Beacon Press.

Hoad, N. (1998). Tradition, modernity, and human rights: An interrogation of contemporary gay and lesbian rights claims in Southern African nationalist discourses. *Development Update*, 2(2), 32-43.

Hoad, N. (1999). Between the white man's burden and the white man's disease: Tracking lesbian and gay human rights in Southern Africa. *GLQ: A Journal of Lesbian and Gay Studies*, 5(4), 559-584.

Holmes, R. (1995) 'White rapists made coloureds (and homosexuals)': The Winnie Mandela Trial and the politics of race and sexuality. In M. Gevisser and E. Cameron (Eds.), *Defiant desire: Gay and lesbian lives in South Africa* (pp. 284-294). New York: Routledge.

James, D. (1996). I dress in this Fashion: Transformations in Sotho dress and women's lives in a Sekhukhuneland Village, South Africa. In H. Hendrickson (Ed.), *Clothing and difference: Embodying colonial and post-colonial Identities* (pp. 34-65). Durham: Duke University Press.

Klopper, S. (1998). 'I respect custom, but I am not a tribalist': The ANC-CONTRALESA Alliance and 'designer tradition' in 1990's South Africa. *South African Historical Journal*, 39, 129-42.

Klopper, S. (2000). Re-dressing the past: The Africanisation of sartorial style in contemporary South Africa. In A. Brah and A. Coombes (Eds.), *Hybridity and its discontents: Politics, science, culture* (pp. 216-232). New York: Routledge.

Kuper, H. (1973). Costume and identity. *Comparative studies in society and history,* 15(3), 348-67.

Louw, R. (2001). Mkhumbane and new traditions of (un)African same-sex weddings. In R. Morrell (Ed.), *Changing men in Southern Africa* (pp. 287-296). New York: Zed Books.

Mamdani, M. (1996). *Citizen and subject: Contemporary Africa and the legacy of late colonialism.* Princeton: Princeton University Press.

Manalansan, M. and A. Cruz-Malave (Eds.). (2002). *Queer globalizations.* New York: New York University Press.

Mandela, N. (1994). *Long walk to freedom.* Boston: Little, Brown and Co.

Mathieson, S. and D. Attwell (1998). Between ethnicity and nationhood: Shaka Day and the struggle over Zuluness in post-apartheid South Africa. In D. Bennett (Ed.), *Multicultural states: Rethinking difference and identity* (pp. 111-124). New York: Routledge.

Miller, N. (1993). *Out in the world.* New York: Vintage Books.

Moodie, T.D. (1989). Migrancy and male sexuality on the South African gold mines. In M. Duberman, M. Vicinus, and G. Chauncey (Eds.), *Hidden from history: Reclaiming the gay and lesbian Past* (pp. 411-425). New York: Pequin Books.

Morris, R. (1995). All made up: Performance theory and the new anthropology of sex and gender. *Annual Review of Anthropology,* 24, 567-92.

Muñoz, J. (1999). *Disidentifications.* Minneapolis: University of Minnesota Press.

Procter, A. and Klopper, S. (1993). Through the barrel of a bead: The personal and the political in the beadwork of the Eastern Cape. In E. Bedford (Ed.), *Ezakwantu: Beadwork from the Eastern Cape* (pp. 57-66). Cape Town: South African National Gallery.

Reid, G. (1999). *Above the skyline: Integrating African, Christian and gay or lesbian identities in a South African church community.* MA Thesis, University of the Witwatersrand, Johannesburg.

Spruill, J. (2000). A post- with/out a past? Sexual orientation and the post-colonial 'moment' in South Africa. In C. Sychin and D. Herman (Eds.), *Sexuality in the legal arena* (pp. 3-16). London: Athlone.

Thadani, G. (1996). *Sakhiyani: Lesbian desire in ancient and modern India.* London: Cassell.

Tyler, C. (1991). Boys will be girls: The politics of gay drag. In D. Fuss (Ed.), *Inside/out: Lesbian theories, gay theories* (pp. 32-70). New York: Routledge.

Chicks with Dicks, Men in Dresses: What It Means to Be a Drag Queen

Verta Taylor

University of California, Santa Barbara

Leila J. Rupp

University of California, Santa Barbara

SUMMARY. One of the burning questions about drag queens among both scholars and audiences is whether they are more gender-revolutionaries than gender-conservatives. Do they primarily destabilize gender

Verta Taylor is Professor of Sociology at the University of California, Santa Barbara. Leila J. Rupp is Professor of Women's Studies at the University of California, Santa Barbara.

Author note: We would like to thank the American Psychological Foundation; the Coca-Cola Foundation; and the Ohio State University College of Social and Behavioral Sciences and the Departments of History, Sociology, and Women's Studies for financial support for this project. We are also grateful to Betsy Kaminski and Stephanie Gilmore for research assistance, Josh Gamson for help with the focus group research, and Kathleen Blee, Josh Gamson, S.J. Hopkins, Joanne Meyerowitz, Ann Mische, Esther Newton, Birgitte Søland, Steven Schacht, and an anonymous reviewer for thoughtful readings and helpful comments.

Correspondence may be addressed: Verta Taylor, Department of Sociology, University of California, Santa Barbara, CA 93106.

[Haworth co-indexing entry note]: "Chicks with Dicks, Men in Dresses: What It Means to Be a Drag Queen." Taylor, Verta, and Leila J. Rupp. Co-published simultaneously in *Journal of Homosexuality* (Harrington Park Press, an imprint of The Haworth Press, Inc.) Vol. 46, No. 3/4, 2004, pp. 113-133; and: *The Drag Queen Anthology: The Absolutely Fabulous but Flawlessly Customary World of Female Impersonators* (ed: Steven P. Schacht, with Lisa Underwood) Harrington Park Press, an imprint of The Haworth Press, Inc., 2004, pp. 113-133. Single or multiple copies of this article are available for a fee from The Haworth Document Delivery Service [1-800-HAWORTH, 9:00 a.m. - 5:00 p.m. (EST). E-mail address: docdelivery@haworthpress.com].

113

and sexual categories by making visible the social basis of femininity and masculinity, heterosexuality and homosexuality? Or are they more apt to reinforce the dominant binary and hierarchical gender and sexual systems by appropriating gender displays and expressing sexual desires associated with traditional femininity and institutionalized heterosexuality? We address this question through a case study of drag queens at the 801 Cabaret in Key West, Florida. On the basis of life histories, observations of their performances, and focus groups with audience members, we examine the role of gender and sexuality in the process of becoming a drag queen and in the personal identities of drag queens. We find that transgenderism, same-sex sexuality, and theatrical performance are central to the personal identities of these drag queens, who use drag to forge personal and collective identities that are neither masculine nor feminine, but rather their own complex genders. *[Article copies available for a fee from The Haworth Document Delivery Service: 1-800-HAWORTH. E-mail address: <docdelivery@ haworthpress.com> Website: <http://www.HaworthPress.com> © 2004 by The Haworth Press, Inc. All rights reserved.]*

KEYWORDS. Drag queens, gender categories, gender transgression, gender identity, gay sexuality, effeminacy, transgender, performance

One night at the drag show at the 801 Cabaret in Key West, Florida, Sushi reminds the audience, as if it were necessary, "Remember we are drag queens! We do have dicks and two balls!" Another night they call themselves "chicks with dicks, sluts with nuts." At the same time, R.V. Beaumont tells us in an interview, "I'm an actor in a dress," and Margo says, "I'm just a man in a dress." R.V. typically announces at the start of the show: "We may look like women, but we are all homosexual men." These different self-presentations suggest how complicated the question of what it means to be a drag queen can be. In this paper we examine the gender and sexual identities of a troupe of drag queens from Key West, Florida, known as the "801 Girls."[1]

To clarify what we mean by "drag queens," it is important to point out that not all men who dress as women are drag queens. Other categories include transvestites or cross-dressers, generally straight men who wear women's clothing for erotic reasons; preoperative male-to-female transsexuals; and transgendered people who display and embrace a gender identity at odds with their biological sex (Fleisher 1996; Brubach 1999; Meyerowitz 2002; Schacht 2002a). Drag queens, in contrast, are gay men who dress and perform as but do not want to be women or have women's bodies (although some drag performers are "tittie queens" who acquire breasts through either hormones or implants). Within the category of drag queen, there are further distinctions based on performance style. Esther Newton, in her classic study *Mother Camp*, distinguished between "stage impersonators," talented performers who sang in their own voices, and "street impersonators," more marginal drag queens who lip-synched their numbers (Newton 1972). Steven Schacht identifies four styles of drag as performance (Schacht 2002a). For our purposes, the most important distinction is one the 801 Girls make between "female impersonators" who generally do celebrity impersonation and keep the illusion of being women, in contrast to drag queens who regularly break it in order to accentuate the inherently performative nature of gender and sexual meanings. Drag queens create their own–often multiple–personae and, in the case of the 801 Girls, adopt an "in-your-face" style.

One of the burning questions about drag queens–among both scholars and audiences–is whether they are more gender-conservatives than gender-revolutionaries, recognizing that there are elements of both in operation. Some scholars view drag as primarily reinforcing dominant assumptions about the dichotomous nature of gender presentation and sexual desire because drag queens appropriate gender displays associated with traditional femininity and institutionalized heterosexuality (Frye 1983; Dolan 1985; Tewksbury 1993, 1994; Gagné and Tewksbury 1996; Schacht 1998, 2000, 2002a, 2002b). Others treat drag in the context of the gay community as more a transgressive action that destabilizes gender and sexual categories by making visible the social basis of femininity and masculinity, heterosexuality and homosexuality, and presenting hybrid and minority genders and sexualities (Butler 1990, 1993; Garber 1992; Lorber 1994, 1999; Halberstam 1998; Muñoz 1999). Despite the fact that many observers see both processes at work in complex ways, the question remains: what, ultimately, is the impact of drag? Whereas the overwhelming majority of writings by queer theorists have explored this question by examining the gender and sexual representations conveyed in drag performances (Butler 1990, 1993; Garber 1992), we address this debate by analyzing the way gender and sexuality shape the personal and collective identities of drag queens.

Our analysis relies upon a social constructionist perspective that treats gender and sexuality as historically variable categories of difference overlaid onto external markers, behaviors, bodies, desires, and practices that typically function to reinforce major structures of inequality (West and Zimmerman 1976; Plummer 1981; Connell 1987; Greenberg 1988; Lorber 1994; Nardi and Schneider 1998; Murray 2000). Most research on gender and sexuality focuses on the processes that create and maintain a binary and hierarchical gender system composed of two genders, male and female, and a heteronormative sexual system consisting of two sexual identities, heterosexual and homosexual (Gagnon and Simon 1973; Goffman 1979; Kessler and McKenna 1978; West and Zimmerman 1987; Plummer 1981; West and Fenstermaker 1995; Butler 1990, 1993; Howard and Hollander 1997; Schwartz and Rutter 1998; Ferree, Lorber, and Hess 1999). Recent writings by gender scholars, influenced by the thinking of queer theorists, have called attention to a wide range of "performative" gender transgressions such as drag, cross-dressing, female masculinity, and other boundary-disruptive tactics used by feminist, queer, transgender, and other social movements (Taylor and Whittier 1992; J. Gamson 1997; Lorber 1999; Foster 1999). In such protests, the body of the performer highlights the social basis of gender and sexuality and becomes a weapon to contest dominant heterosexual gender codes.

We draw on this approach in our empirical study of the 801 Girls, but we use the extended case method (Burawoy 1991) to add to and revise queer theory by focusing on the personal identities of the performers. Queer theorists, most notably Judith Butler (1990,1993), postulate the performative nature of gender, siding with sociologists who argue that social identities are always produced within prevailing normative and structural contexts (Stryker 1987; West and Zimmerman 1987; Howard and Hollander 1997). Queer theory, however, has a tendency to adopt what sociologists think of as a strong structuralist bias that ignores the subjectivity and identities of actors as well as the role that individuals play in producing as well as resisting and altering systems of gender and sexual inequality. We draw upon queer theory's view of gender as a performative act. But we expand our understanding of drag as it is actually practiced by examining drag queens' self-conceptions with respect to gender and sexuality and by showing how these are shaped by and, in turn, shape their collective identities as drag performers.

Our study draws from life histories of a troupe of drag queens, observation of their performances, and focus groups with audience members. We begin by exploring the processes through which the 801 Girls became drag queens, pointing to the central role of effeminacy, same-sex desire, and the use of masquerade to engage in gender crossing. We then analyze the personal identities and public performances of the drag queens to show how transgenderism and theatrical performance are used as blatant and deliberate acts to create a collective drag queen identity that establishes new and more fluid gender and sexual meanings. We see drag queens as neither feminine nor masculine but rather presenting their own complex genders (Schacht 2002b).

SETTING AND DATA

The data for this study come from field research conducted from 1998-2001 in a popular drag cabaret in Key West, Florida. Key West is an internationally known gay tourist destination and something of a mecca for drag queens. The 801 Cabaret sits on upper Duval Street, the center of Key West's dynamic gay life. The 801 Girls are full-time drag queens who, joined by occasional guests, perform different lip-synched shows nightly in the cabaret to anywhere from fifty people on an off-night to several thousand people during festivals, holidays, and other celebrations. The audience is mixed, consisting of men and women, gays and heterosexuals, tourists and locals.

Our research is based on multiple sources of data which we analyzed using qualitative methods. We conducted, tape-recorded, and transcribed semi-structured life histories of twelve performers. We coded the interviews thematically and analyzed them inductively to determine which features of their and others' self-concepts the drag queens accentuated. We rely heavily on these interviews in describing drag queen identity, since perhaps the best source of data on identity work is narrative (Baumeister and Newman 1994). In addition, we attended weekly drag queen meetings and observed the performers in their dressing room. All of the drag queens, who ranged in age from twenty-five to sixty-two, identified as gay men. We also observed, tape-recorded, and transcribed fifty performances, including the dialogue, music, and audience interactions. We supplemented these with photographs and field notes. In addition, we conducted twelve focus groups with forty audience members who attended the performances, and we held informal conversations and short interviews with fifty-five additional spectators. Finally, to assess the role of the 801 performers in the larger gay and lesbian community, we examined over a three-year period all stories that contained references to the performers at 801 in the weekly gay newspaper, *Celebrate!* and in the mainstream Key West media. (Fuller description of these drag queens, the political aspects of their performances, and audience reactions to the shows is available in Rupp and Taylor 2003.)

THE 801 GIRLS

We see the 801 Girls as somewhat unusual, since they perform in a gay tourist destination, but we are also convinced that the commonalities and differences among these drag performers, who come from different racial, ethnic, regional, and national backgrounds, can tell us something about what it means to be a drag queen more generally. They certainly see themselves as part of what they proclaim as "Queen Nation."

Sushi, whose mother is Japanese and late father a GI who met and married her in Japan, has a beautiful tall slender body, with thin but muscled arms and a dancer's legs. She is the house queen. Sushi never really looks totally like a man, even when he is dressed as Gary.

Milla is also beautiful as both a man and woman. Dean's mother is Italian and his father a military man from Florida. He has short wavy black hair, beautiful eyes, and kissable full lips. With her olive skin and dark eyes, and her fondness for Erykah Badu and similar numbers, Milla is often taken onstage for African American.

Kylie, Sushi's best friend from high school, is much shorter than Sushi and Milla. Kevin is a very handsome preppy man with straight blondish hair that falls over his eyes. The other drag queens are convinced that Kylie could go in drag to one of the straight bars at the other end of Duval Street and easily pass herself off as a woman, although most of the women in our focus groups were unconvinced.

R.V., who grew up in a small town in Ohio and used to split the year between Key West and Provincetown, is short and stocky. The other girls call her "fat girl" on stage. He has a redhead's complexion with short curly bleached-blond hair. He wears tee shirts that say "I'm not an alcoholic, I'm a drunk" or "Betty Ford Clinic Alumnae."

Margo is a sixty-two-year-old New Yorker with a deep voice. David is painfully thin and not in good health, having suffered a recurrence of bladder cancer and a heart attack during the latest surgery, for which he had to be airlifted out of Key West as Hurricane Georges hit. He is a local celebrity both as Margo, "the oldest living drag queen in captivity," and as David, a columnist for the local gay newspaper.

Scabola Feces, from Providence, Rhode Island, has no intention of looking beautiful, although as Matthew he is a handsome man. He is very thin, has large expressive eyes, a raspy smoker's voice, and a big evil-sounding laugh. He puts together outlandish costumes and elaborate headdresses which he superglues onto his shaved head.

Inga, the "Swedish bombshell," really is from Sweden, and she is big, tall, blond, soft, and adorable, with beautiful dimples. Out of drag as Roger, he favors long baggy shorts and tee shirts, wearing his hair in a thin ponytail. Inga is curvaceous and icy, prone to giving audience members the finger.

When Inga moved to a club down the street, Gugi, who was an occasional performer, took over Inga's show. Gugi is Puerto Rican, from Chicago, and as Rov he's stunning, with black curly hair, beautiful dark eyes, and an unbelievably sweet face. He is shy, while Gugi is aggressive and outgoing.

This was the roster of the 801 Girls at the time we conducted our research. We talked to all of them about how they became drag queens to ascertain common themes in their life histories.

BECOMING A DRAG QUEEN

In telling stories about growing up, the drag queens recounted three ways in which gender and sexual identity influenced how they came to do drag: *gender transgression, masquerade,* and *same-sex sexuality.* As other ethnographic studies of gender crossing have found (Kulick 1998), beginning even before their early teens the drag queens interviewed for our study began to engage in *gender transgression* through dressing in feminine or androgynous clothing, experimenting with makeup, and playing with what would conventionally be seen as "girls' toys." Several of the 801 Girls tell stories about dressing in their mothers' clothes when they were boys. Milla says, "Growing up, Mom and Dad would leave the house for a second and I just had that hour to get in her drawer and put on her panty hose and put her shoes on." Scabola interjects, "Oh, girl, I used to do the same thing!" Gugi, too, admits to liking to dress in his mother's clothes, although he did not do it as regularly as Milla and Scabby. Milla connects his desire to wear women's clothing to wanting to distance himself from his father, who was abusive. Gugi is not sure why he liked to dress up. "I guess I felt comfortable. That's what I wanted to be."

Effeminacy of some kind or other plays a part in all of the girls' stories. Milla told us, "I don't want to say that I was a sissy, but . . . I always played with Barbies, I wanted to make everybody pretty." Scabby always wanted to take the female roles in play, and Margo, who grew up in the 1940s, remembers tossing away the baseball glove his father gave him. R.V., like Milla, played with Barbie dolls and loved to bake in his sister's Easy Bake Oven as well. He says his mother "knew when I was a kid what I was going to be."

Drag also developed out of the use of flamboyant dressing as a *masquerade* or disguise that allowed the drag queens to flaunt femininity and embrace gender fluidity by performing a separate identity that they could put on and take off. Kylie and Sushi, growing up in Oregon in the 1980s, both began by imitating Boy George. After Sushi's father died suddenly of a heart attack when Sushi was fourteen, "Kylie came into my life and we just went crazy." They began ratting their hair, wearing eyeliner, and doing crazy things. They dressed up to "have fun" and "be this other person." By his senior year, Sushi was a "flaming queen," wearing full makeup and platform shoes. Kylie says that at first it was not really drag, it was offbeat, but "suddenly I remember one time I was making a dress. And it just dawned on me, 'this is a dress, this is like completely all the way into dressing like a woman.'" Scabby, too, began as a "club kid," wearing women's clothes and a wig and running around the streets, "but I never actually *did* drag." It was *The Adventures of Priscilla, Queen of the Desert* that spurred him to add makeup to his repertoire for the first time.

Paradoxically, drag both created a way to hide and attracted attention. Milla says, "I found a place where I could be, I could hide, I could mask myself behind wacky makeup, crazy hair colors, the wildest outfits, and feel strong, feel good. Overpowering." About the first time Milla dressed in drag in Key West, she says, "people gave me love, I got all the attention, all the things I never got from a man." Kylie says much the same thing: "I wanted attention. I wanted love, really." Inga also talks about dressing in drag to get attention. "When I was younger, I always had a need to get all the attention, so I was dressing in freaky clothes during the day time, hats, capes, but never in drag." But then she realized that performing in drag, "with all this makeup and this fake costume, . . . I got attention this way." Dressing in costume, then, allowed them to play with gender and to reject its supposed authenticity.

Perhaps most important in their stories of becoming drag queens is *sexual attraction to and desire for men*. Inga says directly that she started to do drag because of "coming out being gay." It was striking how many of them answered the question of how they began to dress in drag by talking first about having sex with other males. When we ask Scabby how she started to do drag, she says, "I've always been gay, always been attracted to men." Milla answers, "I always knew what I liked, which was I knew I liked boys." Gugi says, "I've always known I was gay. I always knew I was attracted to men."

Despite the different stories, certain common themes emerge in the making of a drag queen. Effeminacy and gay sexuality play an important role. (Of course, not all effeminate gay boys grow up to be drag queens, but what is significant is that the 801 Girls connect these parts of their histories to their identities as drag queens.) The cultural styles of the 1980s–like the foppish dress of earlier centuries (Rey 1985)–made room for flamboyance that could easily edge into true drag. Dressing in drag allows one to hide, attracts attention, expresses an in-your-face attitude, and makes clear the performative nature of gender. But what does it really mean to be a drag queen?

WHAT IT MEANS TO BE A DRAG QUEEN: PERSONAL IDENTITIES

What it means to be a drag queen is different for the various girls, although in telling stories about themselves the 801 Girls point to two kinds of personal identities linked to the performance of drag as a collective identity and strategy for undermining normative gender arrangements. For some, being a drag queen is about expressing a *transgender identity*. Sushi describes herself as "some place in between" a woman and a man. "I've always been a drag queen," she says another time.

In fact, Sushi's sense of being in between male and female led her to think about becoming a woman for a while. She lived as a woman for about a year and a half, as did Milla. When she was younger, "I thought, 'Oh my god, I look like such a woman, maybe I am a woman' and it sort of confused me." But "I know I'm a drag queen, I finally realized that." Now, she says: "That's who I am, . . . there aren't that many people like me." Yet Kylie says Sushi "has a struggle . . . whether she should be a woman or a man."

That struggle came to the fore in the spring of 2001, when Sushi saw a television show about transgendered people in America. Over dinner, she tells us about this transformative experience: "For some reason, by the end of it I was crying my eyes out. . . . And I finally realized, oh my God, I'm not a drag queen. I'm a closeted transsexual–transgendered person. And I've been harping and hooting and tooting my horn for years now about being a drag queen–an openly, out, drag queen. And here I finally realize, I'm not a drag queen. I'm a closeted transgendered person." We ask about the difference. "A drag queen is someone like Kylie who never has ever thought about cutting her dick off. Ever. I think about it once a day, sometimes more." She says she really wants to do it but never will, partly because "it's a religious thing, . . . I was born this way," and partly because "I've been a drag queen for so long, and my whole persona–I don't want to try to change my whole personality again into Susie." We remind Sushi about telling us about her discovery that she was a drag queen, not a woman-wannabe. "But now I'm realizing that it's not that I realized I was a drag queen, I learned how to become a drag queen," Sushi explains.

Gugi, too, has a sense of herself as transgendered in some ways. She talks about the femininity in herself and says, "What I've always wanted was to be a woman." Making the link to sexual identity, she adds, "I don't know if it is because I wanted to be a woman or because I was attracted to men that I preferred to be a woman . . . Out of drag, I feel like I'm acting. In drag, I feel like myself." The other girls tell us that they worried about Gugi when she went through a phase of never getting out of drag, going out in public all the time as a woman. "That means you've lost your identity," they say, making a distinction between being a drag queen and being on the move toward becoming a transsexual. Gugi herself seems to admit this. "It's just that certain things, I got too extreme with . . . I started going to the straight side of town. In drag." And in fact Gugi has not ruled out becoming a woman. She says she does not want to be a titty queen but, "Yeah, to be honest, I would love" getting breasts. She likes the idea of not having to wear as much makeup. For two months she did take hormones that she got from his best friend, a transgendered person. But she stopped because "It wasn't the right time. I did it for the wrong reasons. I did it to get away from my dad's death and the breakup with my ex bastard husband."

Milla says, "I love being a guy," but as an adolescent, going through problems at home and getting involved in drugs, being sent to what she calls "kiddie jail" and drug treatment, "I decided that I wanted to be a woman." Not just because she liked women's clothes, but because "I didn't like *me*." She got hormones from a counselor she was seeing by threatening to get them from drag queens on the street. She would go out dressed as a woman and "just have the *men fall over*, all over me, and with no clue, no clue." She loved it, "it was so away from everything." For a while she thought that she really had to be a woman and was seriously considering sex-reassignment surgery. But then "I started to love myself. I pulled away from that whole effeminate side . . . and I became a man." Now, she says, "I'm so pleased with my penis and my body."

Others never thought of themselves as between genders or as women. Margo says, "I don't want to be a woman. I don't understand why anyone would want to do it." As a young gay teenager in New York in the 1950s, he read about Christine Jorgensen's famous transformation from a man to a woman. It scared him. "I did not want to be a woman, and here it is in the paper that this may be what I have to do." Yet even Margo, who reluctantly dressed in drag for the first time as part of her job at a guest house, nevertheless relates being a drag queen to earlier gender experimentations and transgressions: "And the funny thing is when I got dressed and I came out, it was, it became very natural . . . And I had never done that since when you're five years old and you put on your mother's high heels and walk around the house." "It's fun!" David writes in *Celebrate!* "One becomes the center of attention and flaunts the feminine side of the psyche" (Felstein 1997).

Being a drag queen also means embracing a *theatrical identity*, and many of them have background in theater. Scabola has been involved in theater since elementary school and always loved it. "I loved creating personas," she says. Although for Milla being a drag queen is more profound, she also identifies as a performer. She, too, was in theater groups from a young age. What she loves is being able to use her feelings, to evoke the pain and anger and love that audience members have felt in their own lives.

Like Milla, Gugi experiences drag both as expressing her trans-gendered nature and as theatrical. Growing up as a child in Chicago, she performed in church and school plays. She says, "It just comes to me . . . I want to be loved by everyone . . . It's just part of my destiny."

R.V. had been in professional summer stock theater as a boy. Two days after he graduated from high school, he took off to Disney World, unwilling to stop smoking marijuana and live by the rules of his family home. Although she is clearly close to and proud of his mother, she describes her home life as dysfunctional and sees the stage as a way that she could create his own little world. She worked for Disney for four-teen years. There she met drag queens who took her to the Parliament House in Orlando, where she started doing drag. She defines herself as an entertainer: "I'm an actor in a dress." But she also identifies as a drag queen.

Inga has been in the theater since she was ten, and she, too, loves per-forming. For her it was a natural transition from *Romeo and Juliet* and *The Inferno* to Marilyn Monroe and Madonna impersonations. In con-trast to some of the other drag queens, she says, "I never had a need to dress as a girl or wanted to have a sex change." Drag, she says, is an act, not a lifestyle. "I would not trade it, even if some nights it's hard, doing the show, being paid to do it, but I would not trade it for anything." "It's fun. It's a game."

With their theatrical experience, the drag queens engage in street the-ater–both in the cabaret and literally on the streets–in a way that brings their work into alignment with their identity politics. At one Saturday night show, Kylie asks a German tourist if he is straight, and the man re-plies that he is normal. "Normal!" cries Kylie. "I'm normal. You're weird." They take delight in arousing straight men by teasing and fon-dling them. Before the show, they pass out flyers on the streets, engag-ing in banter with the people who walk by. "Are you in the show?" a wide-eyed young tourist asks Margo. "Would I be dressed like this if I weren't?" retorts David in his deep smoker's voice. During Bikers' Week, when the town is overrun with Harleys, the drag queens troop down to the straight bars to "sniff the seats"–a ritual they invented– and, as Sushi puts it, "hassle the straight men." If some of this behavior sounds masculine, they view it more as "acting like hookers," deploy-ing the kind of sexual aggressiveness of female prostitutes.

This theatrical identity involves, just as in traditional theater, taking on a new persona. "Sushi is different than Gary," says Sushi. Even Margo, who became a drag queen late in life, describes David as "an en-tirely different person" from Margo, although "now they are coming to-gether more and more." Timothy, too, is shy and describes himself as introverted. Given his stage presence, we thought he would talk our ears off when we interviewed him, but then we realized that that was R.V. and this was Timothy. "That's a whole different person up there. Differ-ent personality," he says.

Roger also takes on a different style. "As Inga I can do things I could never do as Roger, I would never do." Kevin says, "Kylie is me," but ad-mits that, "Kylie is more expressive, . . . when I'm dressed as Kylie I know that I can get away with so much more." Dean describes keeping Dean and Milla separate because he understood that not being able to live apart from your image–he mentions Boy George here–leads to drugs and breakdown. "That's why there's Dean and Milla. For a while there wasn't."

Audience members are curious about why the drag queens do what they do and come up with explanations that mirror those that the girls themselves offer. A gay male couple from New York who have become friendly with the girls say "they're people just like anybody else and that just happens to be their profession." A straight man, touching on the theatrical identity and comparing them to women who become strippers or porn stars, wonders if they wanted to break into show business and

could not do it any other way. A lesbian from New York disagrees, saying, "I think it's a choice . . . There are so many things on earth that they
could be doing that for a man to go as far as to dress up as a woman,
there's a leap." Her lover agrees with her: "I think that is something
very important to them." A gay male physician from Boston loves drag

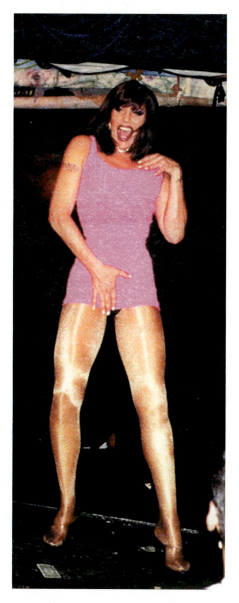

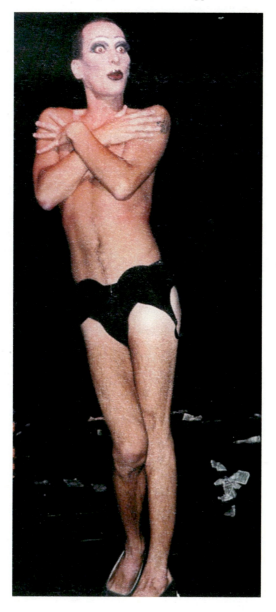

because "it seems to me a pure expression of self . . . They get to project exactly what they want to be." "I think there's an acceptance that they get when they're on stage that they don't necessarily get when they're off stage," says a woman photographer. A gay male lawyer who lives in Key West emphasizes the different motivations: "For some of the performers it's an employment of last resort. For some of the performers it's their pattern. For some of them it's a temporary thing between other things. For some of them it's who they are."

Clearly being a drag queen has different meanings in the 801 Girls' lives, but transgender and theatrical identities emerge clearly from their collective stories. The effeminacy, attraction to masquerade, and same-sex desire that they experienced as boys and young men converge in their drag queen subjectivities. Through their self-presentations and performances, they enact a collective identity that calls attention to the artificiality of gender and sexual binaries. In that sense, they are indeed gender revolutionaries.

CONCLUSION

Watching the transformation that takes place in the dressing room, and listening to the girls' accounts of their gender and sexuality as boys, it is easy to see in concrete terms how unstable the categories of "masculine" and "feminine" and "heterosexual" and "homosexual" really are. The rigidity of the categories in mainstream culture is reflected in the confusion of boys like Sushi, who thought that her sartorial desires meant that she wanted to be a woman. The role of effeminacy and same-sex sexual desires in the girls' stories about becoming drag queens suggests how bound up the identity of drag queen is with deviation from conventional gender expectations and heteronormativity. "Drag queen" emerges as an in-between or third-gender category in a society that insists that there are only two. One gay male audience member captured this when he said that he did not think of them as either men or women, but as "their own thing. I feel like a drag queen is completely different."

In that sense, drag queens are like others who fall between or bridge or challenge the division between masculine and feminine. As other scholars have suggested in considering the butch-fem bar culture of the 1950s or the "female masculinity" of women who look like men on a permanent or temporary basis, such "in-betweens" are not about aping the other side of the divide (Kennedy and Davis 1993; Halberstam 1998). Rather, these are people who create their own authentic genders, suggesting that, rather than eliminating the notion of gender categories, we need to expand the possibilities beyond two or three to a whole range of possible identities, including drag queen.

The case of the 801 Girls supports those who view drag as ultimately transgressive and a challenge to the gender and sexual order. But, by exploring the personal and collective identities of the drag queens at the 801, we go further to show the ways that their gender presentations, performances, and sexual desires play a role in resisting and transforming the gender and sexual systems. Whether "chicks with dicks" or "men in dresses," drag queens create their own transgender and theatrical identities that force their audiences to think in a complex way about what it means to be a woman or what it means to be a man.

NOTE

1. The drag queens generally use drag names and female pronouns in reference to each other, although they sometimes shift to male names and pronouns. There is no correlation to whether they are in or out of drag. In this article, we primarily use their drag names and female pronouns, except when talking about them in their pre-drag past.

REFERENCES

Baumeister, R. and L. Newman. (1994). How stories make sense of personal experiences: Motives that shape autobiographical narratives. *Personality and Social Psychology Bulletin* 20, 676-90.

Brubach, H. and M. O'Brien. (1999). *Girlfriend: Men, women, and drag.* New York: Random House.

Burawoy, M. (1991). Reconstructing social theories. In M. Burawoy (Ed.), *Ethnography unbound: Power and resistance in the modern metropolis* (pp. 8-27). Berkeley: University of California Press.

Butler, J. (1990). *Gender trouble: Feminism and the subversion of identity.* New York: Routledge.

Butler, J. (1993). *Bodies that matter: On the discursive limits of "sex."* New York: Routledge.

Connell, R.W. (1987). *Gender and power: Society, the person, and sexual politics.* Cambridge: Polity in association with Blackwell.

Dolan, J. (1985). Gender impersonation onstage: Destroying or maintaining the mirror of gender roles? *Women and Performance: A Journal of Feminist Theory,* 2, 5-11.

Felstein, D. (1998). Random observations. *Celebrate!* May 29, 3.

Felstein, D. (1997). Face to face with history–Part four. *Celebrate!,* October 24, 9.

Ferree, M., J. Lorber, and B. Hess. (1999). *Revisioning gender.* Thousand Oaks: Sage Publications.

Fleisher, J. (1996). *The drag queens of New York: An illustrated field guide.* New York: Riverhead Books.

Foster, J. (1999). An invitation to dialogue: Clarifying the position of feminist gender theory in relation to sexual difference theory. *Gender & Society* 13, 431-456.

Gagné, P. and R. Tewksbury. (1996). No "man's" land: Transgenderism and the stigma of the feminine man. *Advances in Gender Research* 1, 115-55.

Gagnon, J. and W. Simon. (1973). *Sexual conduct: The social sources of human sexuality.* Chicago: Aldine Publishers.

Gamson, J. (1998). *Freaks talk back: Tabloid talk shows and sexual nonconformity.* Chicago: University of Chicago Press.

Gamson, J. (1997). Messages of exclusion: Gender, movements, and symbolic boundaries. *Gender & Society* 11, 178-199.

Gamson, J. (1994). *Claims to fame: Celebrity in contemporary America.* Berkeley: University of California Press.

Garber, M. (1992). *Vested interests: Cross-dressing and cultural anxiety.* New York: Routledge.

Goffman, E. (1979). *Gender advertisements.* Cambridge, MA: Harvard University Press.

Greenberg, D. (1988). *The construction of homosexuality.* Chicago: University of Chicago Press.

Halberstam, J. (1998). *Female masculinity.* Durham, NC: Duke University Press.

Howard, J. and J. Hollander. (1997). *Gendered situations, gendered selves: A gender lens on social psychology.* Thousand Oaks, CA: Sage.

Kennedy, E. and M. Davis. (1993). *Boots of leather, slippers of gold: The history of a lesbian community.* New York: Routledge.

Kessler, S. and W. McKenna. (1978). *Gender: An ethnomethodological approach.* New York: Wiley.

Kulick, D. (1998). *Travesti: sex, gender and culture among Brazilian transgendered prostitutes.* Chicago: University of Chicago Press.

Lorber, J. (1994). *Paradoxes of gender.* New Haven: Yale University Press.

Lorber, J. (1999). Crossing borders and erasing boundaries: Paradoxes of identity politics. *Sociological Focus* 32, 355-370.

Meyerowitz, J. (2002). *How sex changed: A history of transsexuality in the U.S.* Cambridge, MA: Harvard University Press.

Muñoz, J. (1999). *Disidentifications: Queers of color and the performance of politics.* Minneapolis: University of Minnesota Press, 1999.

Murray, S. (2000). *Homosexualities.* Chicago: University of Chicago Press.

Nardi, P. and B. Schneider. (1998). *Social perspectives in lesbian and gay studies.* New York: Routledge.

Newton, E. (1972). *Mother camp: Female impersonators in America.* Chicago: University of Chicago Press.

Plummer, K. (Ed.). (1981). *The making of the modern homosexual.* London: Hutchinson.

Rey, M. (1985). Parisian homosexuals create a lifestyle, 1700-1750: The police archives. *Eighteenth-century life* 9, n.s. 3, 179-91.

Rupp, L. and V. Taylor. (2003). *Drag queens at the 801 cabaret.* Chicago: University of Chicago Press.

Schacht, S.P. (1998). The multiple genders of the court: Issues of identity and performance in a drag setting. In S.P. Schacht and D.W. Ewing (Eds.), *Feminism and men: Reconstructing gender relations* (pp. 202-24). New York: New York University Press.

Schacht, S.P. (2000). Gay masculinities in a drag community: Female impersonators and the social construction of 'other.' In P. Nardi (Ed.), *Gay masculinities* (pp. 247-68). Newbury Park, CA: Sage.

Schacht, S.P. (2002a). Four renditions of doing female drag: Feminine appearing conceptual variations of a masculine theme. *Gendered Sexualities* 6, 157-80.

Schacht, S.P. (2002b). Turnabout: Gay drag queens and the masculine embodiment of the feminine. In N. Tuana et al. (Eds.), *Revealing male bodies* (pp. 155-70). Bloomington: Indiana University Press.

Schwartz, P. and V. Rutter. (1998). *The gender of sexuality.* Thousand Oaks: Pine Forge Press.

Stryker, S. (1987). Identity theory: Developments and extensions. In K. Yardley and T. Honess (Eds.), *Self and identity: Psychological perspectives.* (pp. 89-103). New York: John Wiley.

Taylor, V. and N. Whittier. (1992). Collective identity in social movement communities: Lesbian feminist mobilization. In A. Morris and C. Mueller (Eds.), *Frontiers in social movement theory* (pp. 104-30). New Haven: Yale University Press.

Tewksbury, R. (1993). Men performing as women: Explorations in the world of female impersonators. *Sociological Spectrum* 13, 465-86.

Tewksbury, R. (1994). Gender construction and the female impersonator: The process of transforming 'he' to 'she.' *Deviant Behavior: An Interdisciplinary Journal* 15, 27-43.

West, C. and S. Fenstermaker. (1995). Doing difference. *Gender & Society* 9, 8-37.

West, C. and D. Zimmerman. (1987). Doing gender. *Gender & Society* 1, 125-151.

"Let the Drag Race Begin": The Rewards of Becoming a Queen

Steven J. Hopkins

Virginia Polytechnic Institute and State University

SUMMARY. Drawing upon my ethnographic experiences in a drag venue called The Park in Roanoke, Virginia, this article explores the experiences of female impersonators in terms of their early motivations for doing drag, how they create and maintain drag personas and identities, and the obstacles to becoming a queen. Departing from previous researchers that have framed female impersonation as a deviant, stigmatizing, and pathological activity, this research analyzes the significant benefits some drag queens garner by donning women's attire. An experiential understanding of drag reveals that the significant rewards from the activity–contextual power and status, self-affirmation and empowerment–are powerful motivating factors. Instead of being deviant and/or partaking in pathological behavior, female impersonators can be seen as operating on an incentive system where the

---

Steven J. Hopkins has a degree in anthropology from Radford University and is currently studying architecture at Virginia Tech.

Author note: I would like to thank all of the people at The Park who participated in this project. Additionally, I would like to thank Steven Schacht and two anonymous individuals for reviewing earlier drafts of this manuscript.

Correspondence may be addressed: 782 Triangle Street, Apt. 494, Blacksburg, VA 24060 (E-mail: sjhopkins@aol.com).

[Haworth co-indexing entry note]: "'Let the Drag Race Begin': The Rewards of Becoming a Queen." Hopkins, Steven J. Co-published simultaneously in *Journal of Homosexuality* (Harrington Park Press, an imprint of The Haworth Press, Inc.) Vol. 46, No. 3/4, 2004, pp. 135-149; and: *The Drag Queen Anthology: The Absolutely Fabulous but Flawlessly Customary World of Female Impersonators* (ed: Steven P. Schacht, with Lisa Underwood) Harrington Park Press, an imprint of The Haworth Press, Inc., 2004, pp. 135-149. Single or multiple copies of this article are available for a fee from The Haworth Document Delivery Service [1-800-HAWORTH, 9:00 a.m. - 5:00 p.m. (EST). E-mail address: docdelivery@haworthpress.com].

http://www.haworthpress.com/web/JH
Digital Object Identifier: 10.1300/J082v46n03_08

benefits of doing drag positively enrich the quality of the performer's life in a context where successful queens are held in the highest regard. *[Article copies available for a fee from The Haworth Document Delivery Service: 1-800-HAWORTH. E-mail address: <docdelivery@haworthpress.com> Website: <http://www.HaworthPress.com> © 2004 by The Haworth Press, Inc. All rights reserved.]*

KEYWORDS. Female impersonation, drag queens, deviance, stigmatization, rewards for doing drag, gay community, transgendered

Through a thick haze of smoke, Anita Mann, the emcee for October's Talent Night competition, takes the stage. She rallies the crowd, "Ladies and gentlemen, let the drag race begin! These bitches are going to come out here . . . they're going to tiptoe through the tulips, do back-flips, somersaults, squirt watermelon seeds out of their ass and plant a garden, right here on the stage." Following Anita's trademark query, "Attitude check?" to which all present respond in unison "Fuck you!" the next hour witnesses a seemingly endless array of colorful queens with equally vibrant names (Fantasia L'Amour, Sinister Abbey, and crowd favorite Maya Divine), two gay male performers that dance and strip (just to underwear) and even a performance by the incomparable Anita Mann herself.

As the spotlight focuses in on the stage, a young, athletic Black male, wearing only a white mask and shiny black pants, lip-syncs the introduction to the Missy Elliott song "Get Your Freak On." As the beat kicks in, Miss Behavin dances out on the stage wearing a white T-shirt adorned with shiny green beads, camouflage pants, and combat boots. Although Miss Behavin is not a celebrity impersonator, in this costume and wig she is the spitting image of Missy Elliott, which adds a great deal of credibility to her performance. Halfway through the show the song abruptly stops and changes to another Missy Elliott song, "One Minute Man," which has the audience chanting the song's refrain "Break me off, show me what ya got, cause I don't want no one minute man." This performance represents Miss Behavin's sixth attempt at winning Talent Night. On this particular evening, she appears to have the right formula (having rehearsed this routine for a solid month), and the crowd is heavily into the performance, forming a line to tip her and her back-up dancer that extends deep into the audience. Although Miss Behavin makes some common mistakes, such as falling out of rhythm with her backup dancer toward the end of the performance when she becomes fatigued, and ceasing to lip-sync as she becomes distracted by taking tips from the audience, her performance is very solid and highly entertaining. Both the audience and the judges acknowledge this fact, and she has her first real victory in the world of female impersonation by tying a more experienced queen (Maya Divine) for the win. Although a tie is never quite as satisfying as an outright win, it is very impressive considering Maya Divine has a reputation for being virtually unbeatable in Talent Night competition and Miss Behavin has only performed a handful of times.

This study focuses exclusively on female impersonators/drag queens, defined in this context as biological males who don women's attire for the purposes of performing for an audience that realizes that they are men. The cross-dressing behavior of female impersonators is limited primarily, if not solely, to performance situations. Congruent with the observations of the majority of researchers, female impersonators in this context clearly define their behavior as different from transsexuals and transvestites (Newton 1979; Tewksbury 1994; Tewksbury and Gagne 1996; Schacht 2000). Throughout this text, I have elected to use the terms "drag queen" and "female impersonator" interchangeably, in order to reflect the usage of this language in the setting. However, many queens do find the term "drag queen" offensive when used by outsiders. More will be said about some additional contextual definitions of the female impersonators at The Park in a moment.

Through an exploration of the process of becoming a queen, this research demonstrates that the significant rewards associated with female impersonation contest stereotypes held by the general public as well as many researchers' assertion that such individuals are stigmatized, deviant, and/or partaking in some sort of pathological behavior (Baker 1994; Elkins and King 1966; Perkins 1996; Tewksbury 1993, 1994; Newton 1972; Benjamin 1966; Docter 1988; Wise and Meyer 1980). To the contrary, there are often significant rewards associated with female impersonation for those who successfully negotiate the process of becoming a queen. Many are empowered by the experience of doing drag, gain contextual status, wield considerable power in their own communities, and, in general, are well-adjusted individuals. Moreover, the odyssey undertaken to become a female impersonator reveals rather common patterns of behavior and that the activity is contextually normal, not deviant. While there are some costs to doing drag (e.g., possible rejection by friends/family, becoming more vulnerable to discrimination, violence, and harassment) the actual contextual experience of doing female impersonation is often quite positive, powerful, and normal.

The following section explores The Park and my role in this setting. I then explore the process of becoming a queen in terms of the early motivations of drag participants, creating and maintaining a drag identity, public presentation of the drag persona, and potential impediments to establishing oneself as a female impersonator. The struggles and rewards associated with becoming a queen demonstrate that, at least for the successful few, drag can be a quite positive and powerful experience. In the concluding section of this paper, I argue that, from an insider's perspective, drag queens contextually are often highly regarded individuals who normatively wield considerable power within the settings they perform.

THE PARK AND MY ROLE IN THE SETTING

Roanoke is an interesting setting for undertaking research on female impersonators. As Roanoke is a relatively small city (population ~95,000), an analysis of its drag scene may help provide an idea of how drag communities emerge in smaller rural areas. Due to the small size of the area, and a corresponding limited tipping audience for drag performers, few if any queens in this area are able to rely on drag as a primary or supplemental source of income. Therefore, as this article will demonstrate, many of the motivations for becoming a female impersonator are not financially related.

The Park is a gay nightclub in downtown Roanoke, Virginia, that features a weekly drag show on Sunday night, with additional shows on special occasions. Firmly entrenched in the so-called "Bible Belt" that runs through much of Virginia, The Park has managed to thrive as a gathering place for gays and lesbians since 1978 even though the majority of the people in the area are highly conservative (there are nearly 450 churches in Roanoke). The only other gay bar in Roanoke is the smaller Backstreet Café, which is located less than a mile from The Park, but it only stages drag shows occasionally.

The following paper draws upon my ethnographic experiences at The Park from August 2000 to the present. My fieldwork was conducted by attempting to capture the experience of becoming a female impersonator. This was accomplished primarily by "hanging out" at the nightclub, interacting with the clientele as peers, and participating in the same activities as the usual patrons (e.g., dancing, drinking, observing and occasionally tipping performers at shows). I was very much a welcomed and accepted participant, even though it was known to many that I am heterosexual and involved in research on the setting. Although I am a regular patron and definitely not an outsider in this setting, I have not been involved to the extent that I can claim a true insider's perspective.

This study is also based upon fifteen informal, semi-structured interviews that were conducted with female impersonators and individuals directly involved in female impersonation (e.g., bar staff and patrons, pageant judges, coordinators, promoters, and owners) and supplemented with information gleaned during countless casual conversations with these and other individuals. Over the course of this research, I took nearly a hundred pages of field notes, collected any literature distributed in the setting (e.g., newsletters, flyers, announcements, promo pictures), took some pictures (when allowed by bar), and was given approximately fifteen hours of video taken of drag shows at the club. Furthermore, I have served three times as a judge for Talent Night. This ethnography attempts to inclusively use all of this various data to construct a holistic image of the setting and its participants.

BECOMING A QUEEN

The Cast

The female impersonators and other individuals noted throughout this paper can be roughly categorized based on their level of experience and relative status in the setting as "veterans," "established queens," and "amateurs." The first category of veterans includes queens such as Ashley Adams and Anita Mann. Both of these individuals have been involved in female impersonation for a number of years, have been successful in many pageants, and are highly esteemed in this setting. Both Anita and Ashley consistently serve as emcees for shows at The Park, a true mark of distinction and status among female impersonators. Included here is also Norman Jones, the owner of the Miss Gay America (MGA) pageant system and veteran female impersonator. Although Jones is not a direct participant in this setting, his pageant system wields considerable influence on the queens in the area. Also included here is Barbara Maberry, a lesbian who operates the largest drag family in this area. Although she is not a female impersonator, she often performs in a drag style and her role as "drag mother" to many (often responsible for developing drag personas, creating costumes/make-up/hair, and creating and choreographing stage shows) has accorded her high status in this setting, equal to many of the veteran queens.

Beyond the initial stages of self-establishment although yet to receive the high status conferred upon what I have termed "veterans," are the "established queens." This includes Phoenix Amber (who has since moved from Roanoke), Taylor Made (a queen from West Virginia who performs at The Park), and Alexis Stone (an experienced queen who now only performs sporadically). These are individuals who are best viewed as up and coming stars in the setting.

The final category is that of the amateur queens, those individuals who have only recently began to appear publicly and have limited status in this setting. Included in this category are Miss Behavin (the queen described at the beginning of this paper), Mercedes, and Paige Valentine (who has since relinquished female impersonation to perform in the male pageant system). It is from the diversity of these and other performers' experiences and backgrounds that I now discuss the process of becoming a female impersonator.

Early Motivations for Becoming a Queen

Queens cite several different motivations for becoming involved in female impersonation. One such motivation is the individual's increased involvement in the gay community by making a further identification with the group beyond that of just homosexual. This represents the opportunity to experience a second "coming out." Others claim that drag offers a chance to be involved in entertaining and receive attention for performing. Mercedes and Miss Behavin both make this claim explicitly, saying that they do drag primarily for the attention they receive performing as females and the subsequent personal benefits. Mercedes expressed, "When I get up on stage, and people are giving *me* money because I look this way . . . it builds your self-esteem."

Many queens state that drag offers a way to become an entertainer in a smaller market. Ashley Adams, an exceptionally talented female impersonator, claimed that she pursued drag because she wanted to be an entertainer but felt that she had little or no conventionally marketable talents. In her case, female impersonation opened up a brand of entertainment that allows men to exercise different, perhaps more unconventional talents.

Another common motivation for being involved in drag is the benefit of being able to personally construct and alter one's persona. Phoenix Amber expressed that drag offers a way of placing a "protective barrier" between herself and the world, by using her character as an intermediary between herself and the people with whom she interacts. She also adds an escapist dimension to her motivations, saying, "I think I do drag sometimes to forget about my problems." Taylor Made highlights the gendered rewards that many queens claim to receive from female impersonation: "When I'm in a dress, I'm a lot more outgoing, and I'm not as shy. But as _____ [male persona], I'd rather be back away." She goes on to say that she is now beginning to assert her male persona so as not to "be in the shadow" of Taylor. Therefore, it is the creation of this female identity that has ultimately given her the courage to negotiate her social phobias.

Some Additional Contextual Norms for Becoming a Female Impersonator

Other than as children, many drag queens are adamant that they have never experimented with wearing female garments until they became interested in becoming a female impersonator. Nor do any of the drag queens dress as females outside of a performance situation (except to rehearse). The participants of this setting have frequently reminded me of their primary role as entertainers, and many have expressed that being a successful entertainer is more important than appearing realistically female. As such, female impersonators often go to great lengths to differentiate themselves from transvestites and transsexuals, which is an important concept in the definition of the female impersonator as a performer.

Beyond these identity aspects of being a female impersonator, there are regional norms that focus on "natural" drag, i.e., no hormones or surgery. This has created an environment that is strongly focused on the illusory aspect of drag. Transsexual performers are often viewed as "cheaters," and are expressly prohibited from participating in the local pageants, most of which are affiliated with the Miss Gay America system. Norman Jones, the owner of this pageant, expresses common sentiments with regard to transsexuals (both pre-operative or post-operative) that become involved in female impersonation in this area:

> I have a hard time going into a bar restroom and a "thing"–something is in there with boobs bigger than I have ever seen with their skirt hiked up peeing. I just have a problem with that. The art of illusion is to be a man and make yourself look like a woman. If you go and have that done, you're not illusion anymore, you're fact.

Female impersonators in this area have long been viewed as socially deviant from much of heterosexual society and even face stigmatization from some gay individuals, and often attempt to establish hierarchies that present themselves as different from, and "more normal" than, transvestites and transsexuals (Tewksbury 1994). When Mercedes recounted the story of when she revealed to her co-workers that she was a female impersonator, she expressed a common sentiment by placing special emphasis on her role as a performer, saying to her friends "I *only* do this for stage, I don't go downtown and do it." Implied in this statement is that she is an entertainer only, not a transvestite or transsexual, and that female impersonation is seen as more normatively acceptable. Furthermore, use of the term "drag queen" is publicly eschewed by most of the veteran performers precisely because of its association with the transvestite prostitutes that were once very common on Salem Avenue in Roanoke.

This is not to say that female impersonators in this area explicitly look down upon transvestites and transsexuals, but more so that the queens are intent upon having their role in the gay community recognized as distinct. Therefore, female impersonators in this area are often frustrated by the fact the many people attempt to classify them homogeneously with other transgendered groups and people.

Rites of Passage in Becoming a Female Impersonator

The initial public presentation of a female persona is perhaps one of the most difficult steps for the aspiring queen. Some individuals decide to make their first public appearance in drag on regular bar nights and Talent Nights, such as the one described at the beginning of this paper. However, many female impersonators in this context report having their first experiences of publicly dressing as women on Halloween (Tewksbury 1994). Paige Valentine describes her first public drag experience, "For Halloween one time, I dressed up as a woman, and they were having this costume competition, and I walked up there and they thought I was a girl, they said 'You're a cute girl, but what's your costume?' So I thought I could probably be a pretty good impersonator." Functionally, Halloween is similar to the masquerade balls that originally inspired the first drag shows, providing an environment of costumes and anonymity that is highly conducive to the needs of one seeking an acceptable outlet to try drag for the first time.

Obviously, appearing in drag on Halloween does not necessarily mean that an individual wants to participate in drag on an ongoing basis. For many men, both gay and straight (when done by a heterosexual man, it is perhaps done entirely for comic effect), doing drag is a one-time experience that they have no intentions of ever repeating. For those that do have an interest in doing drag on a more ongoing basis, however, it may be easier for them to start on Halloween. Since it is a special occasion where costumes are expected, the social pressures of appearing as a female are not as great and the individual will not face as much scrutiny from other female impersonators.

This is in contrast to appearing for the first time for a show at the bar or at a competition, where scrutiny from other queens can be intense. These occasions allow aspiring female impersonators a trial run to estimate their own potential success as a queen by gauging the reactions of their peers. According to Ashley Adams, "It is very common for people to try drag on Halloween because there is less chance for scrutiny and criticism. If they receive good feedback, then they proceed from there with their hobby, career."

Drawing upon the critical concept of public performance in the construction of a definition of female impersonators, aspiring queens must next seek out a venue where they can perform. Since club bookings are not given to female impersonators that have not established themselves, the queens must compete against one another for status in the group. This desire for contextual status is a strong motivating factor, and when achieved, cited as one of the most rewarding aspects of female impersonation. At the amateur level, this usually takes place during Talent Night, a monthly event at The Park and one that appears in various manifestations at many other gay clubs (as well heterosexual establishments). True to its name, Talent Night is not an event solely for amateur female impersonators per se, although these novices represent the majority of the contestants. Other types of contestants occasionally glimpsed are male impersonators, and "real" men and women, who simply perform as themselves, also lip syncing songs or occasionally singing live.

Along with the prestige of winning the event, there is also a cash prize of $100. However, since it usually costs contestants much more in costumes and preparation time, it is unlikely that anyone enters the event solely for the money (an arduous commitment since most of the performers also hold full-time jobs). Tewksbury (1995) observes, "the rewards for which illusionists compete are partially financial, but primarily intangible." These "intangible" rewards are social status and contextual power–two quite tangible things. Furthermore, to most female impersonators in this area money is not a motivating factor. Even in particular contests where the prize money can be substantial, there are still doubts as to whether or not this payoff strongly influences female impersonators. According to Norman Jones, Miss Gay America makes about $32,000 for her yearlong reign, yet Jones insists, "you could take away the money and they'd still enter. All they really want is the prestige."

Participation in Talent Night serves as a major stepping-stone for aspiring female impersonators. Ashley Adams describes her early Talent Night experiences:

> Talent Night played a huge role in my development as a female impersonator. Not many performers, especially new and inexperienced, are given the opportunity to step in front of hundreds of people for four or five minutes and entertain them. So I seized that opportunity and used Talent Night as a means of practicing my craft and fine-tuning the essentials necessary to become a consummate performer.

Many performers who win Talent Night competitions are able to request positions in the normal Sunday night show-cast. However, *not* winning Talent Night can be, at times, equally beneficial, as once one wins Talent Night, that person cannot compete again until the end of the year, at an event called Horizon (the culmination of Talent Night where all previous winners compete against each other). By not winning Talent Night, an impersonator who does not receive bookings has the opportunity to perform at least once a month, and reap the benefits described by Ashley Adams above. Since exposure plays a major role in the success of a queen, even those performers who do not win a Talent Night can obtain bookings by the bar and establish a reputation.

Successfully Creating and Maintaining a Performance Persona

> My stage persona was created out of the creative mind and hands of Lynette Summers. She became my drag mother, taking me under her wings and teaching me everything that she knew about the art form of "drag." In fact, during my early career, I was called "Little Lynette" because I was a spitting image of her. She did my makeup for a few months, I wore her costumes and her hair and I imitated her movements on stage. In fact . . . that ultimately became an obstacle for me because I was constantly being compared to Lynette. I had not created my own identity. I needed to create my own niche, my own look and over time, that's what I've done. (Ashley Adams)

Creating an identity as a female impersonator extends well beyond a cosmetic transformation achieved by applying makeup and costuming. Queens frequently refer to their characters in the third person, as "other," in order to express the existence of that character as a separate entity disparate in presentation from their own as a male, even if interdependent in construction. This change in identity, if successful, is often very apparent. My interviews with female impersonators were all done as their male persona, and I noticed a fundamental change of their demeanor when subsequently speaking with them in the bar as their created female characters. Although this change can be drastic at times, the female persona incorporates aspects of the performer's male persona, and is entirely dependent upon it for formulation.

The resultant personality appears complete yet cannot exist independently of the individual who creates it. The female persona commonly highlights aspects of the male persona that the performer may not feel comfortable expressing as a male, and thus the female persona can serve as a conduit for personal expression, as evidenced by the previous statement issued by Taylor Made. As other researchers have noted (Newton 1979; Schacht 2000; Tewksbury 1994), the drag persona is often used to assert and repair perceived social deficiencies in the performer's male persona.

The creation of a drag identity is a task that is rarely undertaken by an individual acting alone, and all of the aforementioned queens have credited many others with assisting them. Individuals already participating in female impersonation will often help other aspiring queens. Very often, these individuals are veteran performers who function as teachers and mentors–instructing, critiquing, encouraging, and assisting in various ways. These "drag mothers," as they are fondly referred to, are usually older and help the younger performers create and nurture a drag identity.

Phoenix Amber is one of the drag daughters of Anita Mann, the emcee described at the beginning of this paper. Phoenix conceptualizes this relationship as a teacher-student/mother-daughter arrangement, and drag mothers such as Anita Mann may have several "drag daughters" that they are assisting. Often emerging from these arrangements are "drag families," which are larger kinship units that offer a support nexus for female impersonators and present opportunities for strong interpersonal relationships to be forged.

Electing to be involved in a "drag family" has both advantages and disadvantages for young performers, and can shape their subsequent drag career. Family members have a large network to draw on for creative, emotional, and sometimes financial support. However, reliance on the family's support can sometimes prevent a queen from developing a mystique of autonomy that is highly lauded by other impersonators. Phoenix Amber, although receiving some assistance from others, is not part of a drag family and is largely viewed by the community as an independent performer, for which she receives a great deal of respect. Phoenix, crediting a background in art, is very skilled at doing her own (and others') makeup, making her own costumes, and choreographing her own dance routines.

Mercedes, who is also respected as a performer (presenting an impersonation so compellingly real that it made me strongly doubt she was truly a biological male) but relies heavily on others for assistance, has shown some remorse for her dependency, saying, "That's what makes me feel so bad, I feel bad about singing 'Independent Women' because I guess I'm not. I don't depend on anyone else's money . . . but I can't do my own makeup. People don't like that, they want you to do your own makeup. But you get back there [backstage] and half of those bitches are sitting in a chair and some Miss Gay something is doing their makeup." Many queens elect to be largely independent in order to try to avoid many of the conflicts, or "drama," that can so easily arise amongst rival families.

Although autonomy is very respected, there is often a price to be paid. Alexis Stone, an independent performer, has expressed that she is often so busy multi-tasking (making costumes, props, choreographing routines) that there is often little time left to actually rehearse. The result is a catch-22 situation where one can often get to the top more quickly and easily by embracing the assistance of others, often through a family, but may never achieve the same degree of respect that an autonomous individual would at the same level.

Many queens also accuse other performers of attaining status and winning titles based on the political influence of the family of which they are a part (a common accusation whenever competition is involved). Regardless of family affiliation or claims of independence, nearly all queens have received assistance at some point of their drag career. The relationships forged through this common interest have provided many queens with a stronger sense of community and family, and these close relationships and friendships are often cited as one of the benefits of doing drag.

Some Additional Impediments to Becoming a Female Impersonator

Obviously, not all aspiring female impersonators succeed in establishing themselves and fail to achieve a long-term career for a variety of reasons. Queens often relate a common story that when they debuted, they were ridiculed and denigrated based on their stage names, shows, and appearance (most claim that they looked very unconvincing, or "booger," when they started). As a result of this ridicule, Alexis Stone changed her stage name from Gethsemane, after it was repeatedly mispronounced as "get-some-of-me." Most female impersonators are extremely self-conscious, especially in the initial stages of their career, and often these insults can prove fatal to their long-term goals. Even when performers get past this obstacle, often the critique of the judges at various contests is too much for the self-esteem (and ego) of young performers, and even promising individuals cut their careers short.

When dressing as a woman and performing on stage without much experience, mistakes are often made. These mishaps include incorrectly lip-syncing lyrics, falling (reportedly, spiked heels are not easy to dance in), wigs coming off, and even worse. During one show I observed a young performer's genitalia become untucked while wearing a thong, exposing his scrotum to one side of the stage. Mistakes like this can be fatal to those who do not have the determination to overcome them.

Other impediments to becoming a queen include the potentially negative reactions of family members and friends. Most queens express that their families were not initially supportive of their efforts, and the fact that some queens attempt to surreptitiously participate in drag reveals that they anticipate negative reactions. However, once queens are established in the setting it is not uncommon for family members (particularly mothers) and close friends to attend their shows, even those who have previously expressed a strong distaste for drag and the gay community in general.

Once one participates in drag (and even the gay community) that individual becomes more susceptible to discrimination, harassment, and even violence. While I have personally heard no stories of queens here being the target of extremely violent behavior (although I have heard many stories of harassment and close-calls), this sort of thing certainly exists, even if it is only through their involvement in the gay community. Only a few months into undertaking this research, Backstreet Café in Roanoke was the setting for an attempted killing spree by an individual on a mission to "waste some faggots," who succeeded in killing one gay man and injuring many others. In the setting of the bar, queens are relatively safe (barring freak occurrences such as the Backstreet Café incident) and the majority of harassment that has occurred has happened outside of this context.

RETHINKING ISSUES OF DEVIANCE, PATHOLOGY, AND STIGMATIZATION

As previously noted, the preponderance of research conducted with regard to female impersonators has been done from an outsider's point of view. Conducting research in this manner has led researchers to take the various positions that drag queens are stigmatized, deviant, and possibly mentally ill. However, when research is conducted that explicitly attempts to gain an insider's view, a much different picture of drag emerges.

The majority of individuals that attempt to establish themselves as female impersonators fail to ever gain any real status or power in the setting. However, for those that do succeed, the rewards can be immeasurable. The weekly drag shows held at The Park are eagerly anticipated by many of the patrons and are an integral aspect of the club's operation. Therefore, the queens are participating in a contextually normal activity, however deviant their behavior may appear to outsiders.

Although queens are most certainly stigmatized by the heterosexual community as well as in certain segments of the gay community, successful queens are anything but stigmatized in the settings in which they perform. Veteran queens such as Ashley Adams and Anita Mann are held in the highest regard and literally reign supreme while in drag. They are valued by the community as skilled entertainers, role models for up-and-coming queens, effective fund-raisers/advocates for gay-related causes, and are often viewed as "the life of the party."

Despite the commonly held belief that female impersonators are "sick," confused, or mentally ill persons, an experiential understanding of drag reveals that the queens are merely operating on an incentive system where the significant personal benefits gleaned from drag outweigh the costs. These personal benefits (contextual power and status) are so powerful and alluring that the determined queen will persist in spite of any potential impediments, such as bruised egos, rejection by friends/family, becoming more vulnerable to discrimination, violence, or harassment. For successful drag queens, the experience of female impersonation is a positive one that enriches their own lives and fills an important niche in the community.

REFERENCES

Baker, R. (1994). *Drag: A history of female impersonation in the performing arts.* New York: New York University Press.

Benjamin, H. (1966). *The transsexual phenomenon.* New York: Julian.

Docter, R. (1988). *Transvestites and transsexuals: Towards a theory of cross-gender behavior.* New York: Plenum.

Elkins, R. and King, D. (1996). *Blending genders: Social aspects of cross-dressing and sex-changing.* New York: Routledge.

Feinbloom, D.H. (1977). *Transvestites and transsexuals.* New York: Delta Books.

Newton, E. (1979). *Mother camp: Female impersonators in America.* Chicago: University of Chicago Press.

Perkins, R. (1996). The "drag queen" scene: Transsexuals in King's Cross. In R. Elkins & D. King (Eds.), *Blending genders: Social aspects of cross-dressing and sex-changing* (pp. 53-62). New York: Routledge.

Schacht, S.P. (2000). Gay female impersonators and the masculine construction of "other." In P. Nardi (Ed.), *Gay masculinities* (pp. 247-268). London: Sage Publications.

Schacht, S.P. (2002). Four renditions of doing female drag: Feminine appearing conceptual variations of a masculine theme. In P. Gagne and R. Tewksbury (Eds.), "Gendered Sexualities" in *Advances in Gender Research* (pp. 157-180). Boston: Elsevier Science.

Talamini, J. (1982). *Boys will be girls*. Lanham, MD: University Press of America.

Tewksbury, R. (1993). Men performing as women: Explorations in the world of female impersonators. *Sociological Spectrum*, 13, 465-486.

Tewksbury, R. (1994). Gender construction and the female impersonator: The process of transforming "he" to "she." *Deviant Behavior*, 15, 27-43.

Tewksbury, R. (1995). Constructing women and their world: The subculture of female impersonation. In N. Herman (Ed.), *Deviance: A symbolic interactionist approach*. Dix Hills, NY: General Hall.

Tewksbury, R. and Gagne, P. (1996, Nov). Transgenderists: Products of non-normative intersections of sex, gender, and sexuality. *Journal of Men's Studies*, 5, 105-125.

Wise, T. and Meyer, J. (1980). Transvestism: Previous findings and new areas for inquiry. *Journal of Sex and Marital Therapy*, 6, 116-128.

Woodhouse, A. (1989). *Fantastic women: Sex, gender, and transvestism*. New Brunswick, NJ: Rutgers University Press.

Transformance:
Reading the Gospel in Drag

Jeffrey Q. McCune, Jr., MA

Northwestern University

SUMMARY. Despite the large body of scholarship on drag and its performance of misogyny, mimicry, and masculinity, little attention has been paid to the role of musical genres in Black drag performance and its reception. This essay explores drag performances of gospel music and its relationship with the spectator at the Biology Bar, a Black gay drag site in Chicago. By examining the shift from the club "space" to the church "place," this research locates several possibilities for queer gospel performances. Through the introduction of a theory of *transformance*, this essay highlights the contradictions, complications, and complexities of the relationship between the Black church and the Black gay community. *[Article copies available for a fee from The Haworth Document Delivery Service: 1-800-HAWORTH. E-mail address: <docdelivery@haworthpress.com> Website: <http://www.HaworthPress.com> © 2004 by The Haworth Press, Inc. All rights reserved.]*

Jeffrey Q. McCune, Jr., is a PhD student in Performance Studies at Northwestern University.

Author note: I thank Susan Manning, E. Patrick Johnson, Caterria Brown, Christine Dunford, and Steve Schacht for their insights and assistance on this project. Without their support and encouragement, this project would not have been possible.

Correspondence may be addressed: 1942 Wesley Avenue, Evanston, IL 60201.

[Haworth co-indexing entry note]: "Transformance: Reading the Gospel in Drag." McCune, Jeffrey Q., Jr. Co-published simultaneously in *Journal of Homosexuality* (Harrington Park Press, an imprint of The Haworth Press, Inc.) Vol. 46, No. 3/4, 2004, pp. 151-167; and: *The Drag Queen Anthology: The Absolutely Fabulous but Flawlessly Customary World of Female Impersonators* (ed: Steven P. Schacht, with Lisa Underwood) Harrington Park Press, an imprint of The Haworth Press, Inc., 2004, pp. 151-167. Single or multiple copies of this article are available for a fee from The Haworth Document Delivery Service [1-800-HAWORTH, 9:00 a.m. - 5:00 p.m. (EST). E-mail address: docdelivery@haworthpress.com].

Digital Object Identifier: 10.1300/J082v46n03_09

KEYWORDS. Transformance, performance, gospel, drag, space, place, Black drag, Black church, Christianity

> Black gays and lesbians are employing disidentification insofar as they value the cultural rituals of the black worship service yet resist the fundamentalism of its message. (Johnson, pp. 15-16)

After a long hiatus from attending drag performances, I found myself hooked, once again. Close friends had asked me to join them at their favorite club in Chicago, the Biology Bar. This Monday night ritual is often one in which I chose not to participate. Their pleading, however, made it hard for me to resist. This was a night that I had an experience that I shall never forget. Sapphire Blue, one of Chicago's "heavy divas," performed a traditional gospel tune. In my previous experiences with drag, I had seen impersonations from Aretha Franklin to Whitney Houston, but never had I encountered performances of *gospel*. This performance prompted me to question whether I was in a Black club or in a Black church. When I veered to the right and then to the left, it appeared that the Biology Bar had become Bethel African Methodist Episcopal Church. In that moment I felt suspended in a liminal place, caught between my lifetime journey as a Christian and my experience as a member of the Black gay community.

Caught betwixt and between the "sacred" and the "secular," I experienced mixed emotions that were difficult to clearly articulate. There is always a precarious feeling that undergirds each experience. Sapphire Blue's performance is always captivating, but in dialogue with my grandmother's adage "there is a time and place," it also felt out of place. This reminder, in conjunction with the epigraph cited above, not only speaks to the discordance created by these drag gospel experiences, but also explains my own internal dissonance. The mixture of gospel music (the sacred) and the smoke-filled, alcohol-heavy club scene (secular) was a place of contradiction and complexity. This essay explores this confounding situation and all its discourses through a close examination of the *mise en scéne*.

To simply write about drag as a form of entertainment with problematic reifications, reclamations, and resistances is to deny the "art" in its many variances. While these critical sites of engagement have been productive in scholarly discourses on drag, they have often excluded discussions of musical genres that are central to drag "diva" performances. The significance of musical genre to drag performances became most clear at the Biology Bar. This meeting place of gospel and gaydom gave rise to several questions and that could be only expressed through self-reflection, critical writing, and research. In addition, this project was motivated by E. Patrick Johnson's (2001) recent call for "quare" studies, which encourages scholars to look examine more closely the relationships within the "queer" Black community.[1]

I begin this article by locating where this project fits into previous research on drag, focusing particularly on the limits of previous scholarship investigating Black drag performance. However, this essay is not so much about drag; rather, it is more about the cultural production of Black drag performances of gospel. This project interrogates how the performance of gospel in drag *queers* a "queer" space. Thus, this research engages issues of space and place, particularly the role of gospel music and the Black church in the predominantly gay drag scene. Secondly, through the highlighting of the relationship between the spectator and spectacle in this particular space, I introduce a theory of transformation. This theory proposes that performance sites can be significantly altered, as the performer and the spectator's interaction with the performance shifts from place to space–place as being a pre-scripted performance site and space as a polyvalent location. Vivian Patraka elaborates on this shift as "the liberating move that allows us to understand the experience of everyday life" (1996, p. 100). However, it is not bound to this strict binary or a linear transition between these two locations. Finally, this essay explores the ways in which these performances of gospel illuminate transgressive possibilities within the Black church and the Black gay community.

REVIEWING THE OLD, INTRODUCING A NEW BLACK QUEEN GENRE

Recently, drag performance has received much attention within mainstream society, as well as within the academy. The proliferation of talk shows exploring this subject and academic writings has exploded. Over the last decade, American popular press has seemingly taken strong interest in queendom (Feinberg, 1996; Brubach, 1999; Bornstein, 1994). In addition, feature films such as *To Wong Foo*, *The Birdcage*, and *Punks* included drag queens not as peripheral characters, but as central to their production. Indeed, the drag queen has been given a place as a new kind of performance mode that is both appealing and intriguing within mainstream media. Scholars within the academy have also written a great deal about drag performance and the experience of being a witness to this often-dramatic production. These writings on drag, creative and critical, often engage this performance medium as a site from which several scholars can approach issues of gender and sexuality. In this work, critics traditionally discuss areas of gender performativity and problematic or emblematic constructions of gender in drag performance.

Some critical writing has explored drag through a historical approach, examining the origin of drag and its original places of location (Senelick, 2000; Baker, 1995; Slide, 1986). These texts situate themselves as locating drag over time, while being attentive to socio-historical and political moments. In addition, many of these works were specifically interested in drag performance within theatrical productions. These projects were essentially concerned with the intersecting relationships between the theatre, history, and drag performance. They examined the presence of drag in Europe and traced its move into North America and other sites of performance. They were concerned with the politics of the stage, the meanings of drag, and the ways in which spectatorship was being performed and the differences amongst various audiences. This history is very rich and valuable, contributing to our understandings of drag both as an entertainment medium and as a political or highly politicized act.

This subtitle "reviewing the old, introducing a new Black queen," alludes to what seems to have occurred in scholarship as many have collected, critiqued, and cartographed the performance of drag over time. As one begins to review recent work, there is very little in the file marked "Black drag performance." Drag criticism could easily be used interchangeably with queer theory. E. Patrick Johnson states:

> While queer theory has opened up new possibilities for theorizing gender and sexuality, like a pot of gumbo cooked too quickly, it has failed to live up to its full critical potential by refusing to accommodate all the queer ingredients contained inside its theoretical pot. (2000, p. 18)

Hence, Black gay performances of drag are continuously footnoted and their meanings too often overlooked. Investigations of the various forms, meanings, and workings of drag performed by, for, and with Black people needs to be explored. As a critical drag connoisseur, I have observed a wealth of discourses surrounding Black drag, often in direct conversation with contemporary cultural circumstances.

While prior research provides a solid foundation for my work, the research most pertinent to my discussion is work that speaks specifically to the Black drag experience. In this essay, I will explore the performance of Black drag that takes place in predominantly Black gay club settings. The collection of work that explores Black drag performance is limited. Autobiographical work has been the primary place of exploration (Chablis, 1996; RuPaul, 1995). This work is quite focused on the life of the performer and not the performances created through drag. Theorists like José Muñoz have explored Black drag and the cultural critique performed by drag artists like Vaginal Crème Davis (Muñoz, 1999). In his chapter, "The white to be angry," he reveals various cultural politics that inform Davis's performances and give them greater material impact: from her dis-identification with static identity politics and her challenges to all "universals." Likewise, George Chauncey also includes the Black drag queen in his historical sketch of gay history. He contextualizes Black drag performance within the midst of Black homophobia and also discusses the miraculous success incurred beyond these restraints (Chauncey, 1994).

Some of the most productive discussions of Black drag performance have been critical works that look closely at televisual or filmic production. For example, Marjorie Garber (1992), in her investigations of Black drag, uncovers the economic politics and the possibilities that drag as an occupation provides for Black performers in film. This was a noteworthy and valuable discussion that often goes overlooked. Still, many of the analyses of the Black drag performance on the screen have focused on Jennifer Livingston's film documentary, *Paris Is Burning*. Judith Butler's (1999) review of *Paris Is Burning* exemplifies a discussion of drag performance that I find most useful for this project. Her articulation of the "ambivalence of drag" amplifies the importance of critical discussion beyond misogyny and beyond whiteness. Her work illustrates not only the complexity of Black drag, but Black gay life. Butler's research, however, still maintains a focus on Black gay cultural performance with drag at the wings.

While this collection of drag history is critical to understanding queer performance, it frequently elides the experience of Black gays and their contributions to the larger drag tradition. It illuminates a general absence of critical race discussions and the inattention given to various genres that are central to these performance sites. In addition, it fails to fully consider the various cultural and ideological influences that inform "play" and that mark performance as a site of entertainment *and* community, contradiction, and contestation. This silence, often unmarked in the work of drag historians and critics, serves as an impetus for this project. How does race inform drag performances? What role does the audience play in this racialized experience? How do the conversations between race, spirituality, and sexuality enter the club space in drag? These questions have yet to be fully examined. In sum, this project serves to explore the role of genre in drag performance as more than a cursory exercise, but an essential observation.

THE BIOLOGY OF THE BAR:
A SPECTACLE IN THE FLESH[2]

It is Monday night (January 2002) around 12:25 a.m. and I am out on the dance floor of the Biology Bar jamming to the new Michael Jackson remix. I was "cutting a rug," as my great-aunt says. I was grooving all across the 2000 square feet of the dance floor. There were only a few people on the dance floor. I figured it was not customary to dance before the show actually began. But I did not care. I heard the one song I had grown to love by one of the famous musicians of our times. And I was going to dance as long as it played.

After I finished "jookin," I returned to my friends. Trenton, dressed in his baggy jeans and his fitted shirt, is engaged in what seemed to be an intense conversation. I did not interrupt him but instead I kept walking through all the beautiful Black men present. Wow! Is that a lesbian couple? While trying to discern what I was witnessing, I found my friend Julian. He was just wandering around as if he had not been there a hundred times. As soon as we started talking about getting a drink–wine for me–the voice of drag rang. To the theme song "I'm Coming Out," Ms. Ruff N'Stuff, what one could call "manly" drag, appears in her green dress accented by her thick white socks (stockings), her green lipliner, red lipstick and green eye shadow. She also had a full beard and a mysterious bulge in the crotch of her pants? She reminds us that she was just off the plane from her favorite place to visit, "rod-eeeee-o drive." After the audience falls into a cacophony of laughter and verbal outbreaks such as "Girl–you look a mess!" and "Where did you get that shit?" Ms. Ruff N'Stuff screams "What's wrong? Are you talking about me? I know you're not hating. I know I look fierce. You're just jealous!! I don't know what you all are talking about. You wish you looked half this good. Well . . . I'll tell ya . . . I'm here to serve the mother!!" She then moved into the lineup for drag performance. "We have a great show for you tonight. These girls are ready. Are you ready? Are you ready?" The crowd responds with a thunderous scream. "Put it together for our next entertainer, Sapphire Blue!!!!" The audience bursts into thunderous applause. Then silence overcomes them as the music begins.

The stage was bare and the lights are dim. All was calm in the club filled with at least 350 people. The organ began to play slowly, speeding up in rate and feeling more and more like a stampede of chords. Then, over the speakers, you could hear a choir singing, "Jesus can work it out." The phrase in the song is stated several times. Slowly, a woman about five-foot-nine, maybe two hundred and fifty pounds with a big reddish wig and loose-fitting and conservatively designed blue dress walks onto the stage and the audience looks on in reverence. She looks as if she is taking in each word and understanding each note. Then she begins her solo lip-syncing:

> That problem that I had–I just couldn't seem to solve. I tried and I tried, but I kept getting deeper involved. So I turned over to Jesus, and I stopped worrying about it . . . turned it over to the lord he'll work it out.

Hands go up in the air. People shout "all right." You can see people beginning to tap their feet. Sapphire begins to move into the audience. It seems that every phrase is directed toward someone specific in the audience.

In this moment, I travel back to my first experience at Auntie Angie's church–where the church folks would shout, yell, and cry. In her church there was always a big Black woman with a big colored wig who would "lead the church to glory."

People begin to dance and shout. Sapphire begins to dance and shout. One of her legs moves uncontrollably back and forth–but you know she isn't going to lose her balance because "God has control." The music gets stronger, the rhythms are resonating through the room, and I am beginning to feel happy within my own spirit. Then someone places a dollar in her breastline. This disrupts my spiritual upliftment. However, the crowd still dances, sings along, and Sapphire is sweating profusely and allowing her whole body to be used by the "spirit." Sapphire continues to lip sync,

> "How you gonna pay your rent?"And the chorus responds, "work it out!" "All your money spent" . . . "work it out!" . . . "little bit to buy some food" . . . "Jesus will work it out!" . . . "baby need a pair

of shoes" . . . "work it out!" . . . "Didn't he, didn't he work it out!?!"

Sapphire, at the sound of the hard drumbeat, falls to the ground. Some people begin to jump up and down, throwing their hands in the air, shouting, "Yes!! Yes!!!" And then to the reprise, Sapphire rises from the floor, wig in disarray and filled with an exhausted spirit; she then brings in the house and tells the congregation with her last bit of energy one more time, "He will!!" The stage lights suddenly darken and the audience shouts chants of "work it out," "a-ight girl," and "she worked that bitch."

FROM THE BIOLOGY BAR TO THE BLACK CHURCH: OBSERVING DRAG OF A DIFFERENT SORT

The picture, at the biology bar, seems to capture what Thomas Pawley (1971) has written about as some of the behavior patterns of African American spectators in church where people are

> shouting, jeering, hooting, and laughter and a number of non-linguistic vocal reactions indicative of approval or disapproval, enjoyment or dissatisfaction. Physical responses include beating on the seat, stomping on the floor, nudging or kicking companions, clapping or slapping of hands, rock back and forth, and in extreme instances, leaping to one's feet in the manner of a sports crowd. (p. 152)

The context of the Biology Bar is strikingly similar to the above description. Yet Ty,[3] a regular at the Biology Bar, also shared with me that he found it ironic that "people be clappin and people be sayin you work bitch" when watching a show. It is this odd placement of response that I wish to interrogate further. I wish to push further the discussion of drag performance, not only in the sense of exploring race within the performance, but also advancing a discussion of space and place.

Vivian Patraka (1996) utilizes DeCerteau to discuss space and place in a way that I find useful for this research:

> Place refers to "two sorts of stories" or narratives about how meanings are made. Place refers to those operations that makes its object reducible to a fixed location, "to the *being there of something*

dead, [and to] the law of a place" where the stable and the "law of 'proper'" rules. Place "excludes the possibility of two things being in the same location." "Space occurs as the effect produced by the operations that orient it, situate it, temporalize it, and make it function in a polyvalent way." Thus space is created "by the actions of historical subjects." (90)

In this discussion, one could say the Black church is an example of such a place, whereas the club is a primer for space. Although in Patraka's reading she alludes to a fluid shift between space and place, I am employing a discussion that explores the crevices between space and place, where hybridity exists. I argue that this scene of action is much more complicated, more complex, and makes no clear, concrete shifts. Ty, in his citation above, points toward the messiness of this clear divide of space and place, as he reveals the presence of the secular even within the sacred experience. In addition, the historical persecution that gays and lesbians have endured from the church, which houses the gospel tradition, is often informing this exchange at the Biology Bar. In order to fully understand the complexities of this scene, we must further explore the historical site of the Black church.

For the sake of this discussion, I am positing the Black church as a (dys)functional and (de)mobilizing place. The term queer is used in this context to suggest an odd presence, riffing on the queer (in)visibility within the church. The construction of the church place has had dynamic impact on the larger community's view of homosexuality, as well as the Black gay community's view of themselves in relationship to the "gospel." As I enter the discussion of drag performance of gospel, it seems important to look closely at this constructed place to gain a clearer understanding of what is happening in the Biology Bar club space.

It is well known that the Black church served and serves as a great impetus for the Black social and political mobility in America. This sociopolitical role has created what Kelly Brown Douglass (1999) describes as the "impact of the white cultural attack." She suggests that the constant surveillance of Black society has elicited a negative response. The Black community, specifically the Black church, is constantly in the process of cleaning its slate by retaining a code of respectability. Thus, the Black community, always juxtaposed to heterosexual white ideals, self-imposes a hegemonic "civilizing" discourse. Accordingly, the acceptance of homosexuality would risk demobilization. The homophobia and heterosexism prevalent within the Black church serves to preserve a homogenous image of the community, in response to hegemonic notions of family, masculinity, and social stability.[4]

Keith Boykin (1996), in his autobiography, states it plainly, "the black religious experience–a source of compassion for many African Americans–can be a mixed blessing for black gay and lesbians" (p. 124). He affirms my thinking of the Black church as a dysfunctional and demobilizing force for those who are the "abomination" of the church; yet, the opposite is true for those who are the "chosen" of the church. The issues between the Black church and its "queer" congregants are much more complex than this. I am setting the stage for understanding what creates the dis-ease in our travels between space and place. This project teases out the possible tensions that are in place during, before, and after the journey to the Biology Bar.

The presence of contradictions and duplicitous acts is not uncommon within the Black church. This is quite obvious to me, as I am one of the church folk while also being a critical observer in the pew. In my church experience, I have been a witness to moments where the large majority of the musical and ministerial staff was gay. Michael Eric Dyson (1996) contextualizes this observation most effectively:

> A black minister will preach a sermon railing against the ills, especially homosexuality. At the close of the sermon, a soloist, who everybody knows is gay, will rise to perform a moving number, as the preacher extends an invitation to visitors to join the church. The soloist is, in effect, being asked to sing, and to sign, his theological death sentence. His presence at the end of such a sermon symbolizes a silent endorsement of the preacher's message. (p. 105)

However, the gay Christian soloist or congregant usually does not identify with such claims. In fact, he disidentifies with the preacher's polemics. The epigraph in the beginning of this essay reflects what is in action in this holy place. It also re-presents what is happening within the Biology Bar. While the Black gay man identifies with the cultural ritual of "church," he does not support the erasure of his own body and his own subjectivity.[5] In this sense, the gay Black man in church performs a form of "passing" drag. His commitment to silence allows him to be imagined or "seen" as the spectator desires. In this context, his drag performance of heterosexuality is contingent upon following one of the key rules of heteronormativity–silence–and he never names his sexuality. The gay club space, with its gospel performances and gay men, disallows for such erasure and may produce a space of comfort, giving gay Black men access to their own spiritual experiences. These allowances elucidate the possibility for Black gay men to take more pleasure than pain from drag performances of gospel. As Black gay men search for "their church," they beg for a nexus between the club space and church place. It is at this intersection between the sacred and secular that "African-American men have created a self-validating environment in which they possess sexual agency on one hand, and are possessed by the spirit on the other" (Johnson, 2000, p. 98).

TRANSFORMANCE: MORE THAN MEETS THE EYE

Sapphire Blue is the facilitator for this transition between space and place. When Sapphire begins to perform "Jesus will work it out" it has a specific shared meaning that opens doors of possibility. On one hand, she is demonstrating to the audience her own spiritual autonomy and that she is able to worship on her own terms. She carves out her site for worship, independently and unapologetically. Simultaneously, she opens the door for the audience to be transformed, as well. Through her intense engagement with the audience and her closeness to the text she invites gay audiences to participate in a queer spiritual experience. Sapphire Blue's ability to move the audience beyond the club space, both physically and spiritually, through her performance of gospel music can be described as *transformance*.[6]

As a young boy, in the 1980s, I would watch the infamous cartoon *Transformers*. This childhood favorite, with its world of human-like robotic figures, was most captivating and eye-catching because of its action-packed substance. Transformers, through their amazing agility and flexibility, changed not only their bodies but the world around them. In addition, when one transformer would change itself, the others would change with it. The drag performance provides a noteworthy parallel. While the drag performer transforms herself into the "gospel diva," the audience transforms itself into the gospel church.

Transformance, in relationship to the word transform, may suggest something complete that commands change of an entire space. This would be a misreading of what is at work in the spaces where drag queens perform gospel. The gay club space, much like the transformers, transitions into the "church" scene while it sustains characteristics of the club. This often creates a sense of ambivalence. This is what Homi

Bhabha (1984) describes as "almost the same, but not quite" (p. 127). The club space is almost church, but not the same as the church. It registers ambivalence, a reminder that this is not the real thing but close to it.

It is this confounding characteristic that JC expresses when he, in a frank tone, said, "it just don't seem right." Still, JC attends almost every other month and is fully aware of the performance of gospel that has become a tradition at the Biology Bar. JC reveals to us the way in which this performance contains ambiguity and ambivalence that elicits an internal conflict that creates distance. Even though there is a clear tension between the spectator and the spectacle, JC admits that at times he will just tolerate the performance, knowing that it is just that–a performance. This critical comment highlights tensions created by the dual presence of sacred and secular, which creates much of the spectatoral dissonance.

The drag performance of gospel transforms the club space into a hybrid place, where the church and the club can meet. However, when examining the Black church, this scene of hybridity is not so specific to the club. Dyson (1996) explains:

> The black church . . . is full of beautiful, boisterous, burdened, and brilliant black bodies in various stages of praising, signifying, testifying, shouting, prancing, screaming, musing, praying, meditating, singing, whooping, hollering, prophesying, preaching, dancing, witnessing, crying, faking, marching, forgiving, damning, exorcising, lying, confessing, surrendering, and overcoming. There is a relentless procession, circulation, and movement of black bodies in the black church. (p. 88)

This laundry list recognizes the multiple characteristics of the Black church place and the Black bodies within. Likewise, the Black gay club scene has a multicultural dimension.

Aaron, a self-proclaimed Biology Bar drag queen expert, states, "If it's typical of what church folks do . . . [he claps] I'll get with it!!" His use of the descriptive "typical," as the identificatory characteristic, highlights the individual histories that deem these performances as "personal and spiritual" experiences. Through this admission, Aaron identifies his own ability to go where the performer leads him and suspend his own disbelief, so to speak. He describes Sapphire Blue's performance on a specific night as "a sincere routine/performance" and he reiterates, "that's why we were so compelled to give [it was offering time]."

This ability to incite belief is centered in what Judith Butler has discussed as the "realness" in the film *Paris Is Burning* (1999, p. 341). Realness is the ability to produce a naturalized effect. It is the gospel diva's ability to pass, a reiteration of the church norm. Aaron, describing how to delineate sincerity, explains, "what comes from the heart reaches the heart . . . and she got at our deepest most innerselves." This perception of "effectiveness" was a common trope throughout my sessions with men at the Biology Bar. Still, to locate exactly what that "inner most part" was is extremely difficult, as is trying to locate the "true" Holy Spirit manifesting itself in the Black church. Nonetheless, Butler's conception of realness as a "morphological ideal that remains the standard which regulates the performance" (p. 341) explicates how the spectator is able to assess the performances of gospel and engage them, in spite of ambivalence.

The spectator is at the center of transformance. It is the gospel drag spectator who fills the Biology Bar, while the drag queen spectacle provides purpose for their presence within the space. Like church, much of the spiritual and physical energy comes from the multiple bodies that congregate together and allow their spirits to manifest and transform spaces. It appears that "the 'sacred' place of the church where the rhetorical discourse of the service censures and confines the body is revisioned within the secular space of the nightclub so as to liberate the body" (Johnson, 2000, 105). The word "revisioned" in Johnson's description is key for transformance; revisioning is crucial to the transformative process. This is clear not only in the spectacular interpretations of the gospel drag divas, but within the audience's willingness to travel with the spectacle. Their ability to re-vision the church as a safe space for Black gay men allows them to travel to a place where their praise is heard and their presence is validated.

The spectator's move between club and church is not the only transitional moment. I cannot ignore, for instance, when the performance is altered by the audience's changing disposition. Audience members may get so excited, so intensely engaged, that they become as much spectacles as spectators and are very much part of the performance taking place. In the case of the Biology Bar, the club space can only be transformed when the audience transitions into a place where sociocultural tension may exist, but subsides and resolves. Often, these are moments of great improvisations. In these instances, where spectators may begin to "shout" or "yell," the performer acknowledges their admiration. It may also be when a dollar bill is passed to the drag performer and it drops, forcing her to choose to "stay in the spirit" or disrupt the moment.

It is these moments where the most polished performer may be challenged, a point of slippage.

As I revisit church and other performances of gospel in drag, it is important to recognize the communication amongst spectators. JC admits that sometimes as a spectator of drag performances of gospel, "I say it loud, you don't need to be singing that shit . . . and they [other audience members] say 'yeah–you right' and I know it's right." This clarifies not only that there are resistant spectators, but also that individual perspectives on these performances have some direct impact on the experience of other audience members. Through JC's exclamatory remarks, spectators are made conscious of alternative readings for these performances. Thus, JC's eyes become an epistemological frame for spectatorial practice.

Susan Manning discusses this as the effects of "two-way cross-viewing."[7] It is through this practice of spectatorship that much of what happens between the spectators and the spectacle at the Biology Bar gains legitimacy, fluency and "realness." The performances are read through the other, across the other, with the other, and certain attitudes toward the spectacle are achieved or discouraged through this process of cross-viewing. This further complicates the site, but also gives insight to the dynamics of performance. This is a great place for further inquiry into drag performance and spectatorship.

Transformance recognizes what is often a part of the performance analysis periphery. It is what happens to, within, among, and between the spectacle and the spectator. It is praxis and theory. Transformance is a way of seeing and a way of doing. Transformance, as praxis, is an active place where contradictions exist, but transitions are made. As space moves into place, there are several discourses that transform bodies. It is not a smooth or complete operation, but rather one where traces of the initial club form pervade and total transformation is impossible. As theory, transformance is a way of writing that seeks to explore the periphery. Scholarship, invested in transformance, is concerned with acts of change or transition that alters dimensions of space and place. It recognizes multiple discourses and is focused on process more than product. It engages questions of spectatorship, spectacle, and their relationship to the transformative act. It recognizes that transformance is not what happens to the club scene at the Biology Bar, it is the scene.

As one peers around the Biology Bar space on a Monday night, one can see traces of the place also known as the Black church. The presence of the club walls, the alcoholic beverages accompanied by an occasional cigarette, and the gyrating bodies may seem to say we are at a club. However, the spectacle, through her drag magic or her powerful performance may "take us higher." Together, the spectacle and the spectators reveal to us the process of transformance, revealing new dimensions for performance. This site uncovers the very messiness at the heart of all performances. There is no "pure" transformation, no pure performance. Aaron, in his astute and warm baritone voice, at the close of our session repeated the old adage "Ne'er the twain shall meet." My mind reflects on Sapphire Blue and her amazing embodiment, the seemingly honest rejoicing of the spectators, and I smile. I smile knowing that maybe one day the church, which has rejected some of its congregants, will realize that everyone can worship and should be able to engage in reverent acts. Thus, the "Biology Bar" becomes more than a pun, but a model for change.

NOTES

1. In *Quare Studies*, E. Patrick Johnson brings to the table a bold challenge to "queer studies" for its dismissal of issues concerning gay people of color. He calls for revision and demonstrates ways in which white queer scholars and queers of color, both, can advance a much more inclusive and productive discussion of gender and sexuality.

2. This section of the essay is influenced by E. Patrick Johnson's mode of performative writing. This style allows the performance to come alive and engages one in the actual moment and also encourages reflexive practice for the writer and the reader.

3. Ty was one of several men in February 2002 whom I engaged in lengthy discussions of drag performance, specifically drag performances of gospel, the Black church, and their personal relationships within the Black gay club scene. The names of the participants in what I like to call "talk sessions" are identified by pseudonyms. All participants are African American males who had viewed several drag shows (more than 5) and (coincidentally) all identified Sapphire Blue as one of their favorites or most memorable drag performers of gospel. Our "talk sessions" took place in my home or their home; whichever was more convenient for them.

4. Although this logic becomes more faulty and as seemingly progressive views grow within the dominant society; homophobia and heterosexism within the Black church seem more archaic than authentic.

5. José Muñoz speaks of disidentification as a survival strategy to "resist and confound" traditional types of identification. This gets at the heart of what is occurring within the Black church. Black gay men of Christian faith rebel against the traditional identifications and allow themselves to disidentify where it seems necessary in order to claim the church as his own. My interviews reflected this, as they all stated that they would locate their passion in the "choir," "church's ministerial charisma," or in the "women who were catching the Holy Ghost and their breast almost fell out."

6. I offer transformance as a way into the discussion, a tool for inquiry. I do believe that much of this work can be done through performance theory. Transformance, then, is a by-product of performance that has a specific focus on re-vision and transforma-

tion. The language of transformance may assist in our discussions of shifts of space and place.

7. Susan Manning (2001, p. 493) argues that cross-viewing made Negro dance and modern dance more powerful sites for "social and artistic change." Indeed, JC may have created change and prompted a critique of drag practice by other spectators, but the response of the other spectators also seemed to have a clear response on his choice to shout and exclaim discomfort. While Manning argues for the possibilities of learning through "two-way exchange," I suggest that there are also possibilities in this particular moment for two-way coercion.

REFERENCES

Baker, R. (1995). *Drag: A history of female impersonation in the performance arts.* New York: New York University Press.

Bhabha, H. (1984, Spring). Of mimicry and man: The ambivalence of colonial discourse. *October,* 28, 125-133.

Bornstein, K. (1995) *Gender outlaw: On men, women, and the rest of us.* New York: Vintage Books.

Boykin, K. (1996). *One more river to cross.* New York: Double Day.

Brubach, H. (1999). *Girlfriend: Men, women, and drag.* New York: Random House.

Butler, J. (1999). Gender is burning: Questions of appropriations and subversion. In S. Thornham (Ed.), *Feminist film theory: A reader* (pp. 336-349). New York: New York University Press.

Chauncey, G. (1994). *Gay New York.* New York: Basic Books.

Douglass, K.B. (1999). *Sexuality and the Black church.* New York: Orbis Books.

Dyson, M.E. (1996). *Race rules: Navigating the color line.* Reading, MA: Addison-Wesley Publishing Company.

Dyson, M.E. (1993). *Reflecting Black: African American cultural criticism.* Minneapolis: University of Minnesota Press.

Feinberg, L. (1996). *Transgender warriors: Making history from Joan Arc to RuPaul.* Boston: Beacon Press.

Garber, M. (1992). *Vested interests: Cross-dressing and cultural anxiety.* New York: Routledge.

Johnson, E.P. (2001). Quare studies, or (almost) everything I know about queer studies I learned from my grandmother. *Text and Performance Quarterly,* 21, 1-25.

Johnson, E.P. (2000). Feeling the spirit in the dark: Expanding notions of the sacred in the African American gay community. In D. Constantine-Simms (Ed.), *The Greatest Taboo: Homosexuality in Black Communities* (pp. 88-109). California: Alyson Books.

Mannng, S. (2001). Modern dance, Negro dance, and Katherine Dunham. *Textual Practice,* 15, 487-504.

Muñoz, J.. (1999). *Disidentifications: Queers of color and the performance of politics.* Minneapolis: University of Minnesota Press.

Newton, E. (1999). Role models. *Camp.* Ed. In Fabio Cleto (Ed.), *Camp* (pp. 96-109). Michigan: University of Michigan Press.

Patraka, V.M. (1996). Spectacles of suffering: Performing presence, absence, and historical memory at U.S. holocaust museums. In E. Diamond (Ed.), *Performance & Cultural Politics* (pp. 89-107). New York: Routledge.

Pawley, T. (1971). Black theatre audience. *Players*, 257-261.

Rupaul. (1995). *Letting it all hang out: An autobiography.* New York: Hyperion.

Senelick, L. (2000). *Changing room: Sex, drag and theatre.* New York: Routledge.

Slide, A. (1986). *Great pretenders.* Illinois: Wallace-Homestead.

Kind of a Drag:
Gender, Race, and Ambivalence
in *The Birdcage* and *To Wong Foo,*
Thanks for Everything! Julie Newmar

Mary Kirk, PhD

Metropolitan State University

SUMMARY. This paper examines the ways in which two Hollywood films featuring drag queens, *Too Wong Foo, Thanks for Everything! Julie Newmar* and *The Birdcage*, offer a kind of "both/and" look at the complexities of gender, sexuality, race, and culture, simultaneously challenging some institutionalized attitudes (especially heterosexism) while reinforcing others (especially sexism and racism)–making the use of drag as a locus of discovery in both films, at best, ambivalent. *[Article copies available for a fee from The Haworth Document Delivery Service: 1-800-HAWORTH. E-mail address: <docdelivery@haworthpress.com> Website: <http://www.HaworthPress.com> © 2004 by The Haworth Press, Inc. All rights reserved.]*

Mary Kirk is Assistant Professor of Educational Philosophy and Planning at Metropolitan State University.

Paper presented at the annual National Women's Studies Association Conference in Las Vegas, NV, June 2002.

Correspondence may be addressed: Educational Philosophy and Planning Department, Metropolitan State University, 700 East 7th Street, St. Paul, MN 55106 (E-mail: mary.kirk@metrostate.edu).

[Haworth co-indexing entry note]: "Kind of a Drag: Gender, Race, and Ambivalence in *The Birdcage* and *To Wong Foo, Thanks for Everything! Julie Newmar.*" Kirk, Mary. Co-published simultaneously in *Journal of Homosexuality* (Harrington Park Press, an imprint of The Haworth Press, Inc.) Vol. 46, No. 3/4, 2004, pp. 169-180; and: *The Drag Queen Anthology: The Absolutely Fabulous but Flawlessly Customary World of Female Impersonators* (ed: Steven P. Schacht, with Lisa Underwood) Harrington Park Press, an imprint of The Haworth Press, Inc., 2004, pp. 169-180. Single or multiple copies of this article are available for a fee from The Haworth Document Delivery Service [1-800-HAWORTH, 9:00 a.m. - 5:00 p.m. (EST). E-mail address: docdelivery@haworthpress.com].

KEYWORDS. Drag queen, female drag, performing gender, drag in film, racism in film, sexism in film, violence in film, feminist film criticism

INTRODUCTION

Popular culture and media studies scholars have documented the power of media as an institution that teaches us about our perceived social roles in terms of gender, sexuality, race, culture, and all other "categories" (Davis, 1997; hooks, 1992; Gamman, 1989; Kilbourne, 1999; Rapping, 1994). Feminist scholars have focused on "gender as performance" and drag as a possible standpoint from which to challenge simplistic female/male and homosexual/heterosexual dualisms (Bornstein, 1998; Butler, 1993; Feinberg, 1996; Garber, 1992; Liladhar, 2000; Schacht, 2002). Garber (1992) further suggests that if we learn to look *at* drag, rather than looking *through* it toward the binaries of female/male, we can use drag as a locus of discovery. Films featuring drag queens provide an interesting "locus of discovery," and can serve as one location for challenging old social visions and modeling new ones.

This paper examines the ways in which *Too Wong Foo, Thanks for Everything! Julie Newmar* (hereafter referred to as *Foo*)[1] and *The Birdcage* (hereafter referred to as *Cage*)[2] offer a kind of "both/and" look at the complexities of gender, sexuality, race, and culture, simultaneously challenging some institutionalized attitudes while reinforcing others. The following sections describe how both films are more or less successful in achieving their progressive possibilities: (1) using bigots as mirrors upon which to reflect all that is ugly about the dominant culture (successful); (2) confusing and/or conflating "drag" and "passing" (less successful); and (3) indulging in dangerous sexist and racist stereotypes, as well as violence (most unsuccessful).

WHO'S THE UGLIEST OF THEM ALL: BIGOTS AS CULTURAL MIRRORS

Both *Foo* and *Cage* successfully use bigotry (in all of its narrow-minded dimensions, especially homophobia and racism) as a mirror upon which to reflect and hyper-emphasize the rigid limits around the dominant culture's views. The films explore bigotry through two classic caricatures: *Cage*'s Senator Keeley and *Foo*'s Sheriff Dollard.

Keeley and Dollard continue a mass media tradition that Archie Bunker made famous in the 1970s–the bigot as a mirror upon which is reflected the ugliness of racism, sexism and homophobia.

Cage leaves little room for doubt about the absurdity of bigotry in the character of Senator Keeley–a conservative Republican, who is also Vice President and co-founder of the Coalition for Moral Order, and to whom Bob Dole is "too liberal." For Keeley, just about everyone is either too liberal or too controversial, including Billy Graham (too liberal) and the Pope (too controversial). Keeley is the living representative of the ways in which prejudices of all kinds are embedded in dominant cultural views. He is about as narrow-minded as they come, as shown in the following speech where he comments on Armand and Albert (in drag as Val's mother) to his wife, Louise:

> She's a small town girl, and he's a pretentious European–the worst kind . . . Aristotle Onassis was just like this, and all of the French, especially Mitterand, and the English, not Margaret Thatcher, of course. The snobbery, the contempt he has for her. Did you see him when she was talking? He looked almost frightened. He doesn't even let her run the house, and he's in the kitchen, and he serves, and he tells that beige savage what to do.

Translation: it's good for a woman to be naive and innocent; most Europeans are pretentious snobs; women should run the household and the kitchen, and serve the meals; and people of color are uncivilized savages.

Foo's parallel bigot is the hilarious caricature of Sheriff Dullard (whose name says it all). His name is actually Dollard, but his badge has a typo–a fact that he must clarify each time he meets someone. Sheriff Dollard is a classic stereotype of a homophobic bigot all the way from his beer belly to his racist epithets. His first encounter with the drag queens is to pull them over and cite Vida for a moving violation. After he peers into the car window and discovers Noxema and Chi Chi, he says, "We don't go in for white girls riding around with niggers and spics." He asks Vida to get out of the car, and attempts to molest her. When he reaches between Vida's legs, she promptly knocks him unconscious. Furious at being physically bested by a drag queen, Dollard spends the rest of the film trying to find Vida. His investigative skills are another expression of his stereotypical thinking; his list of "Places for Homos" includes "flower shops, ballet schools, flight attendants lounges, restaurants for brunch, and antique stores." Near the end of the story Dollard begs the townspeople to turn the drag queens over to him. When they refuse, the bigoted sheriff's greatest fear is revealed: "Don't protect these freaks; these boys in dresses, corrupting you with their way of life, changing the way things have always been." This represents the underlying fear of all guardians of institutionalized prejudice who will do anything to keep from changing the way things have always been.

DOES S/HE OR DOESN'T S/HE?: PASSING AS PRODUCT OF OPPRESSION

Although both films attempt to use drag as a locus of discovery, they achieve only limited success since they muddy the distinction between drag queens (gay men dressed as women) and passing (men disguised as women, who are often referred to as transsexuals). Schacht (2002) defines "drag queens" as "individuals with an acknowledged penis, who have no desire to have it removed . . . that perform being women in front of an audience that all knows they are self-identified men" (p.159). Feinberg (1996) describes "passing" as "having to hide your identity in fear, in order to live"–making passing a product of oppression, rather than an escape from it (p. 89). In *Cage*, Albert engages in precisely this type of passing when he dresses in women's clothes to pose as Val's mother for the Senator. He is no longer a drag queen when the desired end is to be perceived as a woman, not as a man posing as a woman. When Albert enters in his "dowdy, Republican grande dame" pink suit and blond wig, he comes to life as Val's mother (Ansen, 1996). The neo-conservative version of mother that Albert creates is more than convincing: "I can't get this big lug to buy a new suit. Bless them. That's the way nature made them. Maybe I'm just an old-fashioned girl, but I pity the woman who's too busy to stay home and take care of her man." Translation: Heterosexual men have no fashion sense; gender expression is biologically determined; and a woman's job is to take care of her man. Albert's act is so convincing that neither Senator Keeley nor Louise has any suspicion that he is a gay male in drag. Even Barbara, who knows Albert's true identity, becomes so absorbed in his performance as wife and mother that she forgets:

Barbara: I hope your mother knows I'm going to have a career after we're married.

Val: Barbara, Albert is not my mother. He's a drag queen.

Barbara: That's right. I keep forgetting. He's just so much like a mother.

Another example of passing is evidenced in the scenes where Armand and Albert attempt to practice behaving like "straight" men. While sitting at a restaurant, Albert tries to convince Armand he can play it straight. After Albert uses a spoon to delicately daub mustard on a slice of toast, Armand demonstrates a more "manly" technique: "Don't use the spoon and don't dribble little dots. You take your knife and you smear. Men smear. Hold the knife boldly." Albert attempts this smearing method and squeals, "Oh my God, I smashed the toast." Later in this same scene Armand instructs Albert to walk like John Wayne. Looking quite feminine in a flowing pink blouse, white slacks, and a big floppy straw hat, Albert wiggles across the patio and back with a very authentic John Wayne swagger. When Albert asks if it was okay, Armand replies, stunned, "Yes, it's perfect. I just never realized John Wayne walked like that!" This may be one of the most honest moments in the story; even John Wayne, the last bastion of maleness, is revealed as having a feminine quality to his walk–casting doubt on the rigidity and exclusivity of gender binaries.

In *Foo*, with the exception of two scenes when the men are seen without their wigs, the characters spend nearly the entire film in drag and dressed as women. This makes it questionable whether film viewers are supposed to believe that the characters are drag queens (who appear as women only for performances). The standpoint is unclear, since these characters who are never seen out of female attire might more accurately be depicting preoperative transsexuals. Or, are Vida, Chi Chi, and Noxema "passing" in the sense that Feinberg describes–hiding their identities as gay men to be safe? Throughout most of the story it seems clear that the other characters are completely unaware that the drag queens are men in women's clothes. There is one exceptional moment when the drag queens arrive in Snydersville and Bobby Lee remarks, "For girls, they're sure strong and big." However, the story progresses with no other revelations until the end when Vida starts to tell Carol Ann that he is a man in drag; Carol Ann halts Vida's explanation by saying that she knew on the first night because she observed Vida's Adam's apple and women don't have those. Apparently, Vida was never passing with Carol Ann. During the final scenes, the townspeople rescue the drag queens from being arrested by Sheriff Dollard as each one claims, "No, I'm a drag queen." The confessional begins with Carol Ann, followed by Bobby Lee, followed by the townspeople one by one. No one seems surprised by Carol Ann's revelation, and we are left to wonder whether the whole town always knew that they were three men in drag.

BARBIES, AND MAMMIES, AND SCARES! OH, MY!!

Both films achieve some limited success in challenging cultural stereotypes in relation to homosexuality and gay culture. However, they simultaneously reinforce dangerous sexist and racist stereotypes, which left me concurring with Judith Butler's (1993) assessment that at best "drag is a site of a certain ambivalence" (p. 125). These films stereotype women and people of color in multiple ways ranging from the somewhat trivial to the definitively dangerous.

Let's get trivial. Early in *Foo*, the drag queens reaffirm the notion that "real women" should care more about style and image than substance when they choose to buy an old Cadillac convertible for their cross-country trip rather than the more practical and reliable Toyota Corolla. Later in the film, the drag queens reaffirm the notion of women as "temptresses" who will do anything to "get their man" when they make over Bobby Lee to attract Bobby Ray. First, Bobby Lee is dressed up quite literally like a Barbie doll in a pink cocktail dress with a French twist (looking like a woman in drag as a woman–performing gender). Then, as she's on her way to meet Bobby Ray for their date, Bobby Lee receives the following questionable advice:

> *Vida:* Remember Anne Baxter in *The Ten Commandments* and those are the moves. Her strength, her mystery, and her moves.

> *Noxema:* If you want them to know there is steak for dinner, then you've got to let them hear it sizzle.

> *Chi Chi:* Do the eyes thing I taught you, and be honest with him.

Translation: Women should be mysterious and manipulate men into doing what they want; women should flaunt their sexuality to get what they want; women should be flirtatious; and (perhaps the only advice worth using) be honest.

Chi Chi also reinscribes classic female stereotypes with her first big moment in the film: "The two of you are so pretty, and I am so ugly. Every time I do something I'm doing it wrong and everyone's laughing at me. I'm a loser. Maybe I'll meet somebody nice and they'll rescue me." Translation: Women worry constantly about their appearance; women are inept and have little confidence; and women are waiting to be rescued by a man. Later, when Vida knocks the sheriff unconscious, Chi Chi is the only one willing to check to see if the Sheriff is still alive, but she's too inept to make an accurate determination. After pronouncing him "decea-sed," she dashes off leaving one shoe on the ground in Cinderella-like fashion–setting up an ironic pursuit by the homophobic sheriff/prince for his drag princess.

In *Cage*, Albert (who whether he's in drag or not is more "femme" than most people who are biologically female) sports multiple negative female stereotypes: weeping, martyring, drama queening, all of which could also be viewed as playing the aging diva or prima donna. *Weeping*: After Val announces his wedding, Albert sits weeping aloud over Val's baby book while Armand sits at the piano writing a song. Both female and male gender roles are stereotyped here: Albert (as mother) is emotional while Armand (as father) is outwardly unperturbed. *Martyring*: After Albert realizes that Val and Armand plan to exclude him from the dinner with Barbara's parents, Albert says, "The monster, the freak is leaving . . . Oh, my God, feel my pulse . . . I'm not young. I'm not new and everyone laughs at me. I've been thinking the only solution is to go where nobody is ridiculous and everyone is equal." Here, Albert goes so far as to threaten suicide, which is reinforced by him promising to leave his wigs to Agador. *Drama queening*: Early in the film, while Starina is hiding under a blanket and refusing to go on stage, she says: "Don't look at me, I'm fat and hideous." When Armand tries to calm her down, she replies, "Don't use that tone, that tone that says you know everything because you're a man, and I don't know anything because I'm a woman." Armand retorts, "You're not a woman." It is important that we be reminded because Albert is so convincing as a stereotypical woman that his drag portrayal of Val's mother prompts the conservative Senator Keeley to say, "They don't make women like that anymore." And that's just the problem; they never did!

Cage makes a minor attempt to be more inclusive of race with the supporting character of Agador. However, the attempt largely fails as Agador vacillates between a racist caricature of a "Latina" domestic, a "hot Latino lover," and a Lucy Ricardo knock-off–always begging Armand to "be in the show." When Armand catches Agador in a red wig, pink bikini bra, and denim cut-offs dancing in the kitchen and lip-syncing to Gloria Estefan's "Conga," he quips, "You look like Lucy's stunt double." Agador replies, "I'm a combination of Lucy and Ricky." It's no accident that Agador's character is a reference to Lucy Ricardo and Desi Arnaz. *I Love Lucy* was one of the first television shows to include a Latino character in a leading role. Agador proceeds to ask why Armand won't let him be in the show and defensively whines that his father was a shaman and his mother a high priestess. The irony in this line lies in the fact that many indigenous cultures were goddess-based, and revered the "female" as well as "two spirits" (people who displayed both genders and in some groups were even shamans) (Feinberg, 1996, p. 45). In Guatemala, Agador is a member of the privileged class, but in the United States, he works as a domestic.

Foo attempts to be inclusive of race with two lead characters Noxema and Chi Chi, but ultimately they are portrayed as racist stereotypes. Noxema is stereotyped in at least two ways: the big, black mammy and the hyper-talented black athlete (Collins, 1990; Dates & Barlow, 1990; Dunbar, 1999; Robinson, 1996). Noxema reluctantly agrees to "mother" Chi Chi by teaching her to be a drag queen on the way to the Drag Queen of America pageant in Los Angeles. However, Noxema also reflects the hierarchy of racist oppression when she makes the following comment to Vida regarding taking Chi Chi along with them: "She's Latin. Might turn out to be a Sandinista." To which Vida replies, "Well, I remember a certain ebony enchantress that I helped look a little less like Moms Mabley." The power and privilege of Vida's whiteness is necessary to make both Noxema and Chi Chi "acceptable." Noxema is also stereotyped as the hyper-talented black athlete. She is depicted playing in the Ladies Basketball League in a cheerleader outfit, swishing around "like a girl" until s/he gets the ball, after which s/he aggressively bumps the other women out of the way and leaps up to sink a perfect layup shot.

Chi Chi is also racially stereotyped as the hot-pants Latina bombshell who is sexually exotic (Lester, 1996). Bobby Ray actually tells her she's the "perfect girl" because she's got class, glamour, and she's exotic. Chi Chi is frequently seen reading "bodice-ripper," sexually explicit romance novels aloud to others. At one point during their trip, when Vida will not stop at a hotel, Chi Chi says, "As soon as we get to the next town, I'm jumping on the next man and riding him all the way to New York City." The helpless-woman-waiting-to-be-rescued-by-a-man routine is underlined by Chi Chi's combination baby-doll/slut style of dress (lots of white lace, short skirts, and hot pants) and her over-the-top sexual flirtatiousness. For example, after Bobby Ray speeds up in his truck to rescue her from being gang-raped, she displays her "cleavage" to Bobby Ray and then demurely covers herself again, saying, "They have a mind of their own. What you did was so heroic." This is another dangerous example of the "she really wanted it" stereotype that allows real-world sexual violence to go unreported and unpunished, especially if the victim is a woman of color.

In fact, there is a startling amount of violence in *Foo*. Brookey and Westerfelhaus (2001) see *Foo* as a version of the American monomyth where the hero enters a small town and saves the day. One could certainly liken the plot in *Foo* to a John Wayne movie where there's a new sheriff in town; in this case, the sheriff takes the form of three drag queens and their seemingly improved form of masculinity. In addition, this common Western film genre plot may offer a partial explanation for the violence in *Foo*. However, Vida, Chi Chi, and Noxema's "heroic" solutions to this violence (including two attempted rapes and one case of sexual harassment) require either a great deal of physical strength or being rescued by a man–not very likely solutions for most women. Vida's solution to Sheriff Dollard's attempted rape is to scream, "Get your hand off my dick!" in a loud male voice and to shove Dollard's face to the ground, knocking him unconscious.

When Chi Chi is nearly gang-raped by four white boys in an isolated field, the solution is to have Bobby Ray speed up in his truck to rescue her–the luxury of an instant chauffeur is not an option for most victims of gang rape. The potential seriousness of the scene is undercut even further when Chi Chi quips to her would-be assailants out the truck window as she's speeding off with Bobby Ray: "That's how you pick up a lady." This remark trivializes a very dangerous situation in several ways: it minimizes the seriousness of the situation, it suggests that "real" women want to be rescued/protected by a man, and it suggests (not so subtly) that women "really want it." The latter may be the most insidious message, since it has taken decades of work by feminist activists and legal scholars to attempt to correct this institutionalized belief. I guess we have not come such a long way, baby.

Noxema is also harassed by some boys on the street while walking with a group of women away from the town. The scene begins with the requisite wolf whistles, followed by a threatening comment directed to Noxema: "You're a whole lot of woman, I know what you need." Noxema's response is to walk authoritatively towards him, stand towering over him (Noxema is nearly a foot taller and much more muscular than her potential assailant), and stare directly in his face and reply: "I hardly think you're the man to give it to me. I think you should apologize to me and to those ladies over there." As the boy attempts to say there is no way he is going to apologize, his speech is cut off by Noxema clenching his testicles and asking: "Do you like my nails?" Still clutching his balls, Noxema drags him over to the ladies, introduces everyone, and explains the correct way to greet them. Her last instructions are to "Go home take a bath, comb your hair, and put on a clean shirt." S/he turns to the ladies and sweetly advises: "You just gotta know how to talk to people." Apparently, you've also got to be over six feet tall, muscular, and have very long assertive fingernails.

SOMETIMES THE CLOWN IS TOO SCARY

Like the classic Shakespearean fool (who acts the buffoon and court jester while seeing/revealing all) and the trickster of many indigenous belief systems (who dramatizes our follies and often changes gender) there are some ways in which the bigots and drag queens in *Foo* and *Cage* serve as clowns who dance about waving their arms and making us laugh at our silly binary gender/sexuality obsession and our narrow views on race and culture (Bornstein, 1998; Brant, 1996; Hausman & Rodriques, 1996). Unfortunately for this viewer, however, much of the good that these films do with regard to challenging damaging, institutionalized attitudes regarding gender, sexuality, race, and culture is seriously undercut by sexist and racist stereotypes with violent undertones. Since these two mass-market films target a broad audience, the result is an ambiguous product that ultimately does more harm than good by shaving off the sharp edges of any real social commentary. Bornstein (1998) asks "who as a child saw some circus clown and wasn't frightened?" (p. 275). In the view of this feminist critic, the clowns in the *Foo* and *Cage* "circus" are just too scary, and the joke's still on women and people of color.

NOTES

1. *Foo* features Vida, Noxema, and Chi Chi on a road trip to a drag pageant in California. When the old, convertible Cadillac they are driving breaks down in a small, rural town named Snydersville, the drag queens become embroiled in the affairs of the townspeople. Thus begins the tale of a magical land where women are not raped, women teach men to respect them, women are always dressed in the latest fashion, women rescue other women from their silence and from their abusive husbands–at

least when they are gay men dressed as women, drag queens. The "real" women do not fare quite as well. They seem misguided about who to be and how to dress, a bit lost in the small town of Snydersville, until three drag queens arrive to rescue them. Vida sums it up in her double entendre at the end of the film: "Sometimes it just takes a fairy."

2. *Cage*, a remake of the French original *La Cage Aux Folles*, tells the story of Albert and Armand–a gay couple who must play it straight for a one-night dinner with their son's ultra-conservative future in-laws. Armand owns a drag nightclub called The Birdcage where he and Albert (who as Starina is also the featured attraction at the club) have raised Val, Armand's son from a one-night affair with a dancer turned fitness studio owner named Katherine. The complications begin when Val announces his pending wedding to Barbara, whose conservative father Senator Keeley is also co-founder of the Coalition for Moral Order. Barbara tells her parents that Val's father is a cultural attaché to Greece and his mother is a housewife. The Keeley family goes to Florida to meet Val's parents in order to escape a pending scandal by planning what they think will be a "society" wedding. Albert dresses in drag as Val's mother for the fateful dinner, where all is ultimately revealed.

REFERENCES

Ansen, D. (1996). Gay films are a drag. *Newsweek*, 127, 71.

Ansen, D. & Kuflix, A. (1991). Cross-dressed for success: A gender-bending cult hit breaks into the mainstream. *Newsweek*, 118, 62.

Bornstein, K. (1998). *My gender workbook: How to become a real man, a real woman, the real you, or something else entirely*. New York: Routledge.

Brant, B. (1996). Coyote learns a new trick. In Paula Gunn Allen (Ed.), *Songs of the Turtle: American Indian Literature 1974-1994* (pp. 156-159). New York: Ballantine.

Brookey, R.A. & Westerfelhaus, R. (2001). Pistols and petticoats, piety and purity: To Wong Foo, the queering of the American monomyth. *Critical Studies in Media Communication*, 18, 141-156.

Brown, G.M. (Producer) & Kidron, B. (Director). (1996). *To Wong Foo, Thanks for Everything! Julie Newmar*. [Motion picture]. United States: Universal.

Butler, J. (1993). *Bodies that matter: On the discursive limits of "sex."* New York: Routledge.

Collins, P.H. (1990). *Black feminist thought: Knowledge, consciousness, and the politics of empowerment*. New York: Routledge.

Dates, J.L. & Barlow, W. (1990). *Split image: African Americans in the mass media*. Washington, DC: Howard UP.

Davis, L.R. (1997). *The swimsuit issue and sport: Hegemonic masculinity in* Sports Illustrated. Albany: SUNY Press.

Dunbar, M.D. (1999). Dennis Rodman–"Barbie doll gone horribly wrong": Marginalized masculinity, cross-dressing, and the limitations of commodity culture. *The Journal of Men's Studies*, 7, 317-333.

Feinberg, L. (1993). *Stone butch blues*. Ithaca, NY: Firebrand.

Feinberg, L. (1996). *Transgender warriors: Making history from Joan of Arc to Dennis Rodman*. Boston: Beacon.

Gamman, L. & Marshment, M. (Eds.). (1989). *The female gaze: Women as viewers of popular culture*. Seattle: Real Comet.

Garber, M. (1992). *Vested interests: Cross-dressing and cultural anxiety*. New York: Routledge.

Hausman, G. & Rodriques, K. (1996). *African-American alphabet: A celebration of African-American & West Indian Culture, custom, myth, & symbol*. New York: St. Martin's.

hooks, b. (1992). *Black looks: Race and representation*. Boston: South End.

Kilbourne, J. (1999). *Deadly persuasion: Why women and girls must fight the addictive power of advertising*. New York: Free Press.

Lester, P.M. (Ed.). (1996). *Images that injure: Pictorial stereotypes in the media*. London: Praeger.

Liladhar, J. (2000). From the soap queen to aga-saga: Different discursive frameworks of familial femininity in contemporary "women's genres." *Journal of Gender Studies*, 9, 5-14.

Nichols, M. (Producer & Director). (1996). *The Birdcage*. [Motion picture]. United States: United Artists.

Rapping, E. (1994). *Media-tions: Forays into the culture and gender wars*. Boston: South End.

Robinson, L. (1996). *Media myth, media reality: A primer of racism in America*. Unpublished doctoral dissertation. The Union Institute.

Schacht, S.P. (2002). Four renditions of female drag: Feminine appearing variations of a masculine theme. *Gendered Sexualities*, 6, 157-180.

Racializing White Drag

Ragan Rhyne

New York University

SUMMARY. While drag is primarily understood as a performance of gender, other performative categories such as race, class, and sexuality create drag meaning as well. Though other categories of identification are increasingly understood as essential elements of drag by performers of color, whiteness remains an unmarked category in the scholarship on drag performances by white queens. In this paper, I argue that drag by white queens must be understood as a performance of race as well as gender and that codes of gender excess are specifically constructed through the framework of these other axes of identity. This essay asks whether white performance by white queens necessarily reinscribes white supremacy through the performance of an unmarked white femininity, or might drag performance complicate (though not necessarily subvert) categories of race as well as gender? In this essay, I will suggest that camp drag performances, through the deployment of class as a cru-

Ragan Rhyne is a doctoral candidate in the Department of Cinema Studies at New York University.

The author thanks Lauren Steimer, Lucas Hilderbrand, Leshu Torchin, Rahul Hamid, Peyton McNutt and Steven Schacht, and the anonymous reviewers for their comments and advice in preparing this essay.

Correspondence may be addressed: Department of Cinema Studies, New York University, 721 Broadway, 6th Floor, New York, NY 10003 (E-mail: rar227@nyu.edu).

[Haworth co-indexing entry note]: "Racializing White Drag." Rhyne, Ragan. Co-published simultaneously in *Journal of Homosexuality* (Harrington Park Press, an imprint of The Haworth Press, Inc.) Vol. 46, No. 3/4, 2004, pp. 181-194; and: *The Drag Queen Anthology: The Absolutely Fabulous but Flawlessly Customary World of Female Impersonators* (ed: Steven P. Schacht, with Lisa Underwood) Harrington Park Press, an imprint of The Haworth Press, Inc., 2004, pp. 181-194. Single or multiple copies of this article are available for a fee from The Haworth Document Delivery Service [1-800-HAWORTH, 9:00 a.m. - 5:00 p.m. (EST). E-mail address: docdelivery@haworthpress.com].

cial category of performative femininity, might indeed be a key site through which whiteness is denaturalized and its power challenged. Specifically, I will read on camp as a politicized mode of race, class and gender performance, focusing on the intersections of these categories of identity in the drag performance of Divine. *[Article copies available for a fee from The Haworth Document Delivery Service: 1-800-HAWORTH. E-mail address: <docdelivery@haworthpress.com> Website: <http://www.HaworthPress. com> © 2004 by The Haworth Press, Inc. All rights reserved.]*

KEYWORDS. Drag, camp, white drag, whiteness, drag queen, race drag, class drag, Divine, gender performance

It's beige! *My* Color! (Elsie De Wolfe, on facing the Parthenon for the first time, as quoted by Andrew Ross, 1989, p. 1)

Though drag has most often been understood as gender performance, scholars have begun to recognize drag's meaning as constituted by a matrix of performative categories like race, class and sexuality. But while drag theorists have forged these connections between the performances of gender, race and class by drag queens of color, few, if any, connections have been made between gender performance and the performance of whiteness by white drag queens.[1] Whiteness, as a performative category, has become increasingly centered as an object of inquiry by critical race scholars, and though scholars and performers have engaged in vigorous debates regarding the performance of white femininity by drag queens of color, little attention has been paid to the ways that white performers perform whiteness. Yet, as this essay will argue, the performance of whiteness by white drag queens is a crucial area of inquiry. A failure to interrogate the ways that white bodies perform whiteness threatens to reiterate its normalization and implies that while gendered whiteness might be performed by people of color, whiteness and its power are a natural condition of white bodies.

Or, as Richard Dyer explains, "Whites are everywhere in representation. Yet precisely because of this and their placing as norm they seem not to be represented to themselves *as* whites but as people who are variously gendered, classed, sexualized and abled" (Dyer, 1997, p. 3). An inquiry into the performance of whiteness and the performance of gender by white drag queens can illuminate the ways in which gender and race are coded and decoded as marked and unmarked. Is the performance of whiteness by white drag queens always an exception to the subversive potentials of drag as gender performance or can whiteness be divested of its power? Does the performance of whiteness by white drag queens necessarily reiterate the power embedded in whiteness, or does it have the potential to challenge structures of racism that protect whiteness as an unmarked category? This essay will seek to racialize white drag performance, and, rather than argue for or against the subversive potentials of "whiteness" itself, it will locate a space in which we might understand the performance of gender, race and class as a process of negotiating the boundaries of each. I will argue that camp is one political mode of critical performance through which the categories of race, gender and class are interrogated and that few performers complicate these matrices of identity as thoroughly as camp star Divine.

DRAG POLITICS

In the last decade, scholars, activists and performers have begun to insist upon the recognition of drag performance as a political act. To be sure, not all drag is progressive and in fact, many drag performers define themselves strictly as entertainers. However, there is a growing sense that drag is a political form and that drag performers are responsible to progressive politics. With this reclamation of the political potentials of drag has come a renewed interest in the political potentials of camp.

Early work on camp (Sontag, 1961; Babuscio, 1993) understood camp as an aesthetic and stylistic mode. Contemporary queer theorists, such as Moe Meyer, have revised this understanding, arguing that camp cannot be understood merely as entertainment or sensibility but rather that it is the mode by which queer performance is politicized (Meyer, 1994). Camp, Meyer argues, is at the center of a queer political challenge to gay and lesbian identity politics, and the discourse of drag has reflected this shift in understanding of queer cultural production. As former director of the National Gay and Lesbian Task Force Robert Bray suggests, the political potentials of drag and camp are intimately connected. "The camp and irony evoked by drag have carried our movement through some rough times. We're seeing more and more participation of drag queens on the front lines of the movement" (quoted in Hilbert, 1995, p. 465). That is, drag, as a mode of camp performance, has come to be recognized as a specifically political performative formation. And, as director John Waters suggests, camp drag as political commentary is not confined to queer politics alone.

> Basically, drag had to get hipper or else just be so square. The old idea of what drag queens were is incredibly corny and square in the nineties. The ones who do Carol Channing are really like what Uncle Tom used to be. (Quoted in Hilbert, 1995, p. 464)

Waters's evocation of the Uncle Tom stereotype suggests not only this sense that drag is (or should be) primarily political, but also suggests an affinity with other struggles for political justice. This affinity implies an analogy between the civil rights struggles of peoples of color and the gay, lesbian and queer movements, but more importantly draws connections between gender performance and the performance of race.

Drag performer Vaginal Crème Davis makes this political connection between gender performance and racial performance even more explicit. "It's easier to digest [non-politicized drag]. It's safer, and people aren't challenged. But when people see an African American in this feminized role, they realize that there's a whole spectrum of being out there and that the black experience or the queer experience is not just limited to one aspect" (Quoted in Hilbert, 1995, p. 466). Davis asserts that her performance of gender complicates the performativity of African American masculinity.

Other scholars, too, have made this connection between the performance of gender and the performance of race, particularly with regards to Black men. In her groundbreaking work on cross-dressing, Marjorie Garber argues that stereotypes of Black male sexuality as alternately hypersexualized and emasculated produce a racialized and gendered excess that has been channeled into images of Black male transvestitism. Though these representations have most often been produced in the service of white supremacist rhetoric, they are profoundly ambivalent. "The possibility of crossing racial boundaries stirs fears of the possibility of crossing the boundaries of gender, and vice versa" (Garber, 1992, p. 274). Representations of Black male transvestitism, in the examples Garber offers, simultaneously contain and destabilize racist stereotypes of gender and race and provoke an anxiety that not only are both performed, but that both are part of the same performance. The performance of gender is also the performance of racialized codes of gender and, indeed, of race itself.

DRAG AND DISCONTINUITY

> Drag, as Esther Newton suggests, describes discontinuities be-
> tween gender and sex or appearance and reality but refuses to al-
> low this discontinuity to represent dysfunction. In a drag
> performance, rather, incongruence becomes the site of gender cre-
> ativity. (Halberstam, 1998, p. 236)

Whereas Newton envisions drag as performance in which the binari-
zations of gender are challenged (Newton, 1993), other scholars have
revised this estimation, arguing for a more complicated understanding
of drag's revolutionary potentials. Judith Butler, for instance, argues
that drag very often reiterates heteronormative gender codes and instead describes drag as a site of ambivalence, "one which reflects the
more general situation of being implicated in the regimes of power by
which one is constituted and, hence, of being implicated in the very regimes of power that one opposes" (Butler, 1993, p. 125). Thus while
Butler grants that some drag performances may denaturalize idealized[2]
femininity, other drag performances reproduce it, and most do both simultaneously. However, what marks a performance as drag is an intentional and visible discontinuity between the gender performance and
the gendered performer.

As performers like Vaginal Crème Davis illustrate, however, gender
incongruity is not the only component of drag. For Davis, race is very
explicitly a crucial part of gender performance and her drag evokes the
discontinuity not only between her male body and feminine performance, but also between her queerness and Black masculinity. It is
within this space of dissonance that Davis's political drag critiques the
assumptions embedded in these categories. Indeed, as Davis illustrates,
categories of identity such as queerness and Black masculinity are often
at odds with one another, particularly for drag queens of color.

Scholars have brought these questions of racial and gender performance to bear not only on the performance of Blackness by Black drag
queens, for example, but also on the performance of whiteness by drag
queens of color, most notably with the release of Jennie Livingston's
film *Paris Is Burning*. While most scholars recognize the performances
in Livingston's films as politically crucial, many disagree about the implications of the politics being performed. Understanding the documentary subjects' (poor, urban, black and Latino drag queens) performances
of bourgeois femininity as coded via standards of unmarked whiteness,
bell hooks, for instance, argued that the film exploited the ways in

which "colonized black people . . . worship at the throne of whiteness, even when such worship demands that we live in perpetual self-hate, steal, lie, go hungry, and even die in its pursuit" (hooks, 1992, p. 149). hooks argues that the performance of whiteness by drag queens of color, at least in this specific case, is motivated by internalized racism and a desire to be white–a desire achieved through the appropriation of white femininity.

Judith Butler disagrees with hooks's assessment, instead arguing that the drag pageantry in *Paris Is Burning* simultaneously appropriates and subverts "racist, misogynist, and homophobic norms of oppression" (Butler, 1993, p. 128). For Butler, drag performance has the potential to critique these structures of racism and misogyny even as it reinscribes these very structures on the bodies of the performers themselves. Butler suggests that the excesses of drag performance, that is, the excess meanings of gendered and raced bodies that peek through the drag façade, present ruptures in which these idealizations are challenged, if simultaneously reiterated.

While not specifically writing on *Paris Is Burning*, José Muñoz argues that drag performers of color deploy in very deliberate and political ways the tensions between the appropriation and the subversion of "norms of oppression." He argues that the continuities and discontinuities between bodies of color and performative whiteness can create a space for a critical inquiry of whiteness itself (Muñoz, 1999). As Muñoz describes, performers of color must deploy these axes of their identities in very strategic ways in order to reconcile these identities, and their performances, within the meanings they prescribe. Disidentification is a strategic deployment of dominant ideology in an effort to dismantle it. But if drag finds its political efficacy in the spaces of incongruity between the performance and the performer, what are the radical possibilities for white drag by white queens? That is, if there is no apparent space of discontinuity between the white body of a performer and the whiteness he performs, can such performances critique normalized whiteness? Muñoz's theory of disidentification suggests a framework through which we might answer these questions. If minoritarian subjects might deploy particular axes of identity in order to disidentify with other axes of their identity, might white performers do so as well? As I will argue, camp, as a mode of class performance, is often deployed as a disidentificatory strategy by white drag queens and in fact often subverts naturalized whiteness and renders it marked and visible.

CAMP AS A CLASS ACT

Not merely a gendered performance, drag also performs race, class, ethnicity, and all of the other axes around which identity is structured. These identities, though often at ideological odds with one another, are inextricable. The discourse on drag affords primacy to the performance of gender to the exclusion of all other sociopolitical constructions of difference. Scholars rarely acknowledge the degree to which the codes of gender that inform drag are themselves raced and classed. Carole-Anne Tyler (Tyler, 1991) argues that it is not only the gender incongruity between the performer and the performed that marks drag, but that class and the racial, ethnic and sexual connotations therein also serve as primary spaces of rupture. The codes of gender can be read only through these other axes, and gender performances take on very different meanings from different positions. This is not merely to say that subjectivity informs spectatorial epistimes, but also that embedded in the performance are codes of race and class and sexuality, among others, that create gender meaning itself. These axes of identity cannot be understood as modular elements but rather must be considered mutually determining. Gender, in sum, *cannot* exist without race and class and sexuality, and gender performance is simultaneously a performance of these other categories.

These various categories of identification, or what Ella Shohat calls "modalities of oppression and empowerment," may themselves create tensions within an individual, "being empowered on one axis (class, say) but not on another (such as sexuality)" (Shohat, 1998, p. 4). Therefore, if we consider these modalities not as competing axes but as both contradictory and mutually informing, we can begin to unpack the meanings of white drag performance. I argue that it is specifically through a deployment of these "modalities of oppression" that drag performances of whiteness by white queens might challenge the hegemony of whiteness through a complication of idealized femininity.

If idealized femininity is *white*, it is also heterosexual, bourgeois, and homogeneously Euro-American. If these attributes of idealized white femininity and the white supremacist rhetoric implied in such idealizations are always inscribed on the white drag performer, then performances of nonracial differences such as class, sexuality, and ethnicity might serve to denaturalize white femininity and provide the same ambivalence for race that male bodies can provide for gender. Indeed, drag must be understood not only as a performance of race and as gender, but also as a performance of class, ethnicity and sexuality. Certainly, this is not to say that any one of these categories necessarily subverts white supremacy but instead that the strategic deployment and subversion of each of these elements of performance might produce a denaturalized space in which a white performer performing white femininity might divest that whiteness of its power. I argue that the performance of these other axes actually has the potential to denaturalize whiteness. For if we understand the construction of normative whiteness (as Dyer [1997] does) to be specifically through categories of gender, class and ethnicity, and if we understand these categories to be fully integrated, as Shohat (1998) and Butler (1993) do, then we must acknowledge that a rearrangement of these categories has the potential to complicate the naturalization of whiteness.

In other words, imagine normative whiteness as a suspended mobile in which axes of identity represent weights and counterweights in the tentative balance of the structure. Middle class identity on one side balances Western European heritage on the opposite side, which balances a virginal, submissive femininity above, which holds heterosexuality in check. If we were to, for example, queer our mobile, and replace the heterosexuality axis with a lesbian one (which, of course, is a different shape and weight), our mobile's delicate balance would fail. Though we may quickly rebalance these axes and reiterate a normative whiteness within a lesbian identity with little difficulty, in that moment of imbalance we might find a space in which to challenge its dominance. Similarly, we may find these spaces of racial ambiguity in drag performances where class code, for example, complicate idealized femininity, in that moment when our mobile is off balance.

Camp, as a mode of queer performance, renders class visible within these matrices of identity. This connection between camp and class performance is crucial to a racialization of drag performance. While it is certainly important to note that not all drag is explicitly camp, I would argue that camp's preoccupation with the commodity form and access to capital make it a particularly useful example of the ways in which multiple axes of identity are deployed through gender performance. As Matthew Tinckom argues, camp is a strategy by which queer people negotiate the often-contradictory terms of their identity and capitalist value judgments, and therefore, camp is a strategy for queering value (Tinckom, 2002). John Waters's "trash aesthetic" and Divine's imperfect femininity, for example, expose the "work" not only of gender performance, but of whiteness as well. As Dyer argues, whiteness is an essential category of heteronormative, Euro-American ideals of femininity and further, the identification of women with whiteness is crucial to the construction of normative (nonracialized) whiteness (Dyer, 1997). The performance of imperfect femininity and imperfect class implies an imperfect whiteness. Or, as Gaylyn Studlar puts it, "High-born women could be idealized as pure angels, asexual and nurturing, but lower-class women become the signifier of a *dark* and degenerate femininity" (emphasis added) (Studlar, 1989, p. 4).

Divine's performances in *Polyester* and *Hairspray*, for instance, are as much "class drag" as they are "gender drag." According to some feminist critiques of drag,

> A real woman is a real lady; otherwise, she is a female impersonator, a camp or mimic whose "unnaturally" bad taste–like that of the working-class, ethnic, or racially "other" woman–marks the impersonation as such . . . The same can be said of Divine in *Polyester* (1981), whose polyester marks his impersonation as such for those who find it in "unnaturally" bad taste, since Divine never gives any (other) indication that he is "really" a man. (Tyler, 1991, p. 57)

Class therefore becomes the very excess that characterizes Divine's drag; working class femininity, instead of codes of masculinity, is the marker of incongruity. Divine's "images of nonpriviledged femininity suggests a strong affinity between discriminations of high and low evaluations and the problem of consolidating femininity as necessarily one set of gendered performances" (Tinckom, 2002, p. 169). That is, codes of femininity are specifically dependent on class codes.

Indeed, in *Hairspray* (1988), John Waters's film about 1960s race relations in Baltimore, it is this performance of working-class femininity that offers a critique of normative whiteness. As John G. Ives writes, Waters's films "continue to pursue his lifelong satirical examination of the strange behavior of white people in Baltimore" (Ives, 1992, p. 5). Waters's project specifically recognizes and *marks* whiteness as its object of study, and nowhere as explicitly as in *Hairspray*. Indeed, Divine's drag in *Hairspray* re-appropriates the body of white women as a challenge to institutionalized racism. Instead of a site for the reproduction of white supremacy, Edna Turnblad's (Divine) and her daughter Tracy's (Ricki Lake) class-marked, excessive bodies are re-sexualized outside the structures of white supremacy (or, almost outside them), specifically through dance. Indeed, their fat bodies are juxtaposed with the thin, blonde figures of Velma Von Tussle (Debbie Harry) and *her* daughter Amber (Colleen Fitzpatrick), both of whom do, in fact, reproduce structures of racism through their bodies: in Amber's case, through her mother's insistence on her performance of "white" dances, and in Velma's case, through the bomb hidden in her beehive (intended to disrupt civil rights protests). As Renee Curry writes, "Waters deploys dance and hair as revolutionary communication vehicles" (Curry, 1996, p. 166). Fat, as a class marker, comes to be a primary code through which Divine's drag performance denaturalizes the whiteness implicit in normative femininity. In fact, this camp project of reassigning value to the valueless is achieved primarily through the performance of whiteness, or of "white trash" more specifically.

Kathleen Rowe recognizes similar meanings in the relationship between Roseanne Barr, her body and the femininity she performs: "It is [Roseanne] Arnold's *fatness* . . . and the *looseness* or lack of personal restraint her fatness implies, that most powerfully define her and convey her opposition to middle-class and feminine standards of decorum and beauty" (Rowe, 1995, p. 60). The fat female body is specifically classed. Indeed, Divine's performance of fatness disrupts codes of femininity as much as, if not more than, her performance of gender and further lays bare the "work" of embodiment of all of these categories. "As a form of representational labor, the fat woman's work of emblematizing the circulatory embolisms of a culture might be said to fall into the economic category, not of either production or reproduction, but rather of waste management" (Moon, 1993, p. 231). Following Moon and Sedgwick, representations of *white* fat femininity serve as a sort of repository for the excess of whiteness itself.

White women's bodies, as Dyer argues, bear the representation and reproduction of whiteness, not merely in the sense of sexual reproduction, but the reproduction of meaning as well.

> White discourse has often emphasized the importance of white reproduction and especially of white women's responsibilities in its regard . . . White women thus carry–or, in many narratives, betray–the hopes, achievements and character of the race. (Dyer, 1997, pp. 27-29)

If white women are charged with the reproduction of white supremacy, as Dyer argues, *fat* white women bear the burden of embodying the failure and contradiction of white supremacist discourse. Or, to put it another way, fat white femininity indexes the spaces of rupture in which whiteness is no longer an unmarked category. Camp performances like Divine's offer spaces of critique precisely because camp renders cultural production visible. As Andrew Ross argues, "the camp effect" occurs when the conditions of production themselves produce new meaning for the cultural product (Ross, 1989). The camp performance of fat and classed bodies betrays the conditions of cultural production that render those bodies excessive and in violation of the white supremacist narrative.

Pamela Robertson's work on what she calls "feminist camp" provides another framework through which we might understand Divine's camp drag (Robertson, 1993). Robertson argues that rather than reproducing idealizations of womanhood, Mae West's parody based performances challenged its very naturalization and were, in fact, female, female impersonation. West's "drag," Robertson suggests, found its meaning not in a space of gender incongruity, but via her refusal to naturalize the connection between her body and her performance. West performed this rupture through specific codes of working class femininity. Like West's "drag," Divine's drag has often been accused of reiterating misogynist stereotypes. However, as Robertson argues, camp parody, especially as it was performed by West via class codes, was precisely the discontinuity that made her performances critical drag. And just as there are significant difficulties in painting West as a purely revolutionary performer, so too are there difficulties in positioning Divine as such a figure. The point is not that Divine should be considered an activist drag performer in the vein of Vaginal Crème Davis (though such an argument might certainly be made) but rather that Divine's deployment of classed fat femininity offered a space of discontinuity in which white supremacist rhetoric was often challenged both explicitly and implicitly.

Tinckom explores some of these difficulties in reading Divine's drag, specifically in reference to charges that his performances equate femininity with perversity. "Divine's performances are problematic in that because of its allegedly 'male' position, drag is situated as being unable to disrupt conservativizing sexual orderings; this assumes that an essentialized masculine body arises intact beyond Divine's drag incarnation" (Tinckom, 2002, p. 176). These issues of performance and essentialism are equally important to this essay. I began with the question of whether the performance of white femininity by white drag queens could challenge the power embedded within whiteness without a racial discontinuity between the performance and the performer.

This question, too, is problematic on a number of levels. First, it suggests a racial essentialism that dichotomizes "white" and "non-white," implying both a simplistic understanding of racial and ethnic identity, and second, suggesting that these affiliations are based solely on skin color. Finally, the question suggests that at least for the audience, the performer's race is understood as the primary mode of identification. Or, in other words, the question presumes that the continuities between the white body of the performer and performed white femininity are *primary* continuities for the audience. Nevertheless, the strategic essentialisms deployed in this question pose crucial questions about the ways that race, skin color, gender, class, ethnicity, and sexuality operate in drag performance. In fact, camp drag performance's revolutionary potentials lie specifically in this presentation and deconstruction of essentialisms. Not all drag, or even camp drag performances, challenges these essentialisms and the injustices built upon them, and to be sure, even drag performed specifically as social commentary is often not received as such.

Indeed, despite my attempts to carve out a space in which drag parody might disrupt white supremacist rhetoric, it is vital to understand that this space is anything but utopic. It would be naïve to suggest that "such parody has any status outside prevailing social relations, that it is in some sense sealed off and sanitized from them" (Miller, 1993, p. 203). Just as gender drag implicates the very structures of meaning that it challenges, so too do performances of race and class rest in an uneasy relationship to structures of oppression. Therefore, this essay is not so much about heralding white drag as the antidote to white supremacist rhetoric, but rather recognizing that gender performance is far more complicated than gender incongruity alone and that such performance can indeed tell us a great deal about the ways that people perform other modes of identity and the ways that they resist the confines of those identities.

NOTES

1. Though I employ the binarizing terms "white people" and "people of color," I do not wish to reiterate essentialist notions of race, racial characteristics or racial identity. I find these terms useful, however, in working through the implications of drag performance insofar as the medium employs visual discord between the body of the performer and the performance itself. That is, the visual codes of race are often crucial to performances that seek to challenge them.

2. The notion of "idealized femininity" poses significant questions, particularly in terms of drag performance. The idealized femininity I discuss here references Richard Dyer's (1997) survey of the ways that white femininity has been used in patriarchal and racist representations of whiteness as "good and pure." It is, of course, important to

note that while these idealizations have operated as such in the dominant discourse on white femininity, they have not always been the model of femininity for white women, nor have they gone unchallenged. Furthermore, these traditional idealizations are rarely the same femininities performed in drag, which often favors performances of tragic women, such as Judy Garland, or "bad girls," such as Cher.

REFERENCES

Babuscio, J. (1993). Camp and the gay sensibility. D. Bergman (Ed.), *Camp grounds: Style and homosexuality* (pp. 19-38). Amherst: University of Massachusetts Press.

Butler, J. (1993). Gender is burning: Questions of appropriation and subversion. *Bodies that matter: On the discursive limits of "sex"* (pp. 122-140). New York: Routledge.

Curry, R. (1996). Hairspray: The revolutionary way to restructure and hold your history. *Literature/Film Quarterly*, 24(2), 165-168.

Dyer, R. (1997). *White*. London: Routledge.

Garber, M. (1992). Black and white TV: Cross dressing the color line. *Vested interests: Cross dressing and cultural anxiety* (pp. 267-303). New York: Routledge.

Hilbert, J. (1995). The politics of drag. In C.K. Creekmur and A. Doty (Eds.), *Out in culture: Gay, lesbian and queer essays on popular culture* (pp. 463-469). London: Cassell.

hooks, b. (1992). Is Paris burning? *Black looks: Race and representation*. Boston: South End Press.

Ives, J. G. (1992). A garden in Baltimore. *John Waters*. New York: Thunder's Mouth Press.

Meyer, M. (1994). Reclaiming the discourse of camp. M. Meyer (Ed.), *The politics and poetics of camp* (pp. 1-22). New York: Routledge.

Miller, T. (1993). New technologies to form new selves. In T. Miller (Ed.), *The well-tempered self: Citizenship, culture and the postmodern subject* (pp. 173-217). Baltimore: Johns Hopkins University Press.

Moon, M. and E. K. Sedgwick (1993). Divinity: A dossier, a performance piece, a little-understood emotion. In E. K. Sedgwick, *Tendencies* (pp. 215-51). Durham: Duke University Press.

Muñoz, J. E. (1999). *Disidentifications: Queers of color and the performance of politics*. Minneapolis: University of Minnesota Press.

Newton, E. (1993). Role models. In D. Bergman (Ed.), *Camp grounds: Style and homosexuality* (pp. 39-53). Amherst: University of Massachusetts Press.

Robertson, P. (1993). "The kinda comedy that imitates me": Mae West's identification with the feminist Camp. *Cinema Journal*, 32(2), 57-72.

Ross, A. (1989). Uses of camp. *No respect: Intellectuals and popular culture* (pp. 135-170). New York: Routledge.

Rowe, K. (1995). Roseanne: The unruly woman as domestic Goddess. *The unruly woman: Gender and the genres of laughter*. Austin: University of Texas Press.

Shohat, E. (1998). Introduction. *Talking visions: Multicultural feminism in a transnational age* (pp. 1-62). Cambridge: MIT Press.

Sontag, S. (1961). Notes on camp. *Against interpretation* (pp. 275-292). New York: Dell Publishing.

Studlar, G. (1989). Midnight s/excess: Cult configurations of femininity and the perverse. *Journal of Film and Television, 17*(1), 2-14.

Tinckom, M. (2002). *Working like a homosexual: Camp, capital and cinema.* Durham: Duke University Press.

Tyler, C-A. (1991). Boys will be girls: The politics of gay drag. In D. Fuss (Ed.), *Inside/out* (pp. 32-70). New York: Routledge.

Balancing Acts:
Drag Queens, Gender and Faith

Constance R. Sullivan-Blum, PhD

Binghamton, State University of New York

SUMMARY. While engaged in research on the same-sex marriage debate in mainline denominations, I interviewed 23 LGBT Christians, four of whom were drag queens. While it is not possible to generalize from such a small sample, the drag queens in this study insist on maintaining their identity as Christians despite the hegemonic discourse that renders faith and LGBT identities mutually exclusive. They developed innovative approaches to reconciling their gender and sexual identities with their spirituality. Their innovations are potentially liberating not just for them personally, but for LGBT people generally because they challenge Christianity's rigid dichotomies of gender and sexuality. *[Article copies available for a fee from The Haworth Document Delivery Service: 1-800-HAWORTH. E-mail address: <docdelivery@haworthpress.com> Website: <http://www.HaworthPress. com> © 2004 by The Haworth Press, Inc. All rights reserved.]*

Constance R. Sullivan-Blum received her PhD in Anthropology from Binghamton University (SUNY).

Author note: I want to thank Ilyssa Manspeizer and Louise Sullivan-Blum for their comments on earlier drafts of this paper. I also want to thank Steven Schacht, Sandeep Bakshi and the anonymous reviewer for their helpful comments and suggestions.

Correspondence may be addressed: Department of Anthropology, P.O. Box 6000, Binghamton University (SUNY), Binghamton, NY 13902 (E-mail: csullivan3@stny. rr.com).

[Haworth co-indexing entry note]: "Balancing Acts: Drag Queens, Gender and Faith." Sullivan-Blum, Constance R. Co-published simultaneously in *Journal of Homosexuality* (Harrington Park Press, an imprint of The Haworth Press, Inc.) Vol. 46, No. 3/4, 2004, pp. 195-209; and: *The Drag Queen Anthology: The Absolutely Fabulous but Flawlessly Customary World of Female Impersonators* (ed: Steven P. Schacht, with Lisa Underwood) Harrington Park Press, an imprint of The Haworth Press, Inc., 2004, pp. 195-209. Single or multiple copies of this article are available for a fee from The Haworth Document Delivery Service [1-800-HAWORTH, 9:00 a.m. - 5:00 p.m. (EST). E-mail address: docdelivery@haworthpress.com].

KEYWORDS. Drag queens, homosexuality, gay men, spirituality, religion, Christianity, the Black family

> One of my friends, he was homeless and he went down to stay in the Pentecostal church. They found out he was hanging with drag queens and locked him out the church . . . He was homeless. You can't live here because you're hanging with drag queens? So? We praise God the same way you do. I stand up to go pee the same way you do.[1]

These are the words of a 28-year-old African American drag queen named Eddie[2] whom I interviewed while doing research on the same-sex marriage debate in mainline Christian churches. This quote highlights the tension between the religious discourses that condemn homosexuals and drag queens and the way in which religion is sometimes employed to resist these hegemonic discourses. I interviewed 23 LGBT Christians in a small city in Upstate New York, four of whom were drag queens. While Christian discourses generally condemn gay men and drag queens, their insistence on retaining a Christian identity leads to innovative strategies that destabilize the traditional Christian gender and sexuality binaries. While it is not possible to generalize from such a small sample, it is my hope that this essay will reveal the lacuna in the literature concerning the religious expression of drag queens in the contemporary United States.

Much of the analysis of drag queens focuses on cross-dressing as a form of transgender behavior that negotiates the space between the supposedly fixed binaries of gender (Newton, 1979; Butler, 1990; Garber, 1992; Bullough and Bullough, 1993; Butler, 1993; Lorber, 1994; Whittle, 1996; Schacht, 1998, 2000). By disrupting the one-to-one correspondence between gender performance and anatomical sex, drag queens highlight the fluidity and performative aspects of gender thereby challenging the discourses naturalizing gender (Butler, 1990; Garber, 1992; Bullough and Bullough, 1993; Butler, 1993; Lorber, 1994; Whittle, 1996; Fulkerson, 1997). Drag destabilizes the gender/sex construct that is directly linked to heteronormativity (Rubin, 1975; Newton, 1979; Rubin, 1984; Vance, 1989; Lorber, 1994; Fulkerson, 1997; Wilchins, 1997). Like gender, sexuality in the United States is naturalized. Each is understood as first and foremost a physical fact, dictated to us by our bodies. According to this discourse, gender and sexuality are equally innate, stable and outside of our control. We no more choose our sexuality than we chose our genitals (Rubin, 1975, 1984; Vance, 1989; Butler, 1990, 1993; Gavanas, 2001).

Along these lines, conservative Christian discourse constructs heterosexuality as natural and God-ordained while framing homosexuality as either an unfortunate pathology or as intentional sin[3] (Ankerberg and Weldon, 1994). Heterosexuality, according to this view, is natural because it maps completely onto gender constructions that are seen as absolutely tied to biological sex and reproduction (Nugent and Gramick, 1990; Lienesch, 1993; Ankerberg and Weldon, 1994; Helms, 1997; Olyan, 1997; Gavanas, 2001). Homosexuality, according to this model, perverts the mission and purpose of gender/sex (Lienesch, 1993; Helms, 1997; Olyan, 1997; Gavanas, 2001). Conservative Christian condemnation of homosexuality is inextricably linked to the preservation of the gender binary. Drag queens, therefore, are especially confounding to them (Lorber, 1994; Davies, 1997; Fulkerson, 1997).

Conservative Christian discourse is constructed in an oppositional relationship with what they call "secular humanism" or liberal ideology (Herman, 2000). According to this counter discourse, homosexual relations are, like heterosexuality, naturally occurring, in-born, and immutable (Vance, 1989; Dorenkamp and Henke, 1995; Fulkerson, 1997). In this discourse the heterosexual/homosexual binary is naturalized, leaving gender as a stable aspect of the self that is consonant with biological sex (Davidson, 1992; Dorenkamp and Henke, 1995). This is the language of identity politics and the Gay Civil Rights movement (Kitzinger, 1987; Weston, 1991; Wilchins, 1997; Warner, 1999).

While very little has been written about the relationship of drag queens to religion, gay and lesbian Christians, following the model of the Gay Civil Rights movement, have naturalized homosexuality, making the claim that homosexuality is ordained by God (Boyd, 1987; Thumma, 1991; Davidson, 1992; Comstock, 1996; Gorman, 1997; Yip, 1997). Such discourses are key to strategies used by many LGBT Christians, including the drag queens in this research, to contest the condemnation of their gender and sexual identities that they experienced in their churches. Living and negotiating the stigmatism of homosexuality while still claiming a Christian identity requires reconciling what are often framed as mutually exclusive identities (Boyd, 1987; Bauer, 1992; Helms, 1997; Yip, 1997; Herman, 2000; Rodriguez and Ouellette, 2000). Frequently, LGBT Christians retain their claim to a Christian identity while developing an individual, innovative approach to spiritual expression (Boyd, 1987; Dynes, 1992; Comstock, 1996; Yip, 1997).

Drag queens are not usually examined in the literature on LGBT Christianity. It is this gap in the literature that I hope to call attention to with this work. The drag queens in this study use religion, on the one hand, to normalize and legitimize their gender and sexual expression. Simultaneously, religion also provides them with discourses of resistance that, when combined with their marginality in both Christian and gay worlds, makes for interesting innovations. By claiming multiple identities as Christians, gay men and drag queens, these men contribute to the destabilizing of the heteronormativity and rigid gender dichotomy in hegemonic Christianity.

THE PEOPLE

Before continuing, it is necessary to introduce the four drag queens who participated in this study. While not all drag queens are gay, these men identified themselves as such (Garber, 1992). They had either performed in the past or were performing at the time of the interview in a drag contest culminating in a highly publicized finale at a city venue attended by many straight community members. One of the participants was the winner of this show in the year 2000. Despite their success and local celebrity, all of the drag queens I interviewed were amateurs and made money from performing only when they won contests.

Shawn is a 37-year-old, divorced white man and father of two boys. For much of his early adulthood he was a devout Episcopalian. In fact, he had begun the process of seeking ordination in the Episcopal Church. When he came out as a gay man and divorced his wife, his priest would no longer support his efforts at ordination. While he still calls himself Christian he no longer attends any church. Shawn is the oldest participant. In the 1980s, Shawn was known in the gay and drag community as "Mother" and mentored younger gay men and drag queens. Shawn no longer dresses in drag, but he is still known as "Mother" in his circle of friends.

Jacob is a 33-year-old white man and a practicing Roman Catholic. He attends Mass frequently though he is markedly ambivalent towards the leadership of the Roman Catholic Church. Jacob owns a moderately successful business in the city and performs in amateur drag shows.

Eddie is the star drag performer of this group and the winner of the year 2000 drag contest. He is a 28-year-old African-American man and the father of one child. Eddie was raised Baptist and his stepfather is a local minister. Despite being the center of some gossip, Eddie sporadically attends a Black Baptist church in the city where he feels welcome. In fact, both his mother and his stepfather attend his drag performances.

Douglas is a 29-year-old African-American man. He was raised in a Pentecostal church and still adheres to its tenets. Douglas is not permitted to sing in his church choir because he is gay, and this is a source of profound grief for him. Nonetheless, he defends his church's right to prohibit him from singing in the choir by likening it to the rules for the drag show at the gay bar. Douglas performs in amateur drag shows and was a finalist in the local competition. Having introduced these four men, it is now possible to explore some of the innovations on religious discourses they used to resist the condemnation of their sexual and gender expressions.

UPSETTING THE NATURAL ORDER

Most of the drag queens in this study, like many LGBT Christians, discursively naturalize homosexuality in an effort to claim that it is ordained by God (Boyd, 1987; Thumma, 1991; Davidson, 1992; Comstock, 1996; Yip, 1997). Sexual morality in traditional Christian discourse is linked with a naturalized heterosexuality (Nugent and Gramick, 1990; Lienesch, 1993; Ankerberg and Weldon, 1994; Gavanas, 2001). Leaving aside all of the competing discourses in American Christianity which dispute this statement, the drag queens I spoke to for this research understand this to be the basic conflict which they must navigate as gendered, sexual and spiritual people. They understand that within Christianity a sexuality or gender expression that is deemed unnatural is sinful. Their homosexuality and gender expression must, therefore, be constructed as part of the natural design.

Naturalizing homosexuality allows some of the drag queens in this study to counter the discourse of sin and make a claim for a place in the plan of God. Thumma (1991) refers to this line of reasoning among gay evangelical Christians as the "creationist argument," which LGBT Christians use to posit sexual orientation as an immutable attribute assigned by God (p. 341). For instance, Shawn strongly rejects the notion that homosexuality is sin, saying,

> I'm sorry, I have committed no sin . . . I don't think we need to be forgiven . . . but we scare the Church . . . We upset the natural order as Christianity sees it because there's no room for us in creation.

Here, Shawn is referring to the primary theological argument given by Christians who condemn homosexuality. They argue that homosexual activity falls outside of the "orders of creation" revealed in Genesis and is unnatural (Nugent and Gramick, 1990; Ankerberg and Weldon, 1994).

Shawn subverts the argument from creation by arguing that God created a third gender category that has been recognized by other cultures. Shawn calls on anthropological literature to draw a connection between contemporary gay Americans and the "Two-Spirit People" found in Native American cultures.[4] He says,

> One of the Native American belief systems from the Southwest[5] spoke of the third gender type that was established at creation. Within Christianity, you're well aware there's only two genders created so Christians are saying . . . you can only be male or female . . . The Natives have said, "No, this is wrong. There's three. There's men and there's women and then there's this other." And, so what we call homosexuality, they have no understanding of because it's not deviant. It's part of their society.

Shawn elaborates on the idea that there is a natural space for homosexuality in creation if the binaries of masculinity and femininity are destabilized. Arguing that he shares an essentialized identity with an historical and cross-cultural "other" is a discursive strategy that naturalizes homosexuality. By employing this strategy in the context of Christianity, Shawn destabilizes the argument from the "orders of creation."

Not all LGBT Christians accept this strategy. Douglas, for example, rejects the notion that homosexuality is natural or created by God. He asserts,

> I don't think you're born gay . . . that'd be blasphemy. That would make God a hypocrite because God speaks in the Bible and it clearly says in the Bible that . . . God made men and He made women.

When I asked him what God wanted gay men to do about their sexuality, he responded, "Go straight." He understands that some LGBT Christians frame their sexuality as natural and God-ordained, but he clings to the conservative theology of his church.

Douglas was the only one who argued that homosexuality is unnatural. The other three drag queens claimed that their homosexuality was inborn and outside of their ability to change. They, therefore, argued that it was natural and God ordained (Thumma, 1991). In the next section, we shall discuss how sexual behavior rather than sexual orientation complicates their attempts to reconcile gay drag identities with Christianity.

ALL MEN ARE DOGS

Gender and sexuality are tied to faith via the mechanism of sexual morality. Even if one is able to argue that homosexuality is not sinful because it is God-ordained and natural, Christian theology and practice is actively concerned with the morality of sexual behavior. LGBT Christians I spoke with feel they must come to terms with this if they are to reconcile their faith with their sexuality.

Both Eddie and Shawn expressed the belief that in order to have sexual lives in line with God's will, gay men must have monogamous partnerships. In this way, Eddie and Shawn ascribe to a Christian criterion for sexual morality but reframe it to include monogamous gay relationships (Davidson, 1992; Comstock, 1996; Rodriguez and Ouellette, 2000). The perceived sexual promiscuity of gay men, however, is one of the reasons Douglas believes homosexuality is immoral. Gay male promiscuity is constructed as arising inevitably from an essentialized masculinity (Lienesch, 1993; Gavanas, 2001).

Despite exploiting the fluidity of gender when performing as drag queens, Eddie, Douglas and Shawn naturalize male and female sexuality (Whittle, 1996). Men are supposedly aggressive, strong, sexually active and promiscuous. Women are supposedly nurturing, weaker, and more passive. According to this discourse, women have fewer sexual partners than men and inhibit the sexual drive of heterosexual men by demanding monogamy (Rubin, 1975; Lienesch, 1993; Gavanas, 2001). Gay men, however, do not have the constraining influence of women and are, therefore, "naturally" more promiscuous.

Eddie, Douglas and Shawn view their desire for multiple partners as problematic but inevitable. They envy lesbians for what they perceived as an innate ability to maintain long-term, stable and presumably monogamous relationships. For instance, Douglas told me,

Men are more promiscuous than women . . . whether you're a gay male or a straight male . . . [Women] are looking at it for longevity. Men think once you're out of my bedroom, "Who's next?"

They all argued that lesbian and gay sexuality differed because of natural, sex-linked traits (Rubin, 1975; Lienesch, 1993; Gavanas, 2001).

Despite the idea that being a drag queen opened up alternative ways of expressing gender, this was understood as uneven and incomplete (Garber, 1992; Schacht, 1998). For example, these drag queens insisted that all men, including themselves, are interested in sexual conquest and personal pleasure to the detriment of the stability of their love relationships. As Eddie told me, "All men are dogs." In Shawn's words,

> If you look at gay culture . . . [you] see . . . wanton sexuality, fear of intimacy, constant hedonism . . . And the focus is all on sex, not on building relationships . . . Now, what I observe from the lesbian community is the exact opposite of the men . . . I'm gonna take you back to the animals for that. I think that men, regardless of how they find their sexual pleasure are biologically men and. . . . are programmed to spread their seed and be the dominant male . . . So, I think it's a biological thing that started when we lived in caves.

Shawn uses an essentialized construction of gendered sexuality to critique gay male sexual behavior and brings his own sexual morality in line with the dominant Christian dogma (Davidson, 1992; Comstock, 1996; Rodriguez and Ouellette, 2000; Gavanas, 2001).

On the other hand, Jacob challenges the LGBT Christian discourse of monogamy by claiming that sexual attractions are "meant to happen" and are, therefore, intended by God. He claims that sexual exploration is a way of appreciating God's gifts and should not be feared. He said, "I feel that a person can love more than one person in their lifetime and I don't think it's anything against their mate." Jacob elaborates a strategy that naturalizes a pan-sexuality in which people are free to explore sexual relations regardless of gender or identification with a sexual orientation. He remains committed to incorporating sexuality into a discourse of faith in which God intends for each individual to grow to his or her greatest potential. This actualization includes love and sexual relationships.

Exploring the Christian discourse of love is one of the hallmarks of LGBT spirituality (Comstock, 1996; Fulkerson, 1997; Yip, 1997). Jacob's insistence on a queer sexual ethic that resists the Christian condemnation of pleasure is possible because of his marginal status in Christianity. Rather than attempting to normalize his sexual desire, Jacob explores the ramifications of queer desire and same-sex love.

Most of the drag queens I spoke with expressed the belief that in order to have sexual lives in line with God's will, gay men must have monogamous partnerships (Davidson, 1992; Rodriguez and Ouellette, 2000). They decried the shallowness and hedonism of gay sexuality and ascribed to a Christian criterion for sexual morality but reframed it to include monogamous gay relationships (Davidson, 1992; Rodriguez and Ouellette, 2000). Only Jacob rejected this discourse. He was committed to incorporating sexuality into a discourse of faith in which God intended for each individual to grow to his or her greatest potential. This actualization included love and sexual relationships. In the next section, we will examine the familial ramifications of the discourse on love.

GOD'S LOVE AND THE MYTHIC BLACK FAMILY

Comparing their experience of family with that of white drag queens, Douglas and Eddie claim that Black families are more loving and accepting of their LGBT children. In an especially innovative move, the love of their families is employed as a metaphor for the unconditional love of God that provides the grounds to make demands on their families and churches. Eddie claimed that Black families, unlike white families, do not disown their LGBT children, saying,

> I've noticed that white families, I ain't getting racial, but their kids tell them [they're gay] and they kick them out on the streets. How can you disown your own child? I've never seen a Black family say, "I don't want to see you no more. Stay out my house."

Despite his earlier statements about the sinfulness of homosexuality, Douglas agreed with Eddie's assessment of the difference between white and Black families. Responding to Eddie, Douglas added,

> [Black parents will] still support you. You're their child. They'll still be loving and nurturing. A parent has an *agape* love for you, anyway. The love they have for you is an undying love. Their love is an unconditional love.

The use of the term *agape* is very evocative for evangelical and Pentecostal Christians. *Agape* is the Greek word for love coined by the early Christian writers to describe the love of God for humanity. It is an unconditional love. It is understood to be the love that brought Jesus to the cross as the ultimate sacrifice for human salvation. It is particularly interesting that Douglas used this word because it is the *agape* of Christ that Christians believe redeemed them from an inherently sinful nature. Douglas uses this word to elaborate the connection between Black families and the love of God, yet he continues to see himself as condemned by his sexuality.

Eddie continues the conversation, drawing an explicit connection between his parents' love and the unconditional love of God. Eddie elaborates on the metaphor, saying that God is like his stepfather, the Baptist minister, in that both are good, fair and compassionate. Neither of them expects Eddie to change his sexual behavior because it is understood to be innate.

Extending the mythological unconditional love of the Black family into a metaphor of one's relationship with God is an innovative discursive step that allows Eddie to claim the unconditional love of God. This discourse also empowers him to make demands on his family and church. Grounding the unconditional love of God in the mythic Black family ensures a context in which accepting Black LGBT people must be considered. In the next section, we will examine the ways the two white drag queens negotiate their relationships to their faiths.

PIECING TOGETHER FAITH

Jacob and Shawn, the two white drag queens, illustrate two different approaches to their faith. While Jacob has an innovative sexual ethic in which he argues that transient sexual experiences are gifts from God, he, like other LGBT Christians, keeps his gayness hidden in his church (Comstock, 1996; Yip, 1997). Jacob continues to attend Mass even though he must hide his sexual and drag identities because it helps him feel connected to God. He does not want to give that up for he sake of his other identities. He says, "I think that being gay is a part of my life. It's what I am, but it's not all of me."

Shawn, on the other hand, is "out" about his gay identity, but while continuing to espouse a traditional Christian sexual ethic, he does not attend a church. Like other LGBT Christians, Shawn chooses to practice his faith alone (Comstock, 1996; Yip, 1997). He no longer affiliates with a church, saying,

I believe I'm a Christian because I believe in the teaching of Jesus Christ. But what I can't espouse is all the dogma, all the rules mainline denominational Christianity says you have to do in order to be a Christian.

Like other LGBT people, Shawn has gone outside of the religion in which he was raised to produce spiritual meaning in his life (Boyd, 1987; Dynes, 1992; Comstock, 1996). He has not, however, abandoned his Christianity. Acting as a spiritual bricoleur, Shawn makes a claim for a supernatural basis for homosexuality and alternative gender performances.

Shawn argues that LGBT people, contrary to being sinful pariahs, are spiritually closer to God because they have a "duality of spirit" that mirrors the duality of God. He insists that it is the very essence of homosexuality that makes LGBT people spiritually superior to heterosexuals. Turning the hegemonic religious discourse on its head, Shawn says,

> We get to a point where we realize that we're closer to the nature of God than everybody else . . . The way I view God is as *Ying* and *Yang*. If you live your life by Christian principles and live your life like Jesus did, so to speak, you become part of the light, the white side of the *Ying* and *Yang*. I also believe you can put your energy into negativity and live your life contrary to the principles of the good and focus on the darkness of the world. And that in my mind is the duality of God spinning throughout the universe. It's the *Om*, the sound of the whole universe spinning, the conflict between good and evil.

Using Eastern spiritual terminology to describe the duality of God, Shawn acts again as an innovative bricoleur. Extending his concept of duality to include not only gender and sexuality but also good and evil as the nature of God, Shawn highlights the flexibility of discourses of faith when the separation between Christian theology and other spiritualities is broken down. While Shawn's approach to Christian practice and theology is very different from Jacob's, they share a claim on Christianity that they are unwilling to give up. Reconciling their gay drag identities with their faith opens up innovative possibilities that destabilize the rigid binaries in hegemonic Christian discourse.

CONCLUSION

Like much of the larger LGBT community, sometimes these drag queens resist the hegemonic discourses proscribing sexuality, gender and religion and sometimes they reinscribe these discourses within their daily lives. However, extending the iconoclastic challenge of their stage personas into their religious lives, drag queens reveal the complexities, inconsistencies and contradictions embedded in the gender/sex system and the religious discourse that both underscores and relies on it. They employ many of the same strategies that other LGBT Christians use to negotiate the clash between their religion and their gender and sexual identities. The strategies of the drag queens, however, are particularly innovative.

Many LGBT Christians employ naturalizing discourses to normalize homosexuality. Few of them, however, were as articulate and bold in destabilizing what hegemonic Christian discourses posit as the "orders of creation" (Ankerberg and Weldon, 1994). While for the most part the drag queens in this study utilized a traditional formulation of a Christian sexual ethic, one of them was able to argue for a radically different sexual ethic in which all sexual attraction is seen as a gift from God and potentially actualizing. It is my opinion that these bold counter discourses are possible because the men who are making them are actively resisting the hegemonic Christian worldview. Indeed, by linking the African-American family to the love of God, the two African-American drag queens established grounds for making demands of their families and their churches. These men mine the inconsistencies and contradictions in Christian discourses of sin, sexual morality and theology to carve out a space for their spirituality that is reconciled to their gender and sexual identities even if this requires going beyond traditional Christianity.

The private lives that the drag queens in this study negotiate exist in the unstable gaps between the culturally constructed binaries of gender, sexuality and faith. Their lives are fragile as well as flexible, marginalized as well as liminal. However, their success in navigating around these cultural danger zones illuminates liberating possibilities for other people, LGBT or straight.

NOTES

1. All quotes are verbatim and have been transcribed from taped interviews.

2. The names of the drag queens I interviewed have been changed in order to protect their anonymity.

3. By conservative I mean Christians who privilege scriptural authority over science and experience. It is important to note that many Christians in the United States identify themselves as "liberals" and are advocates for the inclusion and affirmation of LGBT Christians. See Hartman (1996).

4. "Two-Spirit People" is a catchall term to describe a variety of Native American alternative genders. Because they were known to dress in women's attire, some scholars

have associated them with drag queens (Williams, 1986; Wieringa, 1989). This association is highly contested, however, because it posits a universal and essentialized category of the homosexual or transgendered person. See Jacobs et al. (1997).

5. Shawn is probably referring to the Zuni culture that had a documented third gender category. See Roscoe (1991).

REFERENCES

Ankerberg, J. and J. Weldon. (1994). *The facts on homosexuality: Scientific research and biblical authority: Can homosexuals really change?* Eugene, Oregon: Harvest House.

Bauer, P. F. (1992). The homosexual subculture at worship: A participant observation study. In W. R. Dynes and S. Donaldson (Eds.), *Homosexuality and religion and philosophy* (pp. 43-56). New York: Garland Publishing, Inc.

Boyd, M. (1987). Telling a lie for Christ? In M. Thompson (Ed.), *GaysSpirit: Myth and meaning* (pp. 78-87). New York: St. Martin's Press.

Bullough, V. L. and B. Bullough. (1993). *Cross dressing, sex and gender.* Philadelphia: University of Pennsylvania Press.

Butler, J. (1993). *Bodies that matter: On the discursive limits of "sex."* New York and London: Routledge.

Butler, J. (1990). *Gender trouble: Feminism and the subversion of identity.* New York: Routledge.

Comstock, G. D. (1996). *Unrepentant, self-affirming, practicing: Lesbian/bisexual/gay people within organized religion.* New York: Continuum Publishing Company.

Davidson, D. (1992). DIGNITY, Inc.: An alternative experience of church. In W. R. Dynes and S. Donaldson (Eds.), *Homosexuality and religion and philosophy* (pp. 152-162). New York: Garland Publishing, Inc.

Davies, C. (1997). Religious boundaries and sexual morality. In G. D. Comstock and S. E. Henking (Eds.), *Que(e)rying religion: A critical anthology* (pp. 39-60). New York: Continuum Publishing Company.

Dorenkamp, M. and R. Henke. (1995). Introduction. In M. Dorenkamp and R. Henke (Eds.), *Negotiating lesbian and gay subjects* (pp.1-6). London: Routledge.

Dynes, W. R. (1992). Introduction. In W. R. Dynes and S. Donaldson (Eds.), *Homosexuality and religion and philosophy* (pp. vii-xx). New York: Garland Publishing, Inc.

Fulkerson, M. (1997). Gender–Being it or doing it? The church, homosexuality, and the politics of identity. In G. D. Comstock and S. E. Henking (Eds.), *Que(e)rying religion: A critical anthology* (pp. 188-201). New York: Continuum Publishing Company.

Garber, M. (1992). *Vested interests: Cross-dressing and cultural anxiety.* New York: Harper Perennial.

Gavanas, A. (2001). *Masculinizing fatherhood: Sexuality, marriage and race in the U.S. fatherhood responsibility movement.* Unpublished doctoral dissertation. Stockholm University.

Gorman, E. M. (1997). A special window: An anthropological perspective on spirituality in contemporary U.S. gay male culture. In G. D. Comstock and S. E. Henking (Eds.), *Que(e)rying religion: A critical anthology* (pp. 330-337). New York: Continuum Publishing Company.

Hartman, K. (1996). *Congregations in conflict: The battle over homosexuality.* New Jersey: Rutgers University Press.

Helms, K. J. (1997). Religion and cross-gender behavior: Wellspring of hope or swamp of despair. In B. Bullough, V. Bullough and J. Elias (Eds.), *Gender blending* (pp. 398-404). New York: Prometheus Books.

Herman, D. (2000). The gay agenda is the devil's agenda: The Christian Right's vision and the role of the state. In C. A. Rimmerman, K. D. Wald and C. Wilcox (Eds.), *The politics of gay rights* (pp.139-160). Chicago: University of Chicago Press.

Jacobs, S. E., W. Thomas, and S. Lang. (1997). *Two-spirit people: Native American gender identity, sexuality and spirituality.* Chicago: University of Illinois Press.

Kitzinger, C. (1987). *The social construction of lesbianism.* Newbury Park, CA: Sage Publications.

Lienesch, M. (1993). *Redeeming America: Piety and politics in the New Christian Right.* Chapel Hill: University of North Carolina Press.

Lorber, J. (1994). *The paradoxes of gender.* New Haven: Yale University Press.

Newton, E. (1979). *Mother camp: Female impersonators in America.* Chicago: The University of Chicago Press.

Nugent, R. and J. Gramick. (1990). Homosexuality: Protestant, Catholic and Jewish issues: A fishbone tale. *Journal of Homosexuality,* 18(3), 7-46.

Olyan, S. (1997). "And with a male you shall not lie the lying down of a woman": On the meaning and significance of Leviticus 18:22 and 20:13. In G. D. Comstock and S.E. Henking (Eds.), *Que(e)rying religion: A critical anthology* (pp. 398-414). New York: Continuum Publishing Company.

Rodriguez, E. M. and S. C. Ouellette. (2000). Religion and masculinity in Latino gay lives. In P. Nardi (Ed.), *Gay masculinities* (pp. 101-129). Thousand Oaks: Sage Publications, Inc.

Roscoe, W. (1991). *The Zuni man-woman.* Albuquerque: University of New Mexico Press.

Rubin, G. (1984). Thinking sex: Notes for a radical theory of the politics of sexuality. In C. S. Vance (Ed.), *Pleasure and danger: Exploring female sexuality* (pp. 267-319). London: Pandora Press.

Rubin, G. (1975). The traffic in women: Notes of the "political economy" of sex. In R. R. Reiter (Ed.), *Toward an anthropology of women* (pp. 157-210). New York: Monthly Review Press.

Schacht, S. P. (1998). The multiple genders of the court: Issues of identity and performance in a drag setting. In S. P. Schacht and D. W. Ewing (Eds.), *Feminism and men: Reconstructing gender relations* (pp. 202-224). New York: New York University Press.

Schacht, S. P. (2000). Gay female impersonators and the masculine construction of the "other." In P. Nardi (Ed.), *Gay masculinities* (pp. 247-268). Thousand Oaks: Sage Publications, Inc.

Thumma, S. (1991). Negotiating a religious identity: The case of the gay Evangelical. *Sociological Analysis, 52,* 333-347.

Vance, C. S. (1989). Social construction theory: Problems in the history of sexuality. In D. Altman, C. Vance, M. Vicinus, and J. Weeks (Eds.), *Homosexuality, which homosexuality?* (pp. 13-14). London: GMP Publishers.

Warner, M. (1999). *The trouble with normal: Sex, politics, and the ethics of queer life.* New York: The Free Press.

Weston, K. (1991). *Families we choose: Lesbians, gays, kinship.* New York: Columbia University Press.

Whittle, S. (1996). Gender fucking or fucking gender? Current cultural contributions to theories of gender blending. In R. Ekins and D. King (Eds.), *Blending genders: Social aspects of cross-dressing and sex-changing* (pp. 196-215). London: Routledge.

Wieringa, S. (1989). An anthropological critique of constructionism: Berdaches and butches. In D. Altman, C. Vance, M. Vicinus, and J. Weeks (Eds.), *Homosexuality, which homosexuality?* (pp. 215-238). London: GMP Publishers.

Wilchins, R. A. (1997). *Read my lips: Sexual subversion and the end of gender.* Ithaca, New York: Firebrand Books.

Williams, W. (1986). *The spirit and the flesh: Sexual diversity in American Indian culture.* Boston: Beacon Press.

Yip, A. K. (1997). *Gay male Christian couples: Life stories.* Westport, CT: Praeger Publishers.

A Comparative Analysis of Hijras and Drag Queens: The Subversive Possibilities and Limits of Parading Effeminacy and Negotiating Masculinity

Sandeep Bakshi

University of Rouen

SUMMARY. Gender studies in general and queer studies in particular have stressed the notion of imitation, play, and performance of gender. In this essay I undertake a comparative analysis of the hijra and the drag queen in terms of the shared and disparate subversive possibilities and

---

Sandeep Bakshi is a PhD candidate in the Department of English at the University of Rouen.

Author note: I thank Harjot Bhatia for reading earlier drafts of this article and giving me valuable suggestions. Many thanks to Kavita and Manish, to my partner Frédéric, to my mother and father, and to Mohammed Sow, whose various forms of support have made this paper possible. Special thanks to Steven P. Schacht for not giving up on me.

Correspondence may be addressed: Sandeep Bakshi, c/o Professor Jean Pierre Maquerlot, Department of English, Faculté de Lettres, University of Rouen, Mont Saint Aignan, 76821, France (E-mail: bakshisandip@aol.com).

[Haworth co-indexing entry note]: "A Comparative Analysis of Hijras and Drag Queens: The Subversive Possibilities and Limits of Parading Effeminacy and Negotiating Masculinity." Bakshi, Sandeep. Co-published simultaneously in *Journal of Homosexuality* (Harrington Park Press, an imprint of The Haworth Press, Inc.) Vol. 46, No. 3/4, 2004, pp. 211-223; and: *The Drag Queen Anthology: The Absolutely Fabulous but Flawlessly Customary World of Female Impersonators* (ed: Steven P. Schacht, with Lisa Underwood) Harrington Park Press, an imprint of The Haworth Press, Inc., 2004, pp. 211-223. Single or multiple copies of this article are available for a fee from The Haworth Document Delivery Service [1-800-HAWORTH, 9:00 a.m. - 5:00 p.m. (EST). E-mail address: docdelivery@haworthpress.com].

limits of the gendered performances they undertake. Studying the hijra alongside the drag queen will in no way mean conflating the two categories. Rather, I explore the cultural nuances involved in the hijra performance, including its ritualistic and religious aspects. While my analysis relies heavily on previously written works about hijras and drag queens, I have also had the opportunity to meet and visit with hijras during several marriage ceremonies of cousins and other relatives from 1992 to 1998 in New Delhi. *[Article copies available for a fee from The Haworth Document Delivery Service: 1-800-HAWORTH. E-mail address: <docdelivery@ haworthpress.com> Website: <http://www.HaworthPress.com> © 2004 by The Haworth Press, Inc. All rights reserved.]*

KEYWORDS. Hijras, drag queens, gender as performance, effeminacy, masculinity, Hindu culture

In the following paper I offer a queer reading of the hijra in terms of the subversive possibilities and limits such individuals pose to established modes of thinking about gender binaries. I analyze the hijra alongside that of the much discussed and debated western figure of the drag queen. However, a comparative analysis of the hijra versus the drag queen does not mean advocating the critical meaningfulness of the one over the other. Rather, in this article, I relocate both of these cultural models as potentially destabilizing to contemporary understandings of gendered and sexed identities. The notion of gender as performance as a transcultural "tool" for dismantling rigidities of the masculine/feminine divide is discussed in detail. I make it clear, however, that the hijra figure is not the Indian counterpart of, nor the Indian answer to, the drag queen. The hijra community is an integrated and inseparable part of the Indian social fabric and is "undoubtedly related to the variety and significance of alternative gender roles and gender transformations in Indian mythology and traditional culture" (Nanda, 1999, p. 20).

HIJRAS AND HINDU CULTURE

Hijras belong to the category of sexually "ambivalent" men–minus man–who dress up as women and perform on auspicious Hindu occasions like weddings and birth ceremonies (O'Flaherty, 1980, p. 297). Official counts of hijras vary significantly from 50,000 to upwards of

1.2 million (Bobb and Patel, 1982; Hall, 1997, p. 431; Jaffrey, 1997, p. 30; *BBC News Online*, 2001). While a few Hijras are born intersexed (which is rare), most are men who undergo voluntary castration and penectomy while "possessed" by the Goddess Bahuchara (Cohen, 1995, p. 276). They consider themselves to be sexually impotent, an important point which I will discuss later in the essay. Hijras have cultural and ritual sanction during wedding and birth ceremonies, and even the colonial rulers in the nineteenth century had to concede to their rights of property and begging for alms that they had hitherto enjoyed under native rulers (Preston, 1987).

Hijras live in large communities in North India and Pakistan, especially near the city of Ahemdabad (Gujrat, India) where they congregate annually at the Bahuchara Mata Shrine. Every new initiate to the community has a guru (mentor) and becomes a part of the hijra community once he has paid the *dand* (fine) to her guru. The amount of the *dand* is decided by the *Panchayat* (the community elders, a structure replicated from mainstream Indian society). The notion of the community is key to understanding hijra existence, as it is to many marginalized subcultures, which helps them to belong to a hierarchical frame and survive as a "parallel society" (Turner, 1977).

One of the more complicated and difficult tasks that gender and sexuality scholars face when investigating hijras is that there are several, sometimes contradictory definitions of what makes one a hijra. They have been defined as "eunuchs" (Mehta, 1945; Hiltebeitel, 1980, pp. 161-5; Bobb and Patel, 1982; Sharma, 1984; Preston, 1987; Jaffrey, 1997), "hermaphrodites" (Opler, 1960) with a " physical defect, natural or acquired" (Opler, 1961, p. 1331), male or boy prostitutes (Ellis, 1921; Carstairs, 1956, p.130), passive homosexuals (Carstairs, 1957, p. 60; Greenberg, 1988), and as a third gender and/or sex (Herdt, 1996, p. 70; Nanda, 1996; Nanda, 1999) with a cultural and ritual function (Opler, 1961, p. 1331; Hall, 1997; Nanda, 1999). This is further confounded by most hijra representations in the popular press and cinema being "superficial and sensationalist" (Nanda, 1999, p. xvii) and failing to consider their subjective perceptions (for examples of this sort, see Bobb and Patel, 1982, and Bedi, 1994). Moreover, hijras, homosexuals, and jankhas/zankhas (transvestites) are often collapsed in the same category (Bakshi, 2002).

Ultimately, any working definition of hijras must take into account their subjective perception as "neither man nor woman" (Nanda, 1999), and as perceived guarantors of fertility whereby their presence at the marriage and birth rituals is legitimated. They belong to the category of third gender but also to that of third sex (a point not much emphasized in hijra representations). In contemporary India, ritual and religious respect is not given to them per se, rather they negotiate and command this respect in order to empower their marginal identities in "resistance to systematic exclusion" (Hall, 1997, p. 431). Given that hijras do not have children, there is no simple and comprehensive register of genealogy that can give us details on their ancestors. This is partially due to the fact that as "neither men nor women" hijras have few political rights even though in recent times they have been given the right to vote in democratic elections (*BBC News Online*, 2000; *Times of India*, 2002). Thus, the only other source for tracing their beginnings is found in the various myths that have been perpetrated by hijras themselves and other folk literature (songs and chants that are sung during various hijra ceremonies and rituals).

It is interesting to note that transvestism has existed in Hindu mythology even before the conception of humankind and often hijras legitimate their right to existence through a careful decoding of various myths. Almost every hijra has a story of mythological origin relating his/her descendence (Nanda, 1999). For example, most prehistorical myths relate the descent of the hijras from the deity of Shiva (the god of destruction and unparalleled anger), who was also called Ardhanariswar, meaning half man and half woman. For many hijras the quality of being half man and half woman is a source of infinite strength that endows on them the divine power to give a *shraap* (curse), just like Shiva cursed the earth (Hiltebeitel, 1980, p. 159; Nanda, 1999, p. 20).

In yet another famous myth, during the great war of Kurukshetra (*Mahabharata*), the most brave and powerful warriors of the Pandava clan Arjun dressed as and became a woman in appearance called Brihannada (Hiltebeitel, 1980, p. 154; Sharma, 1984, p. 384; Nanda, 1999, pp. 30-1). As Brihannada, he participated in the wedding ceremony of his son Abhimanyu with the princess Uttara (Hiltebeitel, 1980, p. 166). It must be pointed out that Arjun's cross-dressing is read by almost all hijras as an instance of voluntary emasculation that opens up avenues of immaculate physical strength.

All hijras stress the notion of impotence as a prerequisite for joining the community and an eventual surgical emasculation for the attainment of divine and physical power. Castration and penectomy are widely practiced as an inevitable requisite for becoming a hijra. Emasculation is looked upon by the hijras as a source of personal fulfillment. Since such practices are illegal and even criminal under the Indian Penal Code, they take place under strict vigilance away from any outside (police) encroachments. Hijras regard castration as a ritual, a religious offering of their penis to the Goddess and as a source of pleasure which "re/members (it) as a bloody act and takes the violence as central to the representations of thirdness" (Cohen, 1995, p. 277). In a similar vein, the Travesties of Brazil perceive "the injection of industrial silicone into (their) body" as "one of the final steps . . . in (their) transformation into travesty" (Kulick, 1998, p. 46).

I will now further explore English translations of the word "hijra." It is true that for cultural and gender definition purposes, hijras have been relegated to the categories of eunuchs and hermaphrodites, i.e., emasculated biological males and intersexed "males" whose sexual organs are ambiguous at birth or who suffer from a genetical malformation. However, such definitions seem, at best, to be as subjective definitions of the term "hijra" in various Hindi and urdu linguistic codes implies impotence and is stressed by hijras themselves and has been highlighted by Nanda (1996, p. 380; 1999, p. 13). The definitional importance of impotence gains further weight if we consider that most hijras are born with normal male sexual organs and voluntarily undergo surgical castration to become a part of the hijra community. Nevertheless, the term "Hijra" can still be read as a "eunuch" in the broadest sense of the word, which refers "not only to an individual who is physiologically incapable of engendering an offspring but also to one who has chosen to withdraw from worldly activities and thus refuses to procreate," and are a *sanyasi* (to use Hindu terminology), someone who voluntarily renounces the world (Ringrose, 1996, p. 86). As I will demonstrate in a moment, definitional understanding of the hijras is quite helpful in better appreciating what sort of gender performance they undertake.

A COMPARATIVE ANALYSIS OF HIJRAS AND DRAG QUEENS

In recent years queer theory scholars have increasingly focused on how gender and sexuality is performed. Judith Butler's works have been influential to the creation and development of critical analyses and emerging understandings of gender as performance (Butler, 1990). She writes about gender identity as a form cultural fiction, that through "a repeated stylization of the body, a set of repeated acts within a highly rigid regulatory frame that congeal over time to produce the appearance of substance, [become] a natural sort of being" (Butler, 1990, p. 33). She also advocates that drag is a parody of fixed and normative conceptualizations of gender. Ultimately, drag for Butler "constitutes the mundane way in which genders are appropriated, theatricalized, worn, and done; it implies that all gendering is a kind of impersonation and approximation" (Butler, 1991, p. 21).

Drag queens, like Hijra performances, often make us think about the various ways in which gender is played out and "naturalized" in society. They help us to realize that gender is a philosophical category and is not "what one is, but more fundamentally, is what one does" (West and Zimmerman, 1987, p. 140). By exaggerating the feminine, drag queens are capable of showing us the fiction of established dichotomous processes of gendering. Stylization of the self by drag can potentially disrupt regulatory notions of the "self" and can subversively reveal the limits of identity. Perhaps notwithstanding a few movie portrayals, however, most drag queens and their subversive potential are largely marginalized from the larger cultural setting, e.g., most perform in gay bars.

Hijras, on the other hand, enjoy religious and cultural legitimacy. The blessings of hijras in Hindu marriage and birth ceremonies are part of a ritual obligation. This means that the potential "denaturalization" of gender binaries that can be seen in the figure of hijras and their presence at various culturally mainstream rituals is part of the larger social framework in which it occurs. In sum, while drag queens operate in private or alternative social spaces (clubs, bars and lesbian and gay prides), hijras, while still culturally marginalized, perform in normative and conventional cultural spaces.

In hijra performances, however, this alternative space is a priori guaranteed and reinforced by religious and social customs even if the presence of hijras is undesired. Unlike drag shows, hijra performances (although seemingly undertaking a similar deconstruction of gender binaries) take place within mainstream institutions like marriage. Almost all Hindu marriages and birth ritual have ceremonies calling for at least one hijra intervention if not more. Sometimes if the hijras are absent from such ceremonies many newlyweds seek the blessings by going to places where they can find the hijra community. As Andrew Whitehead of the *BBC* reports in his personal experiences with the hijras, "an Indian birth (is) hardly complete without the hijras" (Whitehead, 1998).

Let me now explore the relational aspect of hijra shows. The audience of hijra performances usually comprises everyone present at the concerned weddings. It consists of almost all adult male and female relatives, and even children. Unlike the audiences at drag shows, this mainstream public of hijra shows is paradoxically often not fully prepared for a "visible attack" (in the form of a dance-spectacle) on their preconceived notions of rigid gendered and sexed identities. The alternative space which the hijra performs in, and which has the capacity to demythify gender identities, is often negotiated and at times coerced by the hijras in the presence of an involuntary audience who can sometimes refuse that the hijras lift up their *ghagras* (long skirts) or saris.

One of the most fascinating aspects of the audience/hijra interaction is that men in the audience both regulate and control the hijra performance/transgression. Women are relegated to the subordinate rank of mere spectators while the patriarchal figures of the household (father, uncle or a distant male relative) deal with the performers. Men are responsible for negotiating and fixing the boundaries concerning the duration of the shows, the financial compensation of the hijras, and most importantly, the sexual gestures involved in the hijra performance. In this sense, males in the audience (married or otherwise) represent stability and order of gendered identities and are the monolithic guarantors of the continuation of these identities. Nevertheless, they participate in such an exceptional exchange with the hijras (often in a climate charged with sexual dynamics) who represent a challenge to this very notion of normative identity regulation. The hijra performance thus becomes a discursive site of critical negotiations between the symbolic patriarchs and alternatively (inter-)sexed beings. This site reveals the fiction of gendered and sexed realities where gendering and sexualizing forces (in the figure of the patriarchs) play and are played out (in the figure of the hijras, who enact both the feminine and the masculine parts in case the males present in the ceremonies refuse to take part in their song and dance sequences). This dramatic transgression of normativity subsides once the hijra ceremony is over and the males from the audience (who are often the receivers of hijra attention/irony) return to their constructed role of controlling the gender boundaries but not without a sense of pleasure.

Critical commentators on drag have begun to question the attribution of the unproblematic subversion of heteronormative ideals to the figure of drag. Drag, it has been suggested, is not a simple tool of resistance to preexisting gender/sexual dichotomies and, thus, cannot be set up as a uniquely radical and unified category that has the possibility (and the power) to critique identity limits. Even Butler, who proposed drag as a subversive undertaking, has repositioned drag as a potential threat to an exposure of gender fictions rather than being the unquestioned source of resistance to such fictions in itself. In one of her later works she clarifies that drag is never "unproblematically subversive" and it "reflects the mundane impersonations by which heterosexually ideal genders are performed and naturalized." Moreover, she emphasizes that drag has the potential to "reidealize heterosexual norms without calling them into question" (Butler, 1993, p. 231).

Other queer scholars have even inquired into various ways in which discussions on drag in queer theory have significantly centered around "play" and "performance" thus reducing the very "theory of gender" into the "old 'sex roles' framework" (Walters, 1996, p. 854). In the domain of transgender studies scholars have argued that transgender individuals often "reinforce and reify the system they hope to change" and that "female impersonators almost universally present stereotypical and exaggerated images of females" (Gagné, Tewksbury and McGaughey, 1997, p. 478; Tewksbury, 1993, p. 467). Even in studies of third gender, the male/female binary divide is suspected to be reinstated as if it "recuperates social and sexual norms," to borrow a phrase from Garber (Garber, 1992, p. 69; Kulick, 1998, p. 120).

In order to better understand the critical implications of drag in issues of political and social resistance, one needs to (re)view gender and gendering as intellectual sites where the power dynamic of male/female, straight/gay, superior/inferior, original/duplicate is at work. In other words, all contemporary gender relationships are hegemonically structured around the possession of power. Apart from the play and performance that one links to drag, we must also (re-)locate drag in a broader context of the power problematic. I believe that at a non-complex level, drag relies heavily on the ability to shock and scandalize. The techniques for resisting pre-given identity limits used by drag queens mostly consist of an exaggeration and a deliberate overplay of the "feminine." This can certainly be read as an instrument of "male" power so that men can pose as, and seemingly be, "better" women than women themselves. Drag may tell us how gendered identity is constructed by cultural and social conditioning but it also paradoxically often re-legitimates gender as an essential category with its focus on exaggerated forms of the feminine. Drag, as Schacht argues, is often a form of "homosexual embodiment of the heterosexual," whereby a drag performance often fixes and reinstates the gender binary rather than exposing it. Read in this way drag shows "become wholly dependent on the audience's normative expectations about gender and sexuality" and are "frequently more reflective than transgressive of the dominant culture's ideals of gender and sexuality" (Schacht, 2002, p.163).

Thus, while drag is not unconditionally subversive, the hijra paradigm forces us to rethink about the multiplicity of the techniques of resistance to preexisting gender identifications. Shock and scandal are also used in the hijra shows as tools for unsettling gender equations. The audiences are generally involuntary participants in the performances as hijra shows are an unwritten dictate of the cultural context. Once the song and dance sequences are over, the hijras invariably lift up their *ghagras* or saris (unless warned not to do so by the adult male members of the audience), to show that they are male (i.e., possess a male organ) or that they are neither male nor female (i.e., have no sexual organ) as in most cases. This is often done to show that the hijras are "real" hijras (i.e., are castrated), and not fake ones (i.e., men posing as hijras), or just effeminate men, zenanas, for whom the hijra community reserves disdain (Cohen, 1995, p. 276; Jaffrey, pp. 110 and 161; Nanda, 1999, p.11). However, sometimes if the marriage party refuses to pay the desired alms to the hijras, they can use it as a tool to demand their rights. As Cohen puts it, "the sight of the postoperative hole–the seal of the *hijras* impotence–is paradoxically potent, causing impotence in the man who is exposed to it" (Cohen, 1995, p. 296, italics in original).

The lifting of the sari can be accompanied by their *shraap* or other verbal assaults. Various responses can be given to the hijra insults. Some scholars, like Sharma, think that these insults are the result of hijras' "sexual frustration," while others have argued it is a tried and tested technique for extorting money (Carstairs, 1956, p. 130; Sharma, 1984, p. 387). Yet others consider these insults a legitimate replication of societal intimidation and dehumanization (Mehta, 1945, pp. 47-8; Jaffrey, 1997, p. 241). It should nevertheless be noted that hijra linguistic remarks, though strikingly harsh, form a part of the larger background of their performance. Any drag quarrels remain within closed spaces while the hijra "vituperative banter" is often in the presence of non-hijra males with the aim to "embarrass their male listeners and shamelessly collapse traditional divisions of the secret and the known, private and public, home and market, feminine and masculine" (Hall, 1997, pp. 448-9). Moreover, hijras, like other marginalised and liminal entities, can escape from principal conditions of propriety imposed by social control (Turner, 1977).

Once the hijras lift up their saris, the audience who is seduced into believing that they are witnessing a "female" show often experiences a shock. The myth of seeing a seemingly "female performance" ends abruptly with this gesture. The "incongruity" of sexual and gendered identity that is part of identity politics and identity fiction becomes a "visible" reality. What the audience witnesses and participates in is not only the shock of seeing/not seeing the sexual parts (for many prudish

Indians) but also a demonstrative deconstruction of stabilized gender identities.

This effective de-mythification of the "incongruity" of gendered identities becomes all the more meaningful and interesting if we analyze the figure of hijra itself. Unlike many drag queens, many hijras are visible manifestations of the fiction of gender in their person. Some of them do use the masculine attributes when talking of themselves or addressing each other. Some also have masculine names even if this is rare. Almost all of them that I have met or seen always retain their dry and hard masculine voices while at the same time wearing female attires. Even during hijra shows they do not aim at acquiring a high pitched female voice and it is this very disturbing aspect of their appearance that becomes a dynamic tool for resisting the male/female divide and helps them to disrupt in part the semblance of a "female" performance. If the "body" is an essential component of identity through which "we announce our presence to others," then the 'incongruent' hijra body that belongs to third sex poses a real threat to established sexual dimorphism (Gagné and Tewksbury, 1998, p. 85). The fear of this incongruity is pervasive in the film *Darmiyaan*; when Immi the hijra (as a child) unbuttons his trousers to pee, one of the other children remarks: "*Immi ka to nounou hi nahi hai,*" i.e., Immi does not have a penis.

The hijra body and paradigm, so nebulous, can extend anywhere from an emasculated male to a withdrawn or effeminate one right up to a *sanyasi*. It covers the entire spectrum from the holy to the bizarre to the damned! There is so much irony in this spectrum that one form of the hijra is revered as the *sanyasi* and one is marginalised if not always rebuked or ridiculed in the form of the outlandish "eunuch" in urban India. However, in all this irony there lies a grave similarity. In all its forms, the hijra is certainly also feared. In some cases the fear arises out of psychological insecurities, while in some it may arise out of anxiety of the unknown. But it is fear all the same. And yet culturally we tend to associate the archetype of the hijra with the powerless!

GENDERED (IN)SECURITIES

Studying alternative sex and gender matrices of the Orient involves an unsettling of accepted American and Eurocentric ideas as the only available cultural referent, and debunking sexual and gendered dimorphism across cultures. Transgendered communities found across cultures are suggestive of "a continuum of masculinity and femininity, renouncing gender as aligned with genitals, body, social status and/or role" (Bolin, pp. 447-8). Drag queen and hijras performances open up spaces where we as a larger society "can watch a small group and become aware" of ourselves and understand that all "performance is an illusion . . . and might be considered more 'truthful,' more 'real' than ordinary experience" (Schechner, 1988, pp. xiv and 13).

Reading the hijra alongside the drag queen means broadening and enriching the discursive elements of identity (in)congruity and revealing the fiction of all gendering and sexualizing processes of any dominant culture. Gender and sexuality debates, as I have shown, have centered upon drag or hijras as two distinct cultural categories that unsettle our preconceived notions of the masculine and the feminine. Both are subcultural byproducts of Western and Indian societies and have developed in relation to their respective mainstream cultures. The drag queen and the hijra have different modus operandi but both appear to have the same goal of de-legitimizing polarized and normalizing gender categories. While the drag queen typically performs in marginalized settings, hijras have the right to perform in mainstream cultural ceremonies. Yet both have a limited impact on the larger culture. Drag queens are individuals with an acknowledged penis whereas hijras are framed as impotent and eunuchs. Thus, the subversive potential of drag is undermined by limiting their performances to marginalized settings, whereas that of the hijras is limited because of their marginalized status of being impotent and lacking a penis. Ultimately, while both the hijras and the drag queen have a limited subversive impact on the larger dominant culture in which they perform, in practice and image they can forcibly remind us of our own gendered (in)securities.

REFERENCES

Bakshi, S. (2002). Soupçon d'un Espace Alternatif: Etude de Deux Films du Cinéma Parallèle en Inde. *Inverses*, 2, 9-21.

BBC News Online (2000, March 6). Eunuch MP takes seat.

BBC News Online (2001, March 9). India stages Ms World for eunuchs.

Bedi, R. (1994, April 16). The bizarre and dangerous world of India's eunuchs. *Vancouver Sun*.

Bobb, D., and Patel, C.J. (1982, September 15). Fear is the key. *India Today*.

Bolin, A. (1996). Transcending and transgendering: Male to female transsexuals, dichotomy and diversity. In Gilbert Herdt (Ed.) *Third sex/third gender: Beyond sexual dimorphism in culture and history* (pp. 447-486). New York: Zone Books.

Butler, J. (1990). *Gender trouble: Feminism and the subversion of identity*. New York: Routledge.

Butler, J. (1991). Imitation and gender insubordination. In D. Fuss (Ed.), I*nside/out: Lesbian theories/gay theories* (pp.13-31). New York: Routledge.

Butler, J. (1993). *Bodies that matter: On the discursive limits of "sex."* New York: Routledge.

Carstairs, G.M. (1956). *Hinjra and jiryan: Two derivatives of Hindu attitudes to sexuality. British Journal of Medical Psychology*, 29, 128-138.

Cohen, L. (1995). The pleasures of castration: The postoperative status of hijras, jankhas, and academics. In P.R. Abramson and S.D. Pinkerton (Eds.), *Sexual nature, sexual culture* (pp. 276-304). Chicago and London: University of Chicago Press.

Gagné P., and Tewksbury, R. (1998). Conformity pressures and gender resistance among transgendered individuals. *Social Problems*, 45(1), 81-101.

Gagné P., Tewksbury, R., and McGaughey D. (1997). Coming out and crossing over: Identity formation and proclamation in a transgender community. *Gender and Society*, 11(4), 478-508.

Garber, M. (1992). *Vested interests: Cross-dressing and cultural anxiety*. London and New York: Routledge.

Greenberg, D.F. (1988). *The construction of homosexuality*. Chicago: University of Chicago Press.

Hall, K. (1997). Go suck your husband's sugarcane: Hijras and the use of sexual insult. In A. Livia and K. Hall (Eds.), *Queerly phrased: Language, gender and sexuality* (pp. 430-460). New York: Oxford University Press.

Hiltebeitel, A. (1980). Siva, the Goddess, and the disguises of the Pandavas and Draupadi. *History of Religions*, 20(1-2), 147-174.

Jaffrey, Z. (1997). *The invisibles: A tale of the eunuchs of India*. London: Weidenfeld and Nicholson.

Kulick, D. (1998). *Travesti: Sex, gender and culture among Brazilian transgendered prostitutes*. Chicago: University of Chicago Press.

Mehta, S. (1945). Eunuchs, pavaiyas, and hijaras. *Gujarat Sahitya Sabha Part 2*, 3-75.

Nanda, S. (1996). Hijras: An alternative sex and gender role in India. In Gilbert Herdt (Ed.), *Third sex/third gender* (pp. 373-418). New York: Zone Books.

Nanda, S. (1999). *The hijras of India: Neither man nor woman*. Second Edition. Belmont: Wadsworth.

O'Flaherty, W.D. (1980). *Women, androgynes, and other mythical beasts*. Chicago: University of Chicago Press.

Opler, M.E. (1960). The hijara (hermaphrodites) of India and Indian national character: A rejoinder. *American Anthropologist*, 62, 505-511.

Opler, M.E. (1961). Further comparative notes on the hijara of India. *American Anthropologist*, 63, 1331-1332.

Preston, L.W. (1987). A right to exist: Eunuchs and the state in nineteenth-century. *Modern Asian Studies*, 21(2), 371-387.

Ringrose, K.M. (1996). Living in the shadows: Eunuchs and gender in Byzantium. In Gilbert Herdt (Ed.), *Third sex/third gender* (pp. 85-109). New York: Zone Books.

Schacht, S.P. (2002). Four renditions of doing female drag: Feminine appearing conceptual variations of a masculine theme. *Advances in Gender Research*, 6, 157-180.

Sharma, S.K. (1984). Eunuchs: Past and present. *Eastern Anthropologist*, 4, 381-389.

Tewksbury, R. (1993). Men performing as women: Explorations in the world of female impersonators. *Sociological Spectrum*, 13, 465-486.

The Times of India (2002, June 20). Eunuch elected ward councilor in Bihar.

Turner, Victor W. (1977). *The ritual process: Structure and anti-structure*. Chicago: Adline.

Walters, Suzanna D. (1996). From here to queer: Radical feminism, postmodernism, and the lesbian menace (or, why can't a woman be more like a fag?). *Signs*, 21(4), 830-869.

West C., and Zimmerman, D.H. (1987). Doing gender. *Gender and Society*, 1, 125-151.

Whitehead, Andrew. (1998, August 16). The hijras' blessing. *BBC News Online*.

Beyond the Boundaries of the Classroom: Teaching About Gender and Sexuality at a Drag Show

Steven P. Schacht, PhD

Plattsburgh State University of New York

SUMMARY. Like much of the general public, the vast majority of my students strongly hold dichotomous, essentialist outlooks about what the categories female and male/gay and straight are supposed to represent and be. One way that I have found to challenge these oppressive worldviews, and also to queer my classes in the process, is to take my course participants to drag shows and/or to use videotapes of drag queens and drag kings in my classes. As part of an ongoing ethnography of drag performers I am undertaking, I have taken over 300 students to drag shows over the past eight years. Female students have often found attending a drag show to be a fun experience free of the sexual harassment found in most bars, while male students often contextually experience being a social minority for the first time in their life. From both attending drag shows

---

Steven P. Schacht (1960-2003) served as Professor of Sociology at Plattsburgh State University of New York.

Paper presented at the annual National Women's Studies Association Conference in Minneapolis, MN, June 2001.

The author thanks Leila J. Rupp and S. J. Hopkins for their helpful comments and suggestions on an earlier version of this manuscript.

[Haworth co-indexing entry note]: "Beyond the Boundaries of the Classroom: Teaching About Gender and Sexuality at a Drag Show." Schacht, Steven P. Co-published simultaneously in *Journal of Homosexuality* (Harrington Park Press, an imprint of The Haworth Press, Inc.) Vol. 46, No. 3/4, 2004, pp. 225-240; and: *The Drag Queen Anthology: The Absolutely Fabulous but Flawlessly Customary World of Female Impersonators* (ed: Steven P. Schacht, with Lisa Underwood) Harrington Park Press, an imprint of The Haworth Press, Inc., 2004, pp. 225-240. Single or multiple copies of this article are available for a fee from The Haworth Document Delivery Service [1-800-HAWORTH, 9:00 a.m. - 5:00 p.m. (EST). E-mail address: docdelivery@haworthpress.com].

Digital Object Identifier: 10.1300/J082v46n03_14   *225*

and/or watching recordings of them I show in class, students have reported gaining an experiential appreciation of the performed basis of gender, sexuality, and inequality. Or, stated slightly differently, students begin to understand how the stratification system metaphorically makes drag queens of us all. This, in turn, provides the basis of the foremost argument I make in all my classes: equality will not be realized until nondichotomous, truly new ways of relating to others are envisioned and acted upon. *[Article copies available for a fee from The Haworth Document Delivery Service: 1-800-HAWORTH. E-mail address: <docdelivery@haworthpress.com> Website: <http://www.HaworthPress.com> © 2004 by The Haworth Press, Inc. All rights reserved.]*

KEYWORDS. Drag shows, drag queens, pedagogy, gender, sexuality, performing in inequality, performing equality

Perhaps one of the easiest yet at the same time most difficult subjects to teach about is the socially constructed basis of gender. While students often seem to readily understand academic arguments about how the categories of male and female are socially constructed and performed, instilling a visceral appreciation of this cultural reality is far more difficult. This is perhaps not that surprising considering that our culture forcibly insists that everyone must fit into one of two categories, male and female, and severely punishes anyone who resists or cannot. Thus, when logical arguments are put forth about how these two categories are socially constructed, and that other more complex gender outcomes exist (Delphy, 1993; Herdt, 1994; Lorber, 1993; Schacht, 1998; Rupp and Taylor, 2003), the physical reality that surrounds most students does not validate these arguments. Many students can acknowledge that there are social aspects to gender, but a quick glance around most any classroom, where almost always everyone present is easily categorized as a man or a woman, still leaves most students with a gut-level feeling that there are innate, biologically fixed qualities (e.g., appearances and behaviors) to being male and female.

A similar classroom resistance often occurs around discussions of sexuality. While no one definitively knows what "causes" one's sexual orientation, the categories of homosexuality and heterosexuality both reflect and sustain deep-seated, essential conceptions of gender (Progrebin, 1997). Both are directly grounded in an outlook that prescribes that one is inherently attracted to either men or women. Even with the seeming optional category of bisexuality, where one is seen as now having two choices, there still are no third or fourth gender categories to which one could be attracted. Here again, the seeming innateness of male and female, often expressed in homophobic terms, can make for difficult classroom discussions about the socially constructed basis of sexuality.

Since January of 1993, I have been undertaking an ongoing ethnography of drag performers–both drag queens and drag kings.[1] Prior to this, I, like many of my students, had an academic understanding of the socially constructed basis of the categories of male and female (Schacht and Atchison, 1993), but little experiential appreciation of this knowledge. I could easily list any number of ways the categories of men and women were cultural constructs, yet still viewed everyone around me in dichotomous terms, as either male or female, gay or straight, inevitably reifying the very categories I often looked to deconstruct. Perhaps because of this, even though I thought of myself as a very progressive individual, replete with close lesbian and gay friends, I still had many homophobic tendencies, such as being repulsed by another man kissing me. Since attending my very first drag show, I have been forced to reconsider many of my previous outlooks, some of them now acknowledged as quite sexist, and to emotionally explore many of my deepest personal fears (Schacht, 2002a & b). Because of my drag experiences, I believe I am starting to truly develop an intuitive understanding that there are as many genders and sexualities in the world as there are people.

Reflective of my now forever fractured outlook, this paper explores my experiences of bringing students to drag shows as an excellent way to experientially challenge their dichotomous, often oppressive, beliefs about the social categories of male and female, gay and straight.

Recognizing that attending a drag show may be difficult, if not impossible, for some readers of this paper, I also explore some alternative drag based materials, such as movies and videotapes, which can also be used to this end. Before discussing the particulars of either of these teaching strategies, I think it would be helpful to briefly but clearly spell out the foremost underlying themes of all my courses. As these themes are most easily applied to my gender/sexuality related courses, these courses will provide the basis of the rest of this paper's discussion.

PEDAGOGICALLY SETTING THE STAGE

Over the past 18 years of teaching I have increasingly focused on how oppression is the moral fabric of our contemporary society. Ac-

cordingly, the first few class periods in any of my gender/sexuality related courses (i.e., introduction to LGBTQ studies, sociology of
women, sociology of men, and sociology of gender) always involve the
presentation and discussion of Marilyn Frye's (2001) "Oppression" and
Marion Iris Young's (1988) "Five Faces of Oppression." Both of these
gender theorists offer straightforward conceptual definitions of what
oppression is, an ideological outlook that prescribes and justifies societal dominants' exploitive, marginalizing, often violent treatment of societal subordinates, and what it is not, such as simply being miserable.
Building on their insights, I start to introduce the notion that the categorical inequalities that make up our oppressive society are not merely
cultural givens, but rather ultimately found–made possible and real–in
our attitudes and behaviors. That is, as a dominant and/or a subordinate,
each of us has a lifetime's worth of experiences doing oppression (most
it is typically as oppressor and oppressed), and it is our categorical performances of gender, sexuality, race, and class that make inequality and
oppression a lived reality (Schacht, 2000a).

Most of my students seem to academically accept these early arguments that oppression is something done, even something they do, but
almost all of them find it extremely difficult to envision alternatives to
these apparently inevitable outcomes. This is not that surprising, as the
hegemony of present forms of oppression explicitly and implicitly
works to render all "other" perspectives invisible, thus ideologically
making present forms of inequality seem logical, natural, and just.
Herein I believe is found the promise of drag performers. Moving beyond the boundaries of the classroom and entering into the world of
drag queens (and when possible, drag kings) experientially forces many
of my students to reconsider their personal understanding of what gender and sexuality are.

ATTENDING A DRAG SHOW:
SOME PRACTICAL CONSIDERATIONS
AND EXPECTED CONTEXTUAL OUTCOMES

You're born naked and the rest is drag. (RuPaul, 1995, p. iii)

Since my very first drag show, students have frequently accompanied me to many of the performances I have attended over the years.
This perhaps was initially an unconscious way for me to further demonstrate my "straightness" in various gay and lesbian contexts, and a way

to more easily gain access to the research setting (see below on the benefits of bringing large groups of people to drag shows). In 1995, while teaching at Gonzaga University, I was in the process of becoming a full participant in the Imperial Sovereign Court of Spokane (see Schacht 1998 & 2000b for more detailed discussions of the court and my role in it), and I started to invite students to drag shows held at a local gay bar as a form of community outreach for the group. Not only did students who attended shows come back to class letting everyone know how much fun they had, but slowly their drag experiences, combined with mine, started to become important classroom material. It was at this point that I started to explicitly use drag shows as an important pedagogical tool in my classes.

In the subsections that follow I will first offer some suggestions about successfully bringing students to drag shows. Then I will separately explore the shared and differential effects on men and women of attending shows that I have observed over the years. A discussion of the broader more general effects of bringing students to drag shows will be offered in the concluding section of this paper, after alternative means of using drag performances are explored.

Bringing the Classroom to a Drag Show

Of course, the first requisite for bringing students to a drag show is to find a venue where such performances are undertaken. Such places are easily found in virtually any large city, but often are more difficult to find in smaller towns, perhaps explaining the 400 mile treks I have made to attend shows with students while teaching in Montana. Regardless, a visit to any local gay bar or exploring one of the many lgbtq search engines now available online will enable one to find out where drags shows are being held.

Once a venue is located, I strongly suggest that one attend a show there before bringing students. This will allow for arrangements to be made, such as reserved tables, which will in turn make the students' entry into the setting far more comfortable for all parties. As most drag shows are heavily dependent upon on a tipping audience, and the performers themselves often seem to enjoy using the "straights" present as part of their performance (Schacht, 1998 & 2002b), I have always felt extremely welcome in any drag setting to which I have brought students. Moreover, as the group typically gets recognized as the "straight table," or one of the "straight tables" present, I have found this significantly cuts down on possible aggressive sexual overtures from the bar regulars and often makes attendees feel like special guests for the evening.

Once arrangements are made, it is best to let students know what to expect, especially those attending for the first time, and to let them know that they should be respectful visitors of the setting. While I have never had any problems with unruly or disruptive students attending shows, especially considering that many (mostly men) are intimidated the first time they attend, I think it is of utmost importance for the instructor to set the tone for the outing. When bringing students to drag shows, I feel like both an insider and outsider to the setting–a goodwill ambassador of sorts–and ultimately responsible for all parties having a safe, fun time. Finally, unless meeting as a group prior to departing for the show, I would strongly suggest that one should arrive at the drag venue long before any of the students do as a way to ensure that any reserved tables remain such and as a way to cut down on many (mostly male) students' anxieties about entering a gay bar.

For various obvious legal and ethical reasons, I have never required students to attend shows or offered any sort of extra course credit for doing so. Nevertheless, I have found soliciting students to go to drag shows to be a very easy endeavor. Always stated by me as "an invitation not a course expectation," the mere mention of a show piques the interest of many class members, with those who are not 21 often being disappointed that they cannot attend.[2] I would speculate that many of the students who accept my invitation to attend a show also view it as a fun way to spend a night with me, the instructor, in an off campus bar setting. The number of students accompanying me to a show has ranged from 2 to over 15. Because of the explicitly voluntary basis of my invitation, the percentage of course participants who have attended shows with me has varied drastically ranging from upwards of 25 percent in smaller classes to less than 5 percent in larger classes I have taught. Regardless of the actual percentage of students that have accompanied me, I believe that the pedagogical benefits from attending a show are twofold: (1) as discussed below, attendees come to have a different experiential appreciation of gender and sexuality; (2) attendees return to the classroom with these new understandings and, from my experience, are typically quite vocal about sharing their drag experiences with other course participants.

Although a few women have reported previously attending a drag show or been in a gay bar, I can recall only one man who has ever made this claim when attending a show with me. Moreover, perhaps largely the result of the lack of ethnic and cultural diversity on the various campuses where I have taught, almost all of those attending shows with me have been white students and only a small handful have indicated to me that they were gay or lesbian. Finally, note should be made that all of the drag venues I have attended with students, at least the night of the show, have been gay male in focus, and I would speculate that the below observations would be very different if the performers had been predominantly drag kings at a lesbian bar.

Straight Boys[3]

The response to attending a drag show of most "straight boys," as they are most typically referred to in many gay male drag settings, is quite profound yet fairly uniform. For many of these young men, walking into a gay bar is the first experience they have ever had where they have felt like a social minority. Both to me personally and in classes, men who have attended drag shows have reported feeling totally out of place, like a foreigner in a strange land, where the rules of interaction that usually benefit them are no longer present.

Such sentiments are quite consistent with the nervous, sometimes humorous behaviors they manifest while attending a show (especially those attending for the first time). When entering the bar they typically are visibly quite anxious and very relieved once they spot me and see where we are sitting. This is often followed by them quickly consuming several drinks–typically beer, although I have watched shots being drunk too–with the inevitable outcome that they have to go to the bathroom. A new set of fears emerges. Most heterosexual men are somewhat uncomfortable urinating in the presence of other perceived straight men, and the thought of doing so in front of gay men (and drag queens) is often quite unsettling. After many noticeable glances at the bathroom, many of these men reach a point where they can no longer "hold it" and ask if I will go to the bathroom with them, which, after some teasing, I do.

Perhaps equally entertaining are many of these young men's obvious efforts to let everyone present know they are straight. Even though they often attend with girlfriends, or in a group with female friends, and most everyone present knows they are straight, they are quick to explicitly point this out to anyone whom they perceive a sexual threat. For instance, in Spokane, where I was close friends with many of the participants in the setting, drag queens who would stop by to say "hi" to me often provoked comments such as "I came with Steve and am straight," "This is my girlfriend and I am straight," or just plain "I am straight."

These statements were often also accompanied by the given man putting his arm around his girlfriend, or him trying to sit closer to any women who were at the table. Drag queens' response to the obvious discomfort of these men has been to say things like, "That's too bad as you are so cute" or "Sure, isn't everyone."

Once the show begins, and in hopes of indoctrinating newcomers, I always begin tipping the various performers. Tipping at most drag shows involves approaching the performer on stage and typically giving them a single dollar bill with an accompanying nod of appreciation. Some of the braver young men will follow my lead while others have to be explicitly asked to do so with simple but blunt comments like "Aren't you going to tip?" and me sometimes giving them a dollar bill to do so. Perhaps seeing it as a personal challenge, most of these men eventually do end up tipping, but only if they were escorted by a girlfriend or one of the women present. Instead of the traditional gendered image of a woman holding onto a man's loosely offered arm, most young men attending a drag show firmly grab their escort's arm, as if she somehow provides a shield to ward off any unwanted sexual overtures.

Throughout the given evening's activities, young men will ask me, sometimes redundantly with several performers, "Is that really a guy?" As many drag queens are quite adept at capturing culturally idealized images of hyper-feminine beauty–some even go as far as to say they make better women than women–many young men become quite confused. Through the sexist, objectifying lens that many young men use when viewing women, they often find a performer quite sexually attractive. Their initial rhetorical question is usually followed with some frustrated comment like "Man, she . . . he . . . it . . . whatever is hot" or "Damn, Steve, that's fucked up," all the while shaking their heads and/or rubbing their eyes.

In subsequent classroom and personal discussions, many of these men have reported that they now have problems objectifying women's bodies, some for acknowledged homophobic reasons, and some have come to the conclusion that viewing half the population as a sexual "thing" is an unhealthy outlook. Yet others have reported coming to this conclusion because of the often sexually flirtatious comments directed at them by the drag queens, especially those emceeing the show. As an acknowledged social minority in the setting, many have reported that these comments felt like a form of sexual harassment and that they now have a better appreciation of the "sexist crap" women have to put up with when frequenting straight bars.

Another potential benefit many men realize by attending a drag show is that it can lessen their feelings of homophobia. In some cases, this effect can be quite extreme. For one young man, an ROTC member and "cowboy" from Missoula, Montana, his first visit to a show was quite comical to witness. Although he is an individual who was not intimidated by any man (he was also a boxer), he spent the evening with his back against a pole, "so no one can sneak up on me," as he stated, and after one beer, refused to drink any more because he was afraid he would get AIDS from the beer bottle as the waiters were gay. As he never left his seat the entire evening, I am guessing he also limited his liquid intake so he did not have to go bathroom. Even though it was a real hassle babysitting him this night, as I had to constantly reassure him that everything was fine and ask that all the performers to leave him alone, the long-term impact has been significant. Not only did this individual subsequently become a personal friend, he has frequently accompanied me to many drag shows since then, including in his hometown in Missoula, Montana, and in Chicago, Illinois, and now acknowledges that his being homophobic is about his own insecurities and has subsequently also become friends with many of the gay men in the course.

Yet other men, more secure in their own sexuality, have immediately taken to the context and provided fun entertainment for all present. One of the young men I escorted from Montana for a show in Spokane was an Army Ranger, and quite "ripped," as virtually every gay man in the context, queen and king, quickly noted. Unlike most first-timers, he was receptive to the flirtatious attention directed at him by the drag queens and even other gay men. Part of this I believe was the result of him enjoying any attention he received about his body. Combined with an audience of gay men who often idealize images of straight men (Levine, 1998), this made for a quite interesting mix.

By the second night, and to make a long story short, several of the drag queens convinced him to strip to his underwear to a sexually provocative song, "I Am Too Sexy?" In a normally high-energy setting, I thought the bar was going to explode. Drag queens, gay men, women students who were with us for the trip, and even lesbians flocked to the stage to tip him, some putting their dollars into his underwear. Many loudly cheered him on with several of the queens and gay men nervously fanning themselves, as if overexcited from the experience, with "oh my" comments being most typical. Although arrangements were made for him to make a cameo appearance at an upcoming pageant, these fell through, as neither he nor I could attend that weekend. Nevertheless, every time I have returned to Spokane since then, someone will jokingly ask when I am bringing him back to perform.

In sum, and reflective of my own drag experiences, every young man that has attended a show with me has reported it to be not only a fun outing (most have ended up attending more shows with me), but also an experience that has forever changed the way they view and appreciate the social world around them. These young men return to class and often quite freely share their drag experiences with other course participants. Many become team teachers in my efforts to both academically and experientially articulate the socially constructed basis of gender and sexuality.

Straight Women

While attending a show often can also have an important impact on women's social outlooks, in many ways, it is for very different reasons than for men in ways that are often far more subtle. To begin with, while it has almost exclusively been younger men who attended shows with me (i.e., all men their early 20s, with only one man in his fifties), women attendees have been quite diverse in age. Perhaps because of this, women who have attended shows with me have seemed more mature and far less intimidated by the experience (in particular, attending their first show). Some of this is also very much a function, as numerous women have reported to me, of being able to enter a bar and not be sexually harassed. Several have reported that it is quite strange and nice to be able to sit in a bar and be able to truly relax and enjoy a drink versus feelings of always having to be on guard against unwanted sexual advances in straight bars.

Similarly, while the young men often attract the drag queens' attention, because of the gay male focus of the various drag venues attended, straight women are fairly inconspicuous. As long as they do not challenge who is the fairest-in-the-land in feminine image, typically easily accomplished given the casual dress of most women in college, other than a cordial "thank you" given to them when tipping a performer, most drag queens largely ignore their presence in the setting. Even in settings where lesbian women are present, such as at court shows in Spokane, there seems to be little interest or concern about the "straight women" present. Perhaps because of this, and in direct contrast to the young men, I have witnessed few explicit efforts by women to demonstrate their sexual orientation. Thus, most of the reported effects of attending a drag show are observations women make while there, and much less about experiences where they are the focus of the contextual attention, like the young men who attend.

One thing that I have consistently had shared with me by women attendees is that, while their experience is a sexual harassment-free one, they often find it quite enjoyable to see the "straight boys" get hit on. As they correctly have noted, most men are clueless about what it feels like to be the recipient of unwanted sexual advances, and to be witness to their discomfort as a social minority is quite fun. Many have also noted how surprising it is to see how homophobic and insecure many men are about their own sexual orientation. The image of intimidated, uncomfortable, sometimes even scared men concerning sexual matters is in direct contrast to the cocky overconfidence they usually see exuded by most men in straight bars.

While many women are truly impressed and often quite taken with many drag queens' fashion sense and attention to feminine detail, this is also unsettling to many. Understandably, many find troubling the drag queens' oft-stated assertion that they make better women than women do. Through the sexist lens of most men's (both straight and gay) outlook of what is feminine beauty, which is very much internalized by many women in our society, when many of these women compare themselves to the queens up on stage, they often conclude that the queens are correct. Physically speaking, I would also hold that there is actually some truth to the queens' sexist statement, e.g., men are far more likely to be taller and have skinny but shapely legs. Regardless, many have also reported to me that they now better understand how a woman's worth in our sexist society is often based on how attractive she is, and many vow to search for different criteria for their own personal self-worth. In many ways, the drag queens tarnish many women's ideals of hyper-feminine beauty.

In sum, while the effects of attending a drag show for women are less obvious, perhaps somewhat a function that men are far more obvious in their response, several have subsequently attended drag shows without me, with some becoming friends with the drag queens. In contrast, I am aware of only two young men who have gone on to attend shows without my escort, one who is now an openly gay man. Women often seem to be quite taken and appreciative of the various female impersonators' performances. Perhaps this is not that surprising, as to varying degrees they are quite familiar with doing female drag themselves. In general terms, attending a drag show for women has always been reported to me as a fun experience, in an environment largely free of unwanted sexual advances; most of what is learned comes from observing the perfor-

mances of the drag queens and the young men's often entertaining responses to being in the setting. Moreover, like men who attend shows,
these women return to the classroom and often share their drag experiences with course participants and also become important team teachers
in discussions of the socially constructed basis of gender and sexuality.

BRINGING DRAG PERFORMANCES INTO THE CLASSROOM

Since leaving Spokane in the fall of 1997 to first teach at Montana
State, and now at Plattsburgh State, my geographical location has made
it much more difficult to bring students to drag shows, and I have only
done so on a half a dozen occasions since then (three times entailing
fairly long road trips with overnight stays). Nevertheless, I have continued to frequently use performances of drag queens as learning materials, albeit now in the form of videotapes and movies. For those who do
not have steady access to drag venues, I have found that videotape recordings are a viable alternative to teach about many of the things I have
observed students who attended drag shows have learned.

Over the years I have collected over 50 hours of recordings of drag
shows I have attended and participated in. One of these videotapes is
from a night I emceed a drag show where fifteen of my students were in
attendance, and provides the basis of a previous article I wrote on how
there were multiple genders (at least six) present this evening (Schacht,
1998). Every semester for the past four years I have used this videotape
as a fun way of making real my arguments that there are more than two
genders in the world. Although they are not actually attending a drag
show, after reading my article on the topic, the students have consistently told me that watching the videotape made my argument of there
being multiple genders literally come alive for them.

Accordingly, should only infrequent opportunities exist for one to
take students to an actual show, I would strongly suggest videotaping
the outing for future classroom use. However, since a few drag venues
ban any photographs or videotaping, it is best to secure permission before doing so. Nevertheless, most of the drag venues I have been in are
quite open to one recording shows, and most drag queens love to perform for any sort of camera. In fact, most of my videotapes were gra-
ciously given to me by the participants in the setting, which can be
another possible way of getting recordings of shows.

In the mid-1990s nearly every daytime talk show featured drag
queens. I have found that these shows are frequently shown as repeats,

and periodically new ones also appear (one recent Ricki Lake show was about drag king performers). Recordings of these shows can be used by those who are unable to find a drag venue to attend, and I have found them to be wonderful supplemental course materials. One Maury Povich episode, where the audience is asked to discern the "true" gender of ten female-appearing performers, is especially thought provoking and now I use it in all my gender related courses. I have the students briefly watch each of the ten performers, and most have real difficulty figuring out who is "really" a man or a woman. Ironically, most students (sometimes 100 percent with one of the performers) think the two "real" women are drag queens, while there often is significant disagreement about the "true" gender–all male–of the remaining performers. More will be said about the breaching effect of drag performers in a moment.

As I written elsewhere (Schacht, 2000), I have also found movies about drag performers to work well in my classes. In particular, near the end of each semester, I have my course participants watch the award winning movie-documentary *Paris Is Burning*.[4] I then have them write reflection papers about how they "do" inequality and oppression through their performances of gender, sexuality, race, and social class. I also ask them to envision ways that they could perform equality. I am always humbled by the insightfulness of the numerous ways course participants realize how they have been oppressed by or oppressive to others and personally pleased to hear the various ways they plan to perform equality in the future.

LEARNING HOW TO PERFORM EQUALITY

> Drag constitutes the mundane way in which genders are appropriated, worn, and done; it implies that all gendering is a kind of impersonation and approximation. If this is true, it seems, there is no original or primary gender that drag imitates, but *gender is a kind of imitation for which there is no original*; in fact, it is a kind of imitation that produces the very notion of the original as an *affect* and consequence of the imitation itself. (Butler, 1991, 21–emphasis in the original)

Insomuch that Butler is correct that gender is a form of imitation for which there is no original script, I believe her important insight is equally applicable to all performances of oppression and inequality. While sentiments such as these often seem quite logical to participants of my gender-related courses (I always discuss the above quote in the terms just outlined in one of the first class periods), most initially still find it quite difficult to envision alternative outcomes to the dichotomous world they find so familiar, one exclusively populated with men and women, gays and straights, Blacks and Whites, and rich and poor with corresponding statuses of dominant and subordinate. In spite of all the typical classroom logic offered otherwise, these hegemonic, socially prescribed categories still often feel innate in existence and inevitable in outcome to many of my students.

As I have argued in this paper, one way that I have found to successfully contest the seemingly fixed basis of oppression is by bringing students to drag shows and/or supplementing classroom discussions with recordings of drag shows. I have found that drag performers, especially drag queens, who successfully "do" their "opposite" gender frequently challenge most course participants' behavioral and appearance expectations of what is the basis of being female and male in our society. I have also found that queering my classes in this manner often lessens the homophobic feelings of course participants, especially those of young men, and forcibly demonstrates that there are no absolute criteria for defining who is male or female, gay or straight. This, in turn, has allowed me to fruitfully suggest that since inequality and oppression are ultimately performances–all firmly grounded in socially constructed categories that prescribe roles of dominance and subordination–for which there are no original scripts, new, non-dichotomous ways of being in the world will have to be envisioned and acted upon if an egalitarian future is to be made possible. Those explicitly attempting to undertake performances of equality will play vitally important roles in the construction of a non-oppressive future.

NOTES

1. While over 90 percent of the over two dozen drag venues I have frequented have exclusively featured drag queens, my most in-depth participation of a setting has been in the Imperial Sovereign Court of Spokane, where there are both gay drag queens (primarily) and lesbian drag kings present. As a result, over fifty percent of the students I have escorted to drag shows have seen both types of performers. Nevertheless, since lesbian drag king performers are somewhat of a rarity, unless otherwise noted, this paper will primarily focus on students' responses to attending shows where drag queens are performing.

2. While not a big supporter of the age requirement (21) to legally drink in the United States, I try to make sure all students are 21 to protect the drag venue we

are attending, as gay bars are the frequent targets of police raids for underage drinkers.

3. Although written for a different purpose, several of the observations I list in this section, and the one that follows about straight women, are drawn from a previous article I wrote about the multiple genders present at a drag show (Schacht, 1998).

4. *Wigstock* is another movie-documentary of this sort that can be used to similar ends as *Paris Is Burning*. Dependent on the given instructor's tastes and needs, I am guessing other movies about drag queens, such as *Priscilla* or *To Fong Woo*, could also be used as pedagogical tools to deconstruct dichotomous outlooks of gender.

REFERENCES

Butler, J. (1991). Imitation and gender insubordination. In D. Fuss (Ed.), I*nside/out: Lesbian theories, gay theories* (pp. 13-31). New York: Routledge.

Delphy, C. (1993). Rethinking sex and gender. *Women's Studies International Forum* 16, 1-9.

Frye, M. (2001). Oppression. In L. Richardson, V. Taylor, and N. Whittier (Eds.), *Feminist frontiers V* (pp. 6-8). New York: McGraw-Hill.

Herdt, G. (1994). *Third sex, third gender: Beyond sexual dimorphism in culture and history.* New York: Zone Books.

Levine, M.P. (1998). *Gay macho: The life and death of the homosexual clone.* New York: New York University Press.

Lorber, J. (1994). *Paradoxes of gender.* New Haven, CT: Yale University Press.

Progrebin, L.C. (1997). The secret fear that keeps us from raising free children. In L. Richardson, V. Taylor, and N. Whittier (Eds.), *Feminist frontiers IV* (pp. 171-176). New York: McGraw-Hill.

RuPaul. (1995). *Letting it all hang out: An autobiography.* New York: Hyperion.

Rupp, L.J. and Taylor, V. (2003). *Drag queens at the 801 Cabaret.* Chicago: University of Chicago Press.

Schacht, S.P. (1998). The multiple genders of the court: Issues of identity and performance in a drag setting. In S.P. Schacht and D.W. Ewing (Eds.), *Feminism and men: Reconstructing gender relations* (pp. 202-224). New York: New York University Press.

Schacht, S.P. (2000a). *Paris is Burning:* How society's stratification systems makes drag queens of us all. *Race, Gender & Class,* 7(1), 147-166.

Schacht, S.P. (2000b). Gay female impersonators and the masculine construction of 'other.' In Peter Nardi (Ed.), *Gay masculinities* (pp 247-268). Thousand Oaks, CA: Sage.

Schacht, S.P. (2002a). Four renditions of doing female drag: Feminine appearing conceptual variations of a masculine theme. In P. Gagne and R. Tewksbury (Eds.), "Gendered Sexualities" in *Advances in Gender Research* (pp. 157-180). Boston: Elsevier Science.

Schacht, S.P. (2002b). Turnabout: Gay drag queens and the masculine embodiment of the feminine. In N. Tuana et al. (Eds.), *Revealing male bodies* (pp. 155-170). Bloomington: Indiana University Press.

Schacht, S.P. (2002c). Lesbian drag kings and the feminine embodiment of the masculine. *Journal of Homosexuality,* 43(3/4).

Schacht, S.P. and Atchison, P.H. (1993). Heterosexual instrumentalism: Past and future directions. *Feminism & Psychology*, 3, 37-53.

Young, M.I. (1988). Five faces of oppression. *Philosophical Forum*, XIX, 270-290.

Index

Gay People, Sex, and the Media, edited by Michelle A. Wolf, PhD, and Alfred P. Kielwasser, MA (Vol. 21, No. 1/2, 1991). *"Altogether, the kind of research anthology which is useful to many disciplines in gay studies. Good stuff!" (Communique)*

Gay Midlife and Maturity: Crises, Opportunities, and Fulfillment, edited by John Alan Lee, PhD (Vol. 20, No. 3/4, 1991). *"The insight into gay aging is amazing, accurate, and much-needed. . . . A real contribution to the older gay community." (Prime Timers)*

Male Intergenerational Intimacy: Historical, Socio-Psychological, and Legal Perspectives, edited by Theo G. M. Sandfort, PhD, Edward Brongersma, JD, and A. X. van Naerssen, PhD (Vol. 20, No. 1/2, 1991). *"The most important book on the subject since Tom O'Carroll's 1980 Paedophilia: The Radical Case." (The North America Man/Boy Love Association Bulletin, May 1991)*

Love Letters Between a Certain Late Nobleman and the Famous Mr. Wilson, edited by Michael S. Kimmel, PhD (Vol. 19, No. 2, 1990). *"An intriguing book about homosexuality in 18th-Century England. Many details of the period, such as meeting places, coded language, and 'camping' are all covered in the book. If you're a history buff, you'll enjoy this one." (Prime Timers)*

Homosexuality and Religion, edited by Richard Hasbany, PhD (Vol. 18, No. 3/4, 1990). *"A welcome resource that provides historical and contemporary views on many issues involving religious life and homosexuality." (Journal of Sex Education and Therapy)*

Homosexuality and the Family, edited by Frederick W. Bozett, PhD (Vol. 18, No. 1/2, 1989). *"Enlightening and answers a host of questions about the effects of homosexuality upon family members and the family as a unit." (Ambush Magazine)*

Gay and Lesbian Youth, edited by Gilbert Herdt, PhD (Vol. 17, No. 1/2/3/4, 1989). *"Provides a much-needed compilation of research dealing with homosexuality and adolescents." (GLTF Newsletter)*

Lesbians Over 60 Speak for Themselves, edited by Monika Kehoe, PhD (Vol. 16, No. 3/4, 1989). *"A pioneering book examining the social, economical, physical, sexual, and emotional lives of aging lesbians." (Feminist Bookstore News)*

The Pursuit of Sodomy: Male Homosexuality in Renaissance and Enlightenment Europe, edited by Kent Gerard, PhD, and Gert Hekma, PhD (Vol. 16, No. 1/2, 1989). *"Presenting a wealth of information in a compact form, this book should be welcomed by anyone with an interest in this period in European history or in the precursors to modern concepts of homosexuality." (The Canadian Journal of Human Sexuality)*

Psychopathology and Psychotherapy in Homosexuality, edited by Michael W. Ross, PhD (Vol. 15, No. 1/2, 1988). *"One of the more objective, scientific collections of articles concerning the mental health of gays and lesbians. . . . Extraordinarily thoughtful. . . . New thoughts about treatments. Vital viewpoints." (The Book Reader)*

Psychotherapy with Homosexual Men and Women: Integrated Identity Approaches for Clinical Practice, edited by Eli Coleman, PhD (Vol. 14, No. 1/2, 1987). *"An invaluable tool. . . . This is an extremely useful book for the clinician seeking better ways to understand gay and lesbian patients." (Hospital and Community Psychiatry)*

Interdisciplinary Research on Homosexuality in The Netherlands, edited by A. X. van Naerssen, PhD (Vol. 13, No. 2/3, 1987). *"Valuable not just for its insightful analysis of the evolution of gay rights in The Netherlands, but also for the lessons that can be extracted by our own society from the Dutch tradition of tolerance for homosexuals." (The San Francisco Chronicle)*

Historical, Literary, and Erotic Aspects of Lesbianism, edited by Monica Kehoe, PhD (Vol. 12, No. 3/4, 1986). *"Fascinating . . . Even though this entire volume is serious scholarship penned by degreed writers, most of it is vital, accessible, and thoroughly readable even to the casual student of lesbian history." (Lambda Rising)*

Anthropology and Homosexual Behavior, edited by Evelyn Blackwood, PhD (cand.) (Vol. 11, No. 3/4, 1986). *"A fascinating account of homosexuality during various historical periods and in non-Western cultures." (SIECUS Report)*

Bisexualities: Theory and Research, edited by Fritz Klein, MD, and Timothy J. Wolf, PhD (Vol. 11, No. 1/2, 1985). *"The editors have brought together a formidable array of new data challenging old stereotypes about a very important human phenomenon . . . A milestone in furthering our knowledge about sexual orientation." (David P. McWhirter, Co-author, The Male Couple)*

Homophobia: An Overview, edited by John P. De Cecco, PhD (Vol. 10, No. 1/2, 1984). *"Breaks ground in helping to make the study of homophobia a science." (Contemporary Psychiatry)*

Bisexual and Homosexual Identities: Critical Clinical Issues, edited by John P. De Cecco, PhD (Vol. 9, No. 4, 1985). *Leading experts provide valuable insights into sexual identity within a clinical context–broadly defined to include depth psychology, diagnostic classification, therapy, and psychomedical research on the hormonal basis of homosexuality.*

Bisexual and Homosexual Identities: Critical Theoretical Issues, edited by John P. De Cecco, PhD, and Michael G. Shively, MA (Vol. 9, No. 2/3, 1984). *"A valuable book . . . The careful scholarship, analytic rigor, and lucid exposition of virtually all of these essays make them thought-provoking and worth more than one reading." (Sex Roles, A Journal of Research)*

Homosexuality and Social Sex Roles, edited by Michael W. Ross, PhD (Vol. 9, No. 1, 1983). *"For a comprehensive review of the literature in this domain, exposure to some interesting methodological models, and a glance at 'older' theories undergoing contemporary scrutiny, I recommend this book." (Journal of Sex Education & Therapy)*

Literary Visions of Homosexuality, edited by Stuart Kellogg, PhD (Vol. 8, No. 3/4, 1985). *"An important book. Gay sensibility has never been given such a boost." (The Advocate)*

Alcoholism and Homosexuality, edited by Thomas O. Ziebold, PhD, and John E. Mongeon (Vol. 7, No. 4, 1985). *"A landmark in the fields of both alcoholism and homosexuality . . . a very lush work of high caliber." (The Journal of Sex Research)*

Homosexuality and Psychotherapy: A Practitioner's Handbook of Affirmative Models, edited by John C. Gonsiorek, PhD (Vol. 7, No. 2/3, 1985). *"A book that seeks to create affirmative psychotherapeutic models. . . . To say this book is needed by all doing therapy with gay or lesbian clients is an understatement." (The Advocate)*

Nature and Causes of Homosexuality: A Philosophic and Scientific Inquiry, edited by Noretta Koertge, PhD (Vol. 6, No. 4, 1982). *"An interesting, thought-provoking book, well worth reading as a corrective to much of the research literature on homosexuality." (Australian Journal of Sex, Marriage & Family)*

Historical Perspectives on Homosexuality, edited by Salvatore J. Licata, PhD, and Robert P. Petersen, PhD (cand.) (Vol. 6, No. 1/2, 1986). *"Scholarly and excellent. Its authority is impeccable, and its treatment of this neglected area exemplary." (Choice)*

Homosexuality and the Law, edited by Donald C. Knutson, PhD (Vol. 5, No. 1/2, 1979). *A comprehensive analysis of current legal issues and court decisions relevant to male and female homosexuality.*